"God provides each and every one of us with the opportunity to experience a journey that is ours, and ours alone. Like every great explorer who leaves a "blaze" to mark his trail, Dale Perkins provides guidance for using God's map and a compass for finding our true destination."

—Michael Kormanicki, Ph.D.
Retired Senior Director, Center for Best Practices, Marriott

"Dale Perkins has a unique gift of weaving stories and painting observations about Scripture. In *Looking Up to See the Bottom*, he has thoughtfully put together practical, honest, biblically grounded insights presented in such a way as to make them as relevant as this morning's newspaper. His writing is colorful and enriched by well-chosen illustrations and metaphors drawn from a wide array of life experiences. I recommend this book highly. It will lead you closer to the God of the Bible."

—Pat Williams
Senior Vice President, Orlando Magic
Author, *Leadership Excellence*

"In *Looking Up to See the Bottom*, Dale Perkins opens up the Scriptures for his readers. He engages the Scriptures in all their richness and helps us to connect our lives with the biblical message so that we can live lives worthy of the gospel."

—Brian D. Russell, Ph.D.
Professor of Biblical Studies, Asbury Theological Seminary

"Once again Dale has utilized his experience as an engineer to look at topics and people in the Bible from all angles, digging deep for a foundation. Dale uses his years of teaching Disciple coupled with his ability as a storyteller to bridge history with contemporary culture. Dale's unique writing style and his personal walk as a Christian make this book thought-provoking, fun, and ideal for Bible study or devotion. His enthusiasm for the Bible is contagious!"

—Mrs. Susan Goff

Looking Up

TO SEE THE

Bottom

*Learning to Live
with Divine Focus*

R. DALE PERKINS

...opment Services, Inc.

...uite 105
..., Florida 32765
(407) 563-4806
www.ahigherlife.com

Unless otherwise indicated, Scriptures are taken from THE HOLY BIBLE, NEW INTERNATIONAL VERSION®, NIV® Copyright © 1973, 1978, 1984, 2011 by Biblica, Inc.™ Used by permission. All rights reserved worldwide.

Scriptures marked RSV are taken from the Revised Standard Version of the Bible, copyright 1952 [2nd edition, 1971] by the Division of Christian Education of the National Council of the Churches of Christ in the United States of America. Used by permission. All rights reserved.

Scriptures marked NRSV are taken from the New Revised Standard Version of the Bible, copyright 1989, Division of Christian Education of the National Council of the Churches of Christ in the United States of America. Used by permission. All rights reserved.

Scriptures marked KJV are taken from the King James Version of the Bible.

Scriptures marked ESV are taken from The Holy Bible, English Standard Version® (ESV®), copyright © 2001 by Crossway, a publishing ministry of Good News Publishers. Used by permission. All rights reserved.

Copyright © 2012 by R. Dale Perkins
All rights reserved

ISBN 13: 978-1-935245-71-1
ISBN 10: 1-935245-71-6

Cover Design: Principle Design Group – David Whitlock

First edition

Printed in the United States of America

12 13 14 15 — 9 8 7 6 5 4 3 2 1

Table of Contents

1.13.13 Sermon
ROOTED

2 trees
tree of life
tree of knowledge of good & evil.
The glory and the central problem of creation —
you and me.
Why? what is the meaning of all this?
Ch 1 creative nature of God
Praise God for the wonder.

Ch 2. Wake up call: Destiny of human
kind is to live in God's world not the
world of our own making.
Adam's personality — lights and darkness.
The first living contradiction, ambiguous.
In the image of God - my destiny can
only be fulfilled in God. relationship w/ God
God's gift - how to begin again.

INTRODUCTION

In the spring of 1987, I first set foot in the sanctuary of First United Methodist Church in Winter Park, Florida. I was there primarily at the insistence of my wife, Sara. She wanted to have a Christ-based marriage and to show our children an example of a Christian home. When I was a child, my family never attended church, so I had no real connection with any church, nor did I have any history of regular attendance at a church or spiritual guidance of any type.

As I look back to those early days attending church, I can clearly see the hand of God in my life had begun. Week after week, while seated in the pew alongside Sara, before the "big church" began, a "children's moment" leader would go to the front and beckon all the children to come forward. Five- through eight-year-olds would scamper from their seats up to the front and sit on the floor around the leader, each child eager to take in what the leader had to say.

The leader normally would have with him an everyday item he would use as a prop, from which he would drive home a scriptural point. The children would sit, their eyes wide open, digesting the story as it unfolded. Unbeknownst to the leader, sitting among the congregation was a thirty-seven-year-old "child," also with his eyes wide open, eagerly awaiting the telling of the story. The leader told the stories in a simplistic way, and not in an "in-your-face" manner, and I looked forward to the following Sunday and the next lesson. After church, I found myself going home and pulling out the Bible to study the Scripture passage he gave to the children during that five- to ten-minute time spent with God—a sermon that was given at MY level. As weeks turned into years, my appetite to learn more became insatiable. I actually found myself understanding the sermon given from the pulpit at "big church."

One day it occurred to me that at that point in their lives, those five-year-old children seated around their leader each Sunday had more Bible knowledge than this thirty-seven-year-old man did.

I wondered, What more will they know about God when they reach my age? I had wasted thirty-two years not growing spiritually, and I was literally looking up to see the bottom. So I decided it was time to get started. I did not have another second to waste. I had finally realized the gift God had given to me.

Twenty-five years later, I find myself still having that insatiable appetite to discover what God would have me do in my life. I may never truly know that answer. However, I do know that I will always remember that life-changing moment when God touched my heart. His touch came with the help of a child and a leader who took the time to speak to me at my level, though never knowing he was doing so. And now it is my turn to give back a small portion of what was first given to me.

I trust that these thirty-two simple chapters will give you new insight to "know [God] more clearly, love [Him] more dearly, follow [Him] more nearly, day by day," as the thirteenth-century English bishop Saint Richard of Chichester prayed, later adapted in the song "Day by Day" from the musical *Godspell.* After all, how we see God has a lot to do with how we experience life. So may you enjoy looking up with fresh eyes to see the bottom!

ACKNOWLEDGMENTS

It is with the utmost pleasure that I dedicate this book to and acknowledge the inspiration of Dr. Thomas Price Jr., my mentor, my minister, my counselor, and my friend of twenty-five years. Tom's guidance from the pulpit and from everyday realities has shown me that the Scriptures are as fresh and pertinent as this morning's newspaper. He has shown me how to take this austere Book—shrouded in a black cover, placed upon a shelf to gather dust—down off the shelf, dust it off, and begin to paint word pictures that a person can understand and to which a person can relate.

It is my prayer that God uses this book to His glory to provide you, the reader, with the clarity of Scripture that I have been blessed to witness through Dr. Price's teaching. Through the writings within this book, I have attempted to share with you the inspired wisdom of God's Servant that so many of us at First United Methodist Church have been blessed to receive.

Thank you, Tom.

Chapter 1

WHAT IS A CHURCH, ANYWAY?

In ancient times, the Greeks and Hebrews didn't look at things in the same way; there was a basic and fundamental difference.

The Greeks came out of the plush Aegean Islands and interpreted life in terms of FULFILLMENT. The Hebrews came out of the bleak Arabian Desert and interpreted life in terms of SURVIVAL.

  The Greeks were theoretical and developed philosophy;
  the Hebrews were pragmatic and developed faith.

   The Greeks thought abstractly and invented mathematics;
   the Hebrews thought concretely and invented history.

    The Greeks had lots of gods. You tried to be just like them.
    The Hebrews had only one God. You tried to get away from Him.

     The Greek gods gamboled on the green and sipped ambrosia;
     the Hebrew God thundered from the mountain or whispered in your ear.

The Greeks tended to be visual; they created sculptures.
The Hebrews tended to be audible; they told stories.

  Greeks produced art; Hebrews produced a chronicle.
  Greeks worried about universals; Hebrews worried about guilt.

   Greeks generalized; Hebrews particularized.
   Greeks created systems; Hebrews isolated instances.
    Greeks were speculative; Hebrews dealt with specifics.
    Greeks talked about mankind; Hebrews talked about this MAN, this . . . church.

Indeed, in ancient times, the Greeks and Hebrews didn't look at things in the same way, and Western civilization is essentially a blending of these two points of view.

Now, I say all this as a preface and as a justification for what follows. I'm not going to try to be a Greek, in the classic, theoretical, system-making sense. I just want to be a Hebrew and talk to you about particulars.

Today, many churches have new members classes, and the church where I worship and serve follows in this tradition. After their respective four weeks of introduction to the doctrine of the church, it accepts these people into the congregation. They'll become part of us . . .
full,
complete,
official members,
with all the rights, privileges, and responsibilities appertaining thereunto.

This process raises the question, "WHAT IS THIS CHURCH THEY'RE JOINING, ANYWAY?" What are they coming into? They'll make some vows and promise, as we all did when we joined, to uphold the church and support it, with their prayers,
their presence,
their gifts,
and their services.
But can we say what it is they're promising to uphold in this way? CHURCH? How do we define church?
Explain it?
Characterize it? What is it all about?

Well, to ask it that way, of course, is to ask it as a Greek. Maybe there would be some value in approaching it that way, in talking about THE church in the broad,
inclusive,
generic,
universal sense.
Hundreds of books have been written on that. I'm certain we all have some of them in our church library.

However, that's an awfully big, generalized statement. That covers a lot of ground, and frankly, I'm not sure I know enough to do it justice.

So instead, let me try to do something more modest, more Hebrew in nature. Rather than talk about THE church, I'd like just to talk about *a* church, one specific church I know. Maybe you'll be able to identify it as we go along. I will just share with you in a concrete, Hebrew way images of the way it seems to me.

What is a church? It's really a funny thing, as it's not easy to define, but it's not hard to point to.

First, and most obviously, it usually includes one or more buildings. In the case of the church I'm thinking about, it has especially beautiful, architecturally impressive buildings. Does that give it away? If you said your own particular church, you're right.

And you're also correct if you think a church is not a building, but a building helps *make* it a church, helps it to . . . *be* church. Winston Churchill used to say, "We shape our buildings, and afterward, our buildings shape us." I think that's an accurate description.

The buildings make a statement;
    they help create a climate—a climate of dignity, mystery, the beauty of holiness.

The way a congregation cares for its building says something about the faith of that congregation. Treating its property with respect suggests the congregation treats God with respect.

Now, you *could* be a church *without* a beautiful building. In fact, you could be a church without a building at all. But how blessed you are if you have one as a starting point. Somehow God seems more accessible, and faith, therefore, seems more possible.

Of course, there's more to a church than a building. If that's where you start, it's *only* where you start. What is a church? A church is a funny thing. It's MEMORIES . . . specific memories, particular memories, gathered and filtered through a community's experience. In a sense, a church is the sum total of all those memories.

In some cases, families in generation after generation have been coming to their respective churches. They have come to worship,
                to pray,
                  to lay down burdens,
                      to make commitments. Sometimes you can almost feel it.

What is a church? Take a whiff . . . or, better yet, listen carefully. Some of the echoes still reverberate.

A church is memories . . . of old, familiar hymns sung,
                  of Sunday school lessons studied,
               of friendships deepened,
                  and even of reminiscences started.

A church is recollections of ice cream socials,
                 of Easter lily decorations,
               of birthday celebrations,
                and of washing dishes after a fellowship dinner.

A church is recalling moments of real agony when nobody knew where the money would come from to pay that month's bills. But we somehow pulled together and pulled through. We learned and remembered what—and WHO—was important, WHY we were there.

A church is your remembering old friends who are no longer around,
 memories of support you received when you were low,
  and insight you received when you were perplexed.

What is a church? In part, it's memories . . . of learning,
                         of sharing,
                           of thinking,
                             of listening,
                               of committing,

of accepting,
of trusting.
A church is the accumulation of ALL these things.

But a church is more than that, isn't it? What is a church? A church is a funny thing. It's FAITH.

A church is believing some things enough to take a chance on them, enough to bet your life on them, even if you can't prove they're true.

A church is believing, however difficult it may be, that there is *not* chaos, meaninglessness, and disorder at the heart of things. Instead, there is a PURPOSE, conscious and incredibly kind, which genuinely seeks the welfare of Its created offspring.

A church is FAITH . . . even if you can't be sure.

A church is believing that the loudest is not necessarily the truest,
that what is most obvious is not necessarily what is most permanent,
that what is most materialistic is not necessarily what is most substantive,
that what is most glittering is not necessarily what is most real,
that greatness is not measured by possessions, but by . . . *service*.

A church is believing that there is meaning in life, in spite of its frequent contradictions,
that there is goodness in life, in spite of its frequent hardships,
that there is a beauty in life, in spite of its frequent ugliness,
that there is joy in life, in spite of its frequent sorrow.

What is a church? A church is a funny thing. It's DREAMS. It's a dream that little children can grow up anywhere, without having to fear abuse, or terror, or crippling disease, or gnawing hunger.

A church is a dream that human beings weren't meant to live fighting,
and hating,
and exploiting one another,
that they weren't created for that kind of insanity. A church is where the dream that "man's chief end is to glorify God and to enjoy him forever," as the Westminster Catechism puts it, is given expression.

Finally, we come to an answer to "What is a church?" A church is a funny thing, consisting of
buildings,
memories,
faith,
dreams . . . yes, all
that in a way, but most fundamentally, most basically, a church is PEOPLE—and it's a funny kind of thing.

Every other organization in the world prides itself on the quality of its personnel . . . but *not the church*. What is a church?

A church is a body of ordinary people called and claimed by an extraordinary TRUTH. That's the essence of it. A church is not made up of perfect people; it's made up of *surprised* people, people who know they are not worthy, but that somehow God has laid His hand on them.

A church is made up of people in transit,
>   in progress,
>   under development,
>   on the road . . . people going from where they used to

be to where they aren't yet but, by the grace of God, are being led.

A church is not an art gallery for the display of saints. Rather, a church is a workshop for the making of them. A church is not a beauty pageant but would be more accurately called a hospital. A church is not a showroom but an assembly line.

As such, membership in the church is not by qualification; it's by *desperation*. Those who need to belong most are not those who are best. Thinking you're best doesn't reveal aptitude, anyway; it only reveals misguidedness. Instead, those who need to belong most are those who simply recognize the need for God's further action in their lives. *THAT* IS THE QUALIFICATION.

What is a church? The answer is, exactly what it's always been—rich men, poor men, beggars, thieves, doctors, lawyers, sinners, the chief of sinners, as Paul put it so unforgettably, the unworthy, the unforgivable . . . MADE worthy and forgiven by the grace of God in Christ.

You see, the greatness of the church is not in its constituency, but in its Lord.

So what is a church? Well, it's not easy to grasp or define.

The church is a funny thing, isn't it?

Chapter 2

1.6.13

HOW CAN A BOOK
KNOW US SO WELL?

*They said to each other, "Come, let's make bricks and bake them thoroughly." They used brick instead of stone, and tar for mortar. Then they said, "**Come, let us build ourselves a city, with a tower that reaches to the heavens**, so that we may make a name for ourselves; otherwise we will be scattered over the face of the whole earth."*
Gen. 11:1-9 (emphasis added)

Suddenly a sound like the blowing of a violent wind came from heaven and filled the whole house where they were sitting. They saw what seemed to be tongues of fire that separated and came to rest on each of them. All of them were filled with the Holy Spirit and began to speak in other tongues as the Spirit enabled them.
Acts 2:2-4 (see also vv. 1, 5-6)

How can a Book know us so well? All this talk about failure to communicate, mix-ups in understanding, and confusion seems familiar today. If that isn't contemporary, what is? Sure sounds like the world I know. These two graphic stories from centuries ago and halfway around the world could almost have been written with any modern city in mind, couldn't they have? How *can* a Book know us so well?

As we would an anniversary or a birthday, in the church, we even set aside a day to celebrate Pentecost, the pouring out of God's Spirit on that little group of followers who were hanging around in the Upper Room, waiting . . . waiting for what God was going to do next.

And boy, did they get more than they bargained for. Mathematician and philosopher Alfred North Whitehead once characterized the development of Western philosophy as essentially a series of footnotes to Plato. In a similar sense, the whole subsequent course of Christian history is essentially commentary on that creative moment . . . that "birth" in the Upper Room back in the first century.

However, the Pentecost experience itself has a background, and it's that *other* story by its very contrast that helps us appreciate what happened in the Upper Room. Also, in an eerie kind of way, it evokes an image of the world right outside our doors.

For just a moment, let's go back to the Old Testament, to the book of Genesis, almost to the very beginning . . . Babel. Or maybe we should pronounce it "babble"—that brings it closer to home.

Now, walk through Orlando International Airport, and listen to the voices around you, or go to the local Publix or another grocery store, or Disney World, for that matter, and tell me the Bible doesn't know what it's talking about. The plain of Shinar could almost as well be Orange Avenue in downtown Orlando, with its noise, clatter, cacophony, different languages, and strange dialects. You can hear them all—Spanish, Vietnamese, Creole, South Georgia, and the lilt of Jamaican *patois*. Don't you love to hear it spoken?

And that's just close by, in Orlando. Go to Miami, and you'll see stores in Little Havana bearing signs that say "Se habla inglés"—ENGLISH SPOKEN HERE. Imagine that, in the United States of America!

You'll see the same thing in New York, Chicago, Los Angeles, and nearly every other big city. It's a modern Babel. And although language is perhaps the best symbol of it, it's more than language.

People from everywhere—the "new immigrants," as *Time* magazine once called them—from all kinds of backgrounds are going in all kinds of directions with all their various needs,

and problems,
and hopes,
and dreams,

and aspirations. And they're all trying to "make it," trying to carve out a place, trying to (may I be so bold?) build a tower of fulfillment and security . . . BABEL.

The symbolism penetrates more cuttingly than that. The biblical scholars tell us, and our hearts confirm, that the point of this primitive Hebrew story—influenced, no doubt, by their association with Babylon (Babel/Babylon); even the tower reflects Babylonian architecture, those ziggurats we used to study about in world history class—is to illustrate vividly the futility of life apart from God.

"Come, let us build ourselves a city, with a tower that reaches to the heavens, so that we may make a name for ourselves," the text reads. Boy, that hurts. There WE are. How *can* a Book know us so well?

Being arrogant enough to think you can do it all on your own,
　being arrogant enough to think you yourself have the resources for a full and complete life,
　　being arrogant enough to think you don't need anything . . . beyond *you*,
　　　priding yourself on your self-sufficiency,
　　　　leaning only on yourself,
　　　　　living just for yourself . . . that's Babel, and the inevitable consequence is chaos and confusion.

Is Babel ancient history only? As Rev. Gary Rideout asks, "ARE YOU KIDDING ME?" Just look around.

Babel means meaninglessness and purposelessness. It means no real direction, no point. It means emptiness, disorientation, whirl, abrasiveness, and discord. In family life, Babel means backbiting, nagging, quarreling, and rivalry. In race relationships, Babel means name-calling and put-downs. It still escalates into violence sometimes.

So is Babel ancient history? On the contrary, it's as contemporary as this morning's newspaper. "Come, let us build ourselves a city, with a tower that reaches to the heavens, so that we may make a name for ourselves…" I tell you, if you don't like looking into a mirror, you better not read the Bible; you better just stay away from it.

How *can* a Book know us so well?

Now, Pentecost is another matter. That's another side of the picture entirely. If Babel is what happens when a person tries to run alone, Pentecost is what happens when God is given a chance to play.

Pentecost is to Babel what a skilled farmer is to an unplowed field,
  what Michelangelo was to a piece of rough marble,
    what Julia Child was to an uncooked soufflé,
      what Robert E. Lee was to Joseph Hooker at the Battle of Chancellorsville.

Pentecost is the solution, Babel is the problem.

If Babel represents the dead end of the purely human, Pentecost represents the open-ended limitlessness of the Divine. If Babel represents the futility of self-sufficiency, Pentecost represents the prodigality of GRACE.

Babel says the height of stupidity is the illusion that you can make it on your own.

Pentecost says, *Thank God I don't have to make it on my own.* It says YOU DON'T HAVE TO PROVE ANYTHING. You couldn't do it, anyway.

There is POWER AND MEANING BEYOND OUR WILDEST IMAGINING . . . and here it is, with the compliments of the Creator.

Well, there are the two stories, the two contrasting and wonderfully complementary lessons we store away so we can extract during some more propitious time. They're equally brilliantly told and powerfully penetrating.

I'll be quick to say I don't even begin to understand all the details of the account as recorded by Dr. Luke in the book of Acts. Frankly, many parts of it baffle me. While wind and fire are used over and over in the Bible to symbolize God's presence and power, I'm enough of a modernist to have my doubts that if we had been there that day physically, in the flesh, we would have seen literal tongues of flame or heard a literal wind blowing through the room. This is religious, not meteorological, language. If Willard Scott had been there, I doubt he would have been able to measure the wind velocity.

If there had been a video camera set up in the room to record the scene, I doubt if it would have picked up anything beyond the norm physically. But I say to you, WHAT DIFFERENCE DOES IT MAKE? We're not talking about natural phenomena; we're talking about experience. What I do understand and think is at the heart of the matter is SOMETHING HAPPENED to those people to turn them on and turn them around—something real and vital. They had an experience. Try to explain it or explain it away, if you like, but that's the bottom line.

They came alive.
 They were changed.
  They were empowered.
   They experienced a Reality that virtually defies description.

It was Babel in reverse. Beyond Dr. Luke's own words, I don't have words for it. How better to describe it than with words like "wind" and "fire"? They were swept up in it and transformed. They were seared by its intensity.

They didn't manufacture the experience. It was something that came to them. They called it the Holy "Pneuma," the Holy "Breath," the Holy Spirit. They weren't the instigators of it; they were observers of it. They didn't produce it; they received it. BUT *THEY* HAD TO SET THE STAGE FOR IT.

After all, it was Ignatius of Loyola who said: "You can never find God by looking for Him. But God rarely finds those who aren't looking for Him." The record in Acts makes it clear as a bell that those people that day were expecting something special to take place.

They had been told to wait for it.
 They had elected another disciple to replace Judas so the circle was complete again.
  They were ready for whatever God was ready to give them.

Can this Pentecost moment still happen, or was it a one-shot deal? How clear it is in the account given in the Scripture text. Who is left out of the Pentecost experience? *NOBODY* . . . WHO WANTS TO BE INCLUDED.

EVERYONE! ANYBODY!

Chapter 3

THE NEED FOR PERSPECTIVE

Lot lifted up his eyes, and saw . . . the . . . valley . . . .
Gen. 13:10 RSV (see also vv. 1-9, 11-13)

Can you imagine? I mean, can you just *IMAGINE?* Could whoever is responsible for the wording have meant that? Could he have known what he was saying? Could he have written it that way on purpose? It's almost too good to be true.

Do you remember this old story? It's in early Genesis. It's early antiquity, early primitive. It goes back to an agrarian setting, a nomadic setting, where almost nothing was more important than good, fertile pasture land.

Back then, Abraham and Lot, uncle and nephew, respectively, were the protagonists. Both of them were men of influence and power. They were important men, prestigious men, wealthy men—at least by the standards of that day. Despite the kinship, despite the close blood relationship, one of the strongest forces in the ancient world, there was trouble in Happy Valley.

The servants of these two men, their underlings, their hired hands, began to squabble amongst themselves. Just like in the Old West, range war was imminent. Abraham knew something had to be done quickly.

So in a magnanimous gesture, a gracious act of high-mindedness, he went to Lot and made him an offer he couldn't refuse. "We'll divide the land between us," he said. "I'll take half, and you take half, and you can have first choice." With this offer, Abraham showed nobility of character, generosity of the first order.

"Take your choice," Abraham said unselfishly, motioning with a broad, inclusive wave of his hand. "Take whatever you like. Pick the area you want, and my entourage and I will go elsewhere so our people can get along in harmony."

Now, the King James Version also states: "Lot lifted up his eyes . . . ." At the time, he was standing on the PINNACLE OF THE HILL, for heaven's sake, way up there, and he "lifted UP his eyes and beheld" the valley . . . way DOWN there. That's not lifting up his eyes very high.

Frankly, I don't know whether it's translated accurately. In the more modern versions, unfortunately, the distinction is not as sharply etched as here. But, I think you would agree, you can't expect a writer to let a little thing like accuracy spoil a good insight.

It's about the need for perspective, the need for seeing things from the long-range view. Lot didn't, and it cost him in the end. HE DIDN'T LOOK FAR ENOUGH, and it cost him terribly. He didn't raise his eyes high enough until, before he knew it, it was too late.

It's a mistake to be so shortsighted that you see value only in what glitters. That's what this story is suggesting. What looks like a bargain at first may *not* be after it hangs around for a while. And in Lot's case, it wasn't.

He thought he had made a smart move, of course.
  He thought he had pulled a real shrewdie.
    He thought he had used his head. HOW COULD HE MISS?

The valley was where it was *at*, as they say today. He saw his chance, and he grabbed it. After all, the entire valley was the fertile part of the land.

The valley was pasture and prosperity;
  the valley was water and wealth;
    the valley was the comfortable place to live. And that was just it.

It was opportunity and bargain;
  it was luxuriant and plush;
    it was soft and easy;
      it was opulent and seductive . . . for it was where the WICKED CITY OF SODOM was located.

Lot didn't think about that; he didn't lift his eyes that high. He got more than he bargained for when he chose to settle in the valley. The perspective makes it plain. He got an environment that almost immediately began to poison what was best and finest in his family life. He moved into an atmosphere that was rotten to the core.

Ideals that formerly were cherished and protected,
  standards that previously were honored and lived by . . .
    ALL OF IT WILTED . . . SUCCUMBED TO THE EROSION OF BAD INFLUENCE.

And it didn't take long. It was only a short time before the filth and sordidness of the city polluted even his closest relationship—that with his own family.

It's not a pretty picture. You can explore the details for yourself, if you have a stomach for it. Not only is it not pretty, but it doesn't have a happy ending. The Bible is a very honest Book. Lot's shortsightedness was enormously expensive.

Oh, he got out himself. He got out with his life . . . barely. But everything else—
all those herds,
  all those flocks,

all those possessions,
 all that money,
   even his wife, finally GONE in one cataclysmic convulsion.

Do you suppose that, in old age, in retrospect, at the end of his life, he ever thought back to the beginning of it? Do you suppose he ever thought back to the day he stood with Abraham on that mountainside and "lifted up his eyes, and saw . . . the . . . valley"? He must have. Surely, he must have wished over and over he'd taken a broader perspective.

Now, there's got to be another side of this story. There just has to be. After all, THERE ARE TIMES WHEN YOU HAVE TO RESPOND TO OPPORTUNITY OR BE LEFT BEHIND. The lesson of Lot is not the folly of responding to opportunity. The lesson of Lot is the folly of responding on the basis of a limited and narrow vision.

But then, aren't a lot of us guilty of it, too? Someone has called it "the cult of instant gratification." We're so obsessed with the immediate . . . in everything, from values to Valium. We can't wait. The lottery appeals to it. Advertising, such as that of Nike, plays to it, sometimes shamelessly.

While perhaps some things come immediately, most of the experiences that really count probably don't. In our hearts, we know that. Abraham knew it. And Lot, I hope, finally did.

The short range can be a chimera.
 The valley is likely to be a mirage.
   The lessons we treasure most,
     the experiences that afford us the deepest satisfaction, rarely happen instantaneously. They may be free, but they're not cheap.

This text from Genesis, this old story of Lot's lifting up his limited gaze on the side of the mountain, has an uncanny pertinence, doesn't it?

As parents and grandparents, we believe in the importance of possessing and passing along our Christian heritage to our children and grandchildren because we believe not only in the church of today, but also in the church of tomorrow.

It's part of our Old Testament heritage, part of what we've received out of our Jewish background. And it continues into Christianity. As Dr. Thomas Price Jr., in a sermon at First United Methodist Church in Winter Park, Florida, once said, "The Christian has a moral obligation . . . to be as intelligent and as well-trained as he or she can be, just as surely as he or she has a moral obligation to be as good as he or she can be."

If we could only see far enough,
 if we could get to the top of that mountain and lift up our eyes high enough,
   if only we could see the need for perspective in our own lives . . .

Chapter 4

A GROANIN' IN
THE DESERT

*"Why do you find fault with me? Why do you put the L*ORD *to the proof?" But the people thirsted there for water, and the people murmured against Moses.*
Exod. 17:2-3 RSV (see also vv. 1, 4-7)

In a long, convoluted story, the Bible tells about God's
 yearning for,
  searching for,
   reaching out for,
    and finally coming down for His wayward children to bring them home.

It's the great rescue story of all time. It begins with Abram way down there in the city of Ur, in the Chaldeans. There he is just standing around, minding his own business, and then the story moves forward through fits and starts,
                up hills and down,
                    through valleys of mindless ignorance and bitter opposition, until at the right time—"the fullness of time," as Paul called it—God directs it to the top of a hill where He plants a cross so mesmerizing the world can't get it out of its mind.

Along the way of this winding, twisting plot line, between Ur and Golgotha, we see events that, in retrospect, make the story, which is now OUR STORY, more meaningful.

Go back thirty-five hundred years, more or less, and go halfway around the world and out into the desert. See a motley, ragtag band of pilgrims trudging through the sand. These are not your everyday, singing-and-whistling-as-they-go happy campers.

Gripe, gripe, gripe! That's all you hear out of them. As they inch their way ponderously and painfully along, all you hear is gripe, gripe, gripe! Talk about nonstop bellyaching. I don't know how Moses took it, continual griping, for forty years . . .
no letup,
 no break,
  no cessation of complaining. It sure seems that way when you read through the narrative.

If we were there, it wouldn't take long for some of us to appoint a Complaint Department and point all those "murmurers" toward it. *WAY-Y-Y* back at the end of the line, surely they would forget what they were complaining about when they waded through more than 2 million people to get there.

From the land of Egypt to the Promised Land,
  from the Red Sea to the Jordan River,
    from the time they left Pharaoh stuck in the mud to the time they finally set foot on dry land in Canaan, with a whole new generation, about the only thing heard out of the troops was an incessant barrage of bickering.

The wonderfully graphic word in the Revised Standard Version that some translations, unfortunately, dilute to the point of insipidness is "murmured." Isn't that a great word in that setting? *MURMURED!*

What vivid images it conjures up. Can't you just imagine those sweaty, dusty wanderers out under the beating sun, skulking around among the sand dunes,
                    leaning over to one another,
  whispering behind cupped hands at the sides of their mouths
    and confiding in conspiratorial tones . . . murmuring.

It's an unforgettable image, and all the more so because it's so . . . *HUMAN*. How easily it translates across the centuries.

For instance, it doesn't take much to bring out the complaint in people. Matthew Arnold, a great nineteenth-century English poet, had a well-deserved reputation for being demonstrably querulous in manner and conduct, what my wife, Sara, would call just an out-and-out ol' poophead. Though he was a genius, he was a notorious complainer. When he died, someone said, "Poor Matthew; he won't like God."

Haven't we all known people like that—chronic complainers? Doesn't it do something to your soul when they get their comeuppances?

Once three women arrived at the Pearly Gates at the same time. Saint Peter came out to meet them, but said he had some pressing business to attend to and asked if they would mind waiting until he could begin their processing.

All three agreed to wait. He was gone for a long time but finally returned, called one of the women in, and asked her if it had bothered her to wait. "Oh, no," she said. "I've looked forward to this for so long. I love the Lord and want to praise Him face to face. I don't mind a little wait." Peter said, "Well, I have one more question: How do you spell 'GOD'?" She said, "Capital G-o-d." "Good," said Saint Peter. "Go on in."

He invited the second woman in and asked her, "Did you mind waiting?" She said: "No, I didn't mind. I've been a Christian for fifty years, and I'll spend eternity here. I didn't mind at all." So Saint Peter said, "Just one more thing: How do you spell 'GOD'?" She said, "g-o-d . . . I mean, capital G-o-d." Saint Peter said that was fine and sent her on in.

Then he brought the third woman in and asked her if she minded waiting. (I don't think this was Mrs. Matthew Arnold; I don't even know if there *was* a Mrs. Matthew Arnold.) Anyway, she said, "Yes, I minded waiting. I've had to stand in line all my life—when I went to the supermarket, when I went to school, when I registered to vote, when I went to the movies . . . EVERYWHERE I WENT, and I resent having to wait in line for heaven."

Saint Peter said gently: "Well, I understand. It's all right for you to feel that way. It won't be held against you. But there's just one more question: How do you spell Czechoslovakia?"

Griping, as a human characteristic, is ubiquitous . . . and there's a lot of it. Elected officials certainly know it. Every day, they face the onslaught of citizen complaints . . . "What are you going to do about those noisy boom boxes?" "What are you doing about those boys wearing their pants down around their knees?"

As well, journalists know complaints . . . "Why can't newspapers be objective?" "The news on TV is about violence and crime. If it weren't for the left-leaning or the right-leaning press, we wouldn't be in the mess we're in."

Recently, I read about a destitute newspaper editor who died after a long illness. The staff members took up a collection for his funeral. One of them approached a man on the street and said, "Could you give me five dollars to bury an editor?" The man pulled out a twenty-dollar bill and said, "Here, bury four of them."

Moses wouldn't have been surprised by any of it. If he were transplanted from his century to ours, he'd feel right at home, at least in that respect. For forty years, he put up with a relentless outpouring of grumbling. Is there anything new under the sun? Now, admittedly, their complaint here was not over a trivial matter. What was at stake was nothing less than SURVIVAL.

They were thirsty out there. Their lips were getting parched;
                              their throats were dry;
                                     the insides of their mouths were beginning to taste like cotton.
Where could they have gone? They were caught in their sandy, miserable hole. IT GOT TO THEM.

And they looked at the severe, bone-dry terrain that surrounded them, realizing they were miles from their old base of operations back in Egypt and even farther from a destination—this so-called Promised Land, which, for all they knew, may have had no more substance than the shimmering mirages they saw on the horizon. The only *real* thing they knew at that moment was that deep-throated thirst.

"Who's responsible for our being out in these scorching sands?" they murmured, fixing their gaze upon Moses. There he was, right in their crosshairs. "He's the one who has done this to us. There's the culprit." They continued to murmur.

"Maybe it wasn't ideal in Egypt;
  maybe it was cruel and harsh;
    maybe we were slaves there, but at least we had a sip of water when we craved it. At least we could moisten our lips once in a while at the water cooler."

"How much longer can we go on this way? You brought us here, Mr. Big Shot Moses. It's all your fault. Did you drag us away from the flesh pots of Egypt so our children and we could die of thirst?"

Frankly, I don't know how the ol' boy took it. He almost didn't! In fact, I think he came close to cashing it in right then. RIGHT THEN may have been the absolute lowest point of the entire forty-year span. Moses very nearly lost it. He was on the verge of breaking . . . on the brink.

He had just about had it!

The words come to us across the centuries, but even from this distance in time, as you read them, you can almost hear his voice crack. The Record says he cried out to God—CRIED OUT, "What shall I do with these people? They are almost ready to stone me!"

Was it his own personal safety he was frantic about—
  this man who had faced down Pharaoh just a few weeks earlier,
    this man who had stood eyeball to eyeball with the most powerful earthly figure of that era?
Was that it? Surely it would have taken more than a few hundred grumbling Hebrew itinerants to intimidate a man of that intensity.

No, that was not *it;* there was something more ominous than a personal threat. The people's bickering sent a shiver like a knife wound through Moses' heart, for he saw the bickering for *exactly* what it was:
                betrayal,
                  faithlessness . . . not just toward him, as a leader, but toward GOD HIMSELF.
No wonder he cried out in anguish; no wonder he exploded.

Like any other time in human history, this grumbling represented the problem behind the problem, the deeper dimension of the situation. It wasn't just about the water; it never is. That was serious enough, but even more serious, and more deadly, was the people's refusal to trust God. That's what *really* hurt.

So the grumbling,
  the griping,
    the murmuring over water revealed an underlying sabotage of loyalty.

Moses knew that God wasn't going to abandon them now. He knew that God would take care of the water problem, just as He had taken care of the Red Sea problem, the Egyptian Army problem, and the hunger problem when He sent the manna. Gracious me, didn't they remember? They were there, for heaven's sake!

Had they so quickly forgotten the deliverance from bondage,
  the march out of tyranny,
    the sweet smell of freedom? Hadn't they been with this Deliverer, God, long enough to know He hadn't brought them all this way to let them end up as a pile of sun-bleached bones at the base of a sand dune? THEY WERE GOD'S PEOPLE, ON THEIR WAY TO THE PROMISED LAND. Didn't they realize it?

No, I don't think Moses was afraid for his own skin. He was a bigger man than that. I think his frustration was over the people's refusal to trust God's capability and readiness to lead them out of an apparently hopeless situation.

Now, we need to be fair here. We shouldn't be overly hard on the people, and we certainly are in no moral position to be smug. We should ask ourselves, *If I had been where they were, would I have acted more maturely?* Of course, I've never been in precisely that predicament, but I can look back with considerable embarrassment on occasions when, to say the least, I established no great record of faithfulness in the face of extremity.

I wonder how many times I have given away my last, or even next-to-last, coat to someone in need, trusting that God would see that I was provided for when the next cold snap came.

I wonder how many times I've gone to the mat for some worthy, but unpopular, cause without calculating what it might do to my image.

I wonder how many times I've completely turned a situation over to God without first checking for a backdoor escape route, just in case. I'm afraid it wouldn't take too long to count those times.

It's a lot easier to be good-natured with full canteens and a shady oasis in plain view. Still, Moses was basically right. Give him a "D" for patience, if you want to, and a "D-" for composure.

But if you do, then you have to give him an "A" for FAITH. THE MAN TRUSTED GOD . . . *really* trusted Him. He didn't know *how* the problem would be solved, but he knew God well enough to be certain it would be. AND HE WAS RIGHT.

Let's take a moment to look at how this Old Testament story of this group of ragtag,
> murmuring,
> exhausted,
> thirsty,
> discouraged,
> broken-down people at the end of their resources,

with no likely prospect of being delivered from their dilemma relates to the great passion narrative that stands at the center of the Christian story.

Of course, it hits you, doesn't it? What the ragtag, murmuring Hebrews thought about their prospect for triumph in the desolate desert was exactly what the followers of Jesus thought about theirs when they watched the Roman soldiers shove their Master up the hill carrying a cross on His back.

It was the end of the world . . . they thought. *After all we've been through, is it to wind up like this?* It sure looked that way. How much would you have bet on God,
> and goodness,
> and righteousness

about three o'clock that Friday afternoon?

But they were wrong. Just as the sagging gloom of the wilderness murmurers was turned to relief and joy by the gushing forth of fresh water from a rock, so the cold, pallid darkness of Good Friday was turned into the most glorious sunrise this old world has ever seen.

The threshold of authentic religion is at the point where the thirsty soul stands before the barren rock and refuses to believe that what is impossible *has* to be.

There are always going to be dry, desolate deserts and gloomy, steep hill moments in life, and grumbling may be awfully easy to do. But the God who *called* and *leads* His people is always faithful. Beyond all those moments, there is water . . . and there is LIFE.

In Heb. 11:1, we read, "Faith is being sure of what we hope for and certain of what we do not see." So in the face of adversity, we must patiently stand with the barren rock at our feet and await the cool, refreshing water that God will bring forth . . . with certainty.

Chapter 5

WHEN GOD DRAWS NEAR

The life of the flesh is in the blood; and I have given it to you for making atonement for your lives on the altar; for, as life, it is the blood that makes atonement.
Lev. 17:11 NRSV

There must be an Advent story in here, lurking around, if we can break it loose and polish it up. I admit, it's not the usual emphasis we think of when we think of an Advent theme. It's not the traditional interpretation. Still, it's part of the picture and maybe, in a sense, the foundation for all the rest.

Hope is the operative word for the day, but we need to be careful when we talk about hope. In Christian parlance, hope is a special kind of thing.
> It's never fluffy optimism
> or idle pipe dreams
> or castles-in-the-air wistfulness.

THAT'S NOT CHRISTIAN HOPE.

Christian hope is a red-blooded confidence that emanates out of open-eyed realism. It's an assurance with a spine, a bare-knuckled kind of belief. It's a faith that has faced the worst, frankly and honestly, and still believes the best. *That's* Christian hope.

If we're not careful, we can gloss over the fullness of it in Advent simply because we already know how the story turns out.

Probably the most misguided approach to Advent we can assume is the sugarcoated approach, and it's so easy to do. To see it simply as sentimental and sweetness, as pastel preparation for a pious prelude for the pure, innocent Babe who never grows up, I think, is the worst mistake we can make.

Once I heard a minister preach an Advent sermon titled "The Trouble With Kittens." You have to know that he's an old huntin' dog man and never one to get emotional over the positive attributes of felines, but he had a point. As a text, he used an Ogden Nash couplet:

The trouble with a kitten is that
Eventually it becomes a cat.

AND THE PARALLEL STINGS. The Kitten of Bethlehem became the Tiger of Jerusalem. Why else do you think they would have bothered to crucify Him? The Advent that prepares us only for manger tranquility is more distortion than revelation.

The word *ADVENT*, of course, means "the coming"; "the coming to." In Latin, it's *adventus*. Our word *adventure* comes from the same root. It's a strong, muscular word, not a bit syrupy. The connotation is one of excitement, tinged with hazard,
                danger,
                and a racing, beating pulse.

And NO WONDER! The coming of God to His world, the divine condescension, the purposeful restraint of unlimited power to share the common life with His people—WHAT CAN YOU CALL THAT BUT ADVENTURE?

We need to see it in its entirety . . . the big picture. He came to redeem us, but before we can claim the gracious acceptance of the forgiving God, the God who removes sin as far as the East is from the West, we must see Him first as THE GOD TO WHOM THAT SIN IS LOATHSOME. That's the ruthless honesty of Advent.

Before we can bask in the warmth of His mercy, we must be seared by the heat of His justice.
  Before we can know Him as Savior, we must know Him as Judge.
  Before we can know Him as Friend, we must know Him as Enemy.

When this God of whom we sing so glibly, "O come, O come, Emmanuel"—how easily the words form on our lips—draws near, what is it like to have Him around? What would it really be like suddenly to have Him on our hands . . . Kitten or Tiger?

I think a clue can be found in the Scripture title in the book of Leviticus chapter 17. It's an early Old Testament story and, quite frankly, a crude,
                primitive,
                militaristic,
                unsophisticated story that comes out
of a time when religion was shaped by geography and one's concept of God was narrowly nationalistic. There's a lot of that in early Old Testament stories.

Don't let it fool you, though. Don't let its rustic nature keep you from catching its truth. HAVING GOD AROUND IS NOT ALWAYS A COMFORTABLE EXPERIENCE.

Let's take a trip back in time for a moment, to the setting of Samuel. This is post-conquest and pre-monarchy. The days of the judges are over, but there is still no king.

As usual, the Hebrews and the Philistines are fighting. They were always fighting in those days. It was sort of an ancient Semitic Hatfields-McCoys relationship,
                or Buckeyes-Wolverines,
                or Orlando Magic-Miami Heat. They were constantly at it.

Sometimes it went one way; sometimes, another.

But this time, doom descended. The Philistines crashed through with unstoppable force. There's a rout of the Hebrew army, almost an annihilation. Dead bodies were everywhere. Survivors were fleeing to the rear. Hophni and Phinehas, the two wicked sons of Eli, the high priest, were slain on the battlefield, and the ark of the covenant, the most sacred, most precious possession of the Hebrews, was captured by the enemy. The ark represented nothing less than the presence of Almighty God in their midst. They had taken it out on the battlefield, thinking it would assure victory.

Nothing worse than that could even have been conceived. The Philistines, cruel and barbaric, hauled it off as booty into captivity. It was the absolute end of the world for God's chosen people, and the Philistines chortled in their joy.

But then came the comic part—that is, if you consider comeuppance comic,
    if you like banana peels and pratfalls,
       depending on your perspective. No sooner did the caravan bearing the ark get to Ashdod than the trouble began. Their chortling turned into choking.

They placed the ark in the Temple of Ashdod, the temple of Dagon, their god. They placed it in a subservient position, at the feet of Dagon, where their own deity could gloat over the glorious victory. But the next morning when the priests came in to check things out, they found the statue of Dagon smashed to smithereens. In the night, it had toppled to the floor and lay broken in pieces before the ark. What kind of manners is this for a guest?

And that's just for starters. Next, a plague broke out, and half the people in town had boils erupt all over their bodies. Then, there were the rats! It's that Hebrew God. They're sure HE'S to blame.

The politicians, the clergymen, the Health Department, the academics, the courthouse crowd, and I suppose even the members of the Chamber of Commerce were so frightened and terrified by this strange thing they had brought to town that they shipped the ark off to Gath just to get it out of their hair.

But the identical phenomenon repeated itself in Gath, so those city fathers sent it to Ekron. And round and round it went. It happened three times: from Ashdod to Gath to Ekron. It almost sounds like a double-play in baseball: Tinker to Evers to Chance.

Everybody passed it to somebody else.
 Nobody wanted it.
  And nobody knew what to do with it.

"What *can* we do with this thing?" they said. "It's too hot to handle. We don't want this Hebrew God hanging around here, shattering the security of our communal life. It's almost the height of the vacation season. No one will come visit if they find out there's a great white in the lagoon. GET HIM OUT OF HERE."

Finally, in chastened desperation, they put the ark on a cart pulled by two cows, pointed it back in the direction of Shiloh, and turned it loose across the mountains for the Hebrews to retrieve.

Of course, it's an unsophisticated story. I know it's bristling with crudities and improbabilities. But we don't have a corresponding Philistine account to give us a more balanced picture.

But really, do you laugh, or do you cry? Is it simply funny, or is it somehow, at the same time, painfully real? Transpose it, modernize it a bit, and what do we have? Each one of us has to look deep inside and see if there is something in our own lives that would be reduced to shambles in the presence of the REAL God if He were suddenly in our midst. Then again, maybe He's already here.

Are there actions,
       or attitudes,
           or thoughts that wouldn't stand up very well under His relentless scrutiny? It's an Advent theme we'd do well not to gloss over.

A Lutheran church in Denmark, I am told, is notable principally because it houses a statue of Christ that the famous artist Bertel Thorvaldsen carved from wood. The size of the statue is larger than life. This statue of Christ stands at the front of the sanctuary, just off center, inside the chancel rail, His head bowed and arms upraised in blessing.

His bowed head and lifted arms hide His face; you can't see the face of Christ from the front. You can't see it from the side. Even if you walk all around the statue, you can't see His face from any point.

There is only one perspective, one place in the church from which you can see Christ's face. To see the face of Christ in Thorvaldsen's representation, you must kneel at His feet and look up. People say there is something palpably gripping about doing that. Maybe it's partly the position you must be in, but it's more than that, they say.

It's the eyes. Through inspiration and his own genius, the artist has rendered them so they seem, virtually, to look right through you. They are not unkind; they are not cold. But there is an austerity, a dignity, an otherness, an unmistakable sense of moral purity that penetrates your very being and shames the dinginess of your soul. You'd better not look up into those eyes, they say, if you want to hold on to your old way of life.

Simon Peter knew what those eyes of Christ could do to a person. That night in the courtyard, after the betrayal, right after he had vigorously denied even being acquainted with Jesus—the pressure of public opinion will make you do strange things—Matthew reports that the old rooster crowed, and the hollowness of Simon Peter's previous boast hit him. They then led the Lord past to the next stage of trumped-up justice. As He went by, Jesus looked at him . . . that's all, He just *looked* at him.

Peter must have carried to his grave the recollection of that gaze that pierced his heart. It's the transcendence we so often miss in our religious life, even in spiritual matters; familiarity can breed a kind of contempt.

We can become chummy with God. We can think of Him almost as a kind of celestial Grandfather...

avuncular and pudgy,
  doting and good-natured,
    Someone we can manipulate and control.

However, God is not any of these things. God is GOD—that's the biblical understanding—holy and almighty. And to have any type of relationship with Him, we must begin by acknowledging that basic fact.

Jacob would never have gotten a new name,
  and a new future,
    and a reconciliation with the brother he had grievously wronged if he had not first wrestled on the riverbank all that night with his unrelenting conscience.

Paul could never have written that rhapsody of love, which almost sings off the pages of his Corinthian letter, if he hadn't first had to fight the battle of his unworthiness in contrast to the purity of what God had called him to be. He says in Romans 7:24, "O wretched man that I am! Who shall deliver me . . . ?" (KJV).

The best way to sum up the nearness of God to His creation—what distinguishes Creator from creation, what unites them—is the miracle that this God who made us, this God who formed us out of the dust and breathed the Breath of His own life into us, this God who is so far above us that we can only begin to catch a glimpse of the outskirts of His ways, this God whom we dare not presume to whittle down to manageable size, has deigned, as it were, to whittle Himself down to manageable size and come to us in terms we can touch.

In the process, He has not diluted His transcendence. He is still the King of Glory. We are not off the hook with respect to moral demand. We are still accountable, still responsible, still subject to an unremitting standard.

But now there is a new element in the story, a new twist in the plot that the divine Dramatist has added. We are not *all by ourselves* in the time of evaluation. God Himself has come to be with us, and His Son is standing by our side. Yes, GOD HAS DRAWN NEAR!

Chapter 6

WHEN TROUBLE COMES

For my sighing comes like my bread, and my groanings are poured out like water. Truly the thing that I fear comes upon me, and what I dread befalls me. I am not at ease, nor am I quiet; I have no rest; but trouble comes.
Job 3:24-26 NRSV

Have you ever asked it, that imposing question? We probably all have.

Why?

Why me?

Why now? Have you ever asked it? Why do certain things happen in life that seem so unfair, so wrong, so nonsensical?

Every one of us could give examples, most of us, from our own experience. Somewhere along the line, you probably have said something like this: "What have I done to deserve this kind of treatment from God?" "Why did this have to happen to us, to our family?" "WHY DID THIS HAPPEN TO ME?"

If we are honest, we'll admit a whole lot of things that happen in the world don't seem fair. I don't believe you can escape that conclusion. Even the most believing Christian is tempted to wonder sometimes if God is really doing His job the way He ought to do it, the way WE THINK He should do it. I mean, how do you justify much that happens? If you believe in God and believe He's moral, you may wonder, *Couldn't He at least be kind to the people who love and support Him and save His wrath for the bad guys, those who deserve it?* Wouldn't that make the cultivation of faith a lot easier?

Someone has said if we could only set up a hospital somewhere and work it so the people in one wing were prayed for and the people in another wing were not prayed for—with no sneak praying allowed—and then show demonstrably and scientifically that the patients in the first wing got better and the patients in the other wing didn't. THAT WOULD BE A POWERFUL BOOST FOR EVANGELISM.

But in the real world, it doesn't work that neatly. In fact, it almost seems to be the opposite. The very worst people often seem to get away with murder, sometimes literally, and the bitterest kinds of suffering—cancer, an automobile accident, the suicide of a family member, and the tragic death of an infant or child—often seem to descend like a flood on the very ones who deserve it least.

Why? How do you explain it? How *can* you explain it? Is there a meaning behind it? Any kind of rationale? How can God, such as Jesus talked about, permit such things to happen? Isn't He powerful enough to prevent them? Or doesn't He care?

At the risk of copping out, I have to say, quite frankly, that I don't know why everything that happens in the world happens. How arrogant I would be even to suggest I do. I simply don't know why.

In his novel *The Plague,* Albert Camus wrote about a medical doctor in Algiers who worked tirelessly and futilely against an absurd situation, an outbreak of bubonic plague, for which there is no higher explanation; it's just a biological reality. The doctor finally lost his own life in the struggle, but before his death, he said: "Don't try to find a meaning in suffering. Just fight against it."

Sometimes it seems that's all we can say. The truth is, no one has ever given a satisfactory answer to the question "Why is there human suffering?" Jesus didn't,
                              Paul couldn't,
                                    and no one else has been able to.

Of course, some suffering we can understand. Sometimes we bring it on ourselves by disregarding moral and physical laws. Sometimes others bring it on us. Even if we don't like it, we comprehend that kind of suffering.

Regardless, it's important that we, as Christians, remember this: Even though it cannot give a reason for suffering, and has never claimed to be able to, the Christian faith does have some extremely important things to say to those who do suffer. Christian resources are available not to solve our suffering problem but to give us strength and support in the midst of our suffering. Maybe that's even better.

Even though we cannot always understand why there is suffering, we can know that God does not intend for us to suffer. Now, that's not to say, as in the case of Job, He doesn't permit suffering, but He doesn't intend for us to suffer. What God permits or allows through His own self-limitation in giving us freedom and what He intentionally wants for us are not necessarily the same.

I cannot agree with those who say suffering is not really bad but is a blessing in disguise. Maybe you remember this old limerick:

There once was a man from Deal
Who said although pain is not real,
When I pick up a pin
and puncture my skin,
I dislike what I fancy I feel.

In the Old and New testaments, pain and suffering are very real, and they are realities to be opposed. The doctor Camus wrote about was right about that. When we read the Gospels, we see that Jesus is always pictured as doing everything in His power to relieve suffering.

Now, I apologize for being so theological here, but I think there's comfort to be found in this. If I know my suffering is not God's purpose for me, not His intention,
    if I know that God is on my side, not against me, then I have a basis for coping when calamity comes my way.

Knowing that God cares, that He is concerned about our suffering, is a TREMENDOUS HELP IN MAKING THAT SUFFERING ENDURABLE.

I'm going to stick my neck out a little bit here by saying that sometimes suffering can be redemptive. Don't hear me wrong on this. I'm not saying suffering is good, but that sometimes good can come from it. That's a very different thing and an encouraging thing when the burden of suffering has fallen on us.

If there is anything worse than a life of suffering, maybe it's a life in which there is no suffering at all. After all, the Arabs have a saying, "All sunshine makes a desert."

The point is, I suppose, that in each life a little rain had better fall, or that life is likely to end up metaphorically like the Dead Sea, which is capable of receiving only unto itself and not of producing anything living that is marketable for export.

A person who has never experienced defeat or suffering, who has always won, is almost certain to be insensitive and self-centered. We all know people like that. They don't always make the best friends. They're not the ones we want around in times of emergency or crisis.

And we also have known people who have overcome incredible obstacles, ones that would have crushed people of lesser grit, who accepted those bad experiences and even used them in the development of their character.

Certainly, the sufferings and tragedies of life are hard to bear. We can't always explain them, and we often can't understand them. But trying to run away from them or wrapping them in resentment or despair is only adding insult to injury.

In Romans 8:35, Paul wrote, "Who shall separate us from the love of Christ? Shall tribulation, or distress, or persecution, or famine, or nakedness, or peril, or sword?" (KJV).

NO! NO! "I am persuaded, that neither death,
               nor life,
              nor angels,
             nor principalities,
            nor powers,
           nor things present,
          nor things to come,
         nor height,
        nor depth . . ." (vv. 38-39).

As he wrote, I can almost see ol' Paul pausing, quill in hand, to think if he'd left anything out. Is there *anything* that can separate us? He continues: ". . . NOR ANY OTHER CREATURE" (v. 39, emphasis added). There! That ought to take care of it! NOTHING "shall be able to separate us from the love of God, which is in Christ Jesus our Lord" (v. 39).

There is a great balm in Gilead, as the old spiritual puts it . . . and a Great Physician waiting to heal and make whole again His wounded children.

No, suffering is not fun. Furthermore, we don't have an adequate explanation for much of it. But it helps to know that God does not intend for us to face suffering. It helps to know that sometimes good can come from it. And perhaps it helps most of all to know that through the already accomplished grace and suffering of Jesus Christ our Lord, it won't last forever, for He Himself, who has gone before us and now awaits us, will wipe it away.

Chapter 7

WHAT IS MAN?

*When I look at thy heavens, the work of thy fingers, the moon and the stars which thou
hast established; what is man that thou art mindful of him, and the son of man that
thou dost care for him?*
Ps. 8:3-4 RSV

When Carl Sandburg finished writing his monumental work on Abraham Lincoln, somebody asked
him what he planned to do next. He said, "I've been spending a lot of time lately with Lincoln.
Now I think I'll spend a little time trying to find something about this fellow Sandburg."

And there it is, the eighth psalm in twentieth-century costume. Who hasn't felt that way? Who
hasn't asked himself or herself:
WHAT AM I?
 WHO AM I?
  *WHAT IS MAN? What, after all, is the truth, the real truth, about this phenomenon the
anthropologists call* Homo sapiens?

When Plato, the peerless Greek philosopher, speaking through Socrates, once asked for a
definition of man, somebody offered this one: "Man is a featherless biped."

Well, that sounds all right, but Socrates saw a loophole. He picked up a chicken, plucked it clean,
and held it up in the face of the definition-giver. "There," he said. "That's a featherless biped. Is
that a man?"

Some years back, in Egypt, I have read, some archaeologists broke into an underground tomb
that had lain, unopened, for centuries, completely sealed off from the outside air. When they
broke in, just for an instant, just for a second or so, they saw the outline of a lovely young
woman, dressed in the clothing of the grave, lying exactly as she had been left hundreds of years
before.

They saw it. But then, the fresh air poured in, and according to the report, the body virtually
disintegrated before their eyes in a cloud of yellow dust. One of the excavators walked over to the
ledge and brushed his hand along it, gathering up all that was left of the body of a human being
. . . just a bare handful of dust.

A clever chemist went to work analyzing the component parts of the human body and came up with this intriguing information. In the average five-foot, ten-inch, 160-pound man, there is enough fat to make seven bars of soap, enough iron to make one tenpenny nail, enough sugar to fill a shaker, enough lime to whitewash a chicken coop, enough phosphorus to make 2,200 match tips, enough magnesium for a dose of magnesia, and enough potassium to explode a toy cannon.

Now, if you mix all those ingredients together in a big vat, would you have a human being? Is that the truth of MAN?

A modern television comic once said, "Listen, I don't like it when people say disparaging things about the human race. My entire family belongs to it . . . and some of my wife's family, too."

What is man, this strange,
                        bizarre,
                           complex,
                              enigmatic being, who in his brief strut across the stage of history has
produced the Parthenon
  and the *Fifth Symphony*
    and the Mona Lisa . . .
      and hospitals and orphanages and universities . . .
       and fantastic examples of courage and sacrifice and nobility, yet who is responsible for
swindles and carnage and corruption . . .
  for concentration camps and ghettos . . .
   plus a thousand other devices to debase and brutalize other human beings?

We can see the answer to this question right here in this Scripture passage: "When I consider thy heavens, the work of thy fingers, the moon and the stars, which thou hast ordained; what is man, that thou art mindful of him?" (Ps. 8:3-4, KJV).

He's nothing compared to that. Why, just looking up at the heavens is enough to cut you down to size. Remember the old story, maybe true, of President Teddy Roosevelt and his friend Dr. Sinclair, who used to like to go hunting together? Each night out under the stars before they turned in, they would stand beside the tent and look up at the heavens. Then Teddy would say, "All right, Doc, recite . . . "

And the scientist would respond, "Mr. President, there are at least a hundred billion stars in our galaxy alone, the nearest of which is four light years away, and nearly all of which are much bigger than our sun, which itself has a diameter of 865,000 miles, or 269 times the distance between New York and Paris." Then the president of the United States would gasp in amazement and say, "Okay, Doc. I feel small enough now. Let's go to bed."

Of course, that's not the whole truth about the human situation, but it's *a truth;* it's *part* of the truth. We're limited, creaturely, finite . . . in and of ourselves not much to write home about.

When I look at myself in an honest way, down beneath the veneer, the aftershave lotion, and the nice things people sometimes say, I know with a painful kind of certainty that I'm not really as patient,

```
    as kind,
        as sympathetic,
            as understanding,
                as generous,
                    or as considerate as I might be.
```

But then, aren't we all guilty of doing things we're not very proud of? Aren't we all filled at times with an overweening sense of pride? Aren't we all rather egotistically impressed with our accomplishments, and anxious, if we can just do it with proper humility, to let everybody know?

It's no new insight I think the psalmist is telling us. He recognized it centuries ago and described it in a way that sounds so remarkably contemporary. It's one side of the truth about MAN. Apart from God, he's nothing—
```
                a creature of the earth,
                        helpless,
                        limited,
                        and vain, who spends his time as a tale that is told and then
returns in the end to the dust whence he came.
```

F. Scott Fitzgerald once wrote that it's not usually until about age twenty-five that a young man wakes up to the realization that he's not going to live forever. And from that point on, there hangs over him the sobering, and sometimes terrifying, reality that his allotted time is grinding inexorably toward the end.

BUT THIS IS LIFE. Man is man, at least in part because he knows this, because he has the capacity to transcend himself to see both what he is and where he's headed. This is what makes him MAN. Not only is he going to die, but he *knows* he's going to die.

Now, enough of all this gloom and doom . . . this is not the whole picture. This is the end of part one, like *The Perils of Pauline*, but it's not the end of the story. This is just half of it. The Bible doesn't deny any of this, but it doesn't leave it there.

IN THE PSALMS, THERE ARE NO ILLUSIONS ABOUT THE INEFFECTIVENESS OF MAN, BY HIMSELF, BUT THERE ARE ALSO NO HESITANCIES ABOUT PROCLAIMING THE GRADE AND GRANDEUR OF GOD.

It's not enough to say that man is a beast. That's probably true—it IS true, but it's not the whole truth. It's not enough to say that man is a creature of the dust. That's probably true—it IS true, but it's not the whole truth.

There's something more, something else the psalmist is trying to tell us, something woven into the picture: THE ATTITUDE OF GOD HIMSELF ABOUT THE WHOLE THING. The psalmist's message is MAN IS NOT SIGNIFICANT BECAUSE OF SOMETHING INNATE, something inside of him; the deeper truth is that he's significant because GOD BELIEVES IN HIM.

And I think that makes all the difference. Man's stature, man's worth, is not an inherent thing; it's a bestowed thing. It's not something he creates; it's something given to him.

WE BELIEVE IN MAN, WE BELIEVE IN OURSELVES, BECAUSE WE BELIEVE IN GOD . . . AND GOD BELIEVES IN US.

In Ps. 8:5-6 (KJV), we read:

Thou hast made him a little lower than the angels,
And hast crowned him with glory and honour.
Thou madest him to have dominion over the works of thy hands;
Thou hast put all things under his feet.

Have you ever watched a person in love just sort of blossom right in front of you? Love, along with belief, will do that to you. IT CHANGES YOUR SELF-CONCEPT. It makes all the difference in the world.

A prominent English clergyman testifies that the changing point in his life came one night as a teenager. His father had sent him to bed without supper because of some infraction of the family rules. It was a terrible experience, he says. He'd been wrong, he knew he'd been wrong, and now there he was, banished into exile, suffering the consequences of his disobedience.

As he lay in the darkness, with both conscience and hunger pangs gnawing away at his insides, his father suddenly appeared at the head of the stairs, carrying a tray of food. He stood there for a moment, just stood there, looking into the darkened room, and then quietly said five words that changed a boy's life: "Son, I believe in you."

What a difference it makes when you know this. What a difference it makes in everything.

I don't have to be perfect,
  or successful,
   or beautiful,
    or smart.
     I don't have to be anything that involves accomplishment.
     I just have to be me and be worth something.

Dietrich Bonhoeffer, the courageous Christian martyr of World War II who was imprisoned and finally killed by Nazis just before the war ended, has written what I believe to be some of the most arresting passages in modern literature.

One of his poems, titled "Who Am I?" wrestles with this problem of identity and comes out exactly where the psalms do.

Writing from his cell, after the fashion of the apostle Paul, he describes in the first part of the poem the favorable impression he has made on both his fellow prisoners and his guards, an impression, he says, of "one accustomed to win."

Then, in the second part, he confesses with humiliation what a miserable creature he is to himself: "Weary and empty at praying, at thinking, at making. . ."

He concludes with: "Whoever I am, Thou knowest, O God, I am thine."

What is man? Not much, alone . . . yet EVERYTHING, for, hard as it may be to believe, he's God's choice. And God Himself BELIEVES IN US.

Chapter 8

THE GOOD NEWS
OF FEARLESSNESS

The LORD is the strength of my life; of whom shall I be afraid?
Ps. 27:1b (KJV)

I've often joked that we should place a special tax on all those physical fitness nuts who jog and frequent their local gyms and have personal trainers. The tax would be imposed on them because they are going to use the world longer than we non-exercising people.

As I slowly slip into the springtime of my senility, I get closer to realizing that I'm simply not going to be around on this planet forever, and I am convinced that the greatest single personal problem, not only for me, but for people in general, has to do with FEAR.

When I say that, I'm not pointing my finger, or fussing; I'm just reporting. I'm not saying it ought to be that way; I'm just saying that's the way it is. FEAR, in some form or another,
in some garb or another,
seems to be the greatest single personal problem with which people today have to cope.

And I can offer some further corroboration. A prominent psychologist conducted a study recently of five hundred ordinary, everyday people, across the board. Among those people whom he interviewed, he discovered seven thousand different fears.

What are you afraid of? We can cover it up, most of us,
most of the time, with a veneer of
sophistication. In fact, we've gotten pretty good at it. We can do our best to look calm and suave and confident—we *are* pretty good at it—BUT WHO AMONG US, REALLY, wouldn't have to admit, in all honesty, that at least a part of our life is shorn of richness because of some nagging, or even immobilizing, fear?

I'm sure not immune. I have a fear of failure, so I hesitate to attempt certain things I know I ought to try. I have a fear of scorn, so I sometimes avoid certain topics with certain people for fear of being the object of ridicule. I know that's not right. I have a fear of being scrutinized too closely, so I try to hide a part of my life from public view.

WHAT ARE YOU AFRAID OF? The boss? The IRS? Being found out? Rejection? The future? Your adequacy for life's demands?

Psalm 27 from the ancient Hebrew hymnbook speaks to the issue of fear. It forms a link between us and the past. It reminds us of our common humanity, even across the centuries. It reminds us that fear is not simply a modern, contemporary phenomenon. No, our generation is not the first one in history to tremble.

These people who lived in a far different culture from ours experienced the same sense of crippling anxiety,
  the same uneasiness,
    the same debilitating clutch in the throat brought on by terror that we know so well.

"The LORD is my light and my salvation; whom shall I fear? The LORD is the strength of my life; of whom shall I be afraid?"

Now, I don't know how that text strikes you. At first blush, it sounds as if the psalmist is implying that if you have God, ALL your fears will be eliminated. That is too neat, and the Bible, a very realistic Book, knows better than that.

Granted, some fears are normal, even good and valuable. While crippling fear,
                    paralyzing fear,
                       and
undiluted terror can be devastating, a healthy fear and respect for danger, for example, is probably a life protectant.

Remember the old line attributed to the Native American Tonto? When Tonto and the Lone Ranger were surrounded by a circle of raging Apaches, the Lone Ranger would say, "Tonto, I think we're in a heap of trouble." Tonto would reply, "What do you mean *we*, white man?"

If you weren't afraid of anything, ever, you wouldn't likely live very long. For example, you learn pretty early not to run out in traffic. And while playing Russian roulette may offer a certain perverse exhilaration, unless you already have a hole in your head, you know better than to pursue that sport with abandon.

I don't think the psalmist is talking about some contrived, magic, spiritual formula that you can pop into your mouth like a pill, which will remove fear from life and leave you in a state of perpetual arrogant euphoria.

When he says, "The LORD is the strength of my life; of whom shall I be afraid?" isn't he really saying something magnificently comforting and sustaining—to TRUST GOD, REALLY TRUST HIM, AND HE WILL GIVE YOU STRENGTH TO FACE YOUR FEARS IN A WAY THAT IS TRULY LIBERATING?

Now, I know there's more here than we can ever do justice to. It appears to me there are two perspectives on one great reality on the subject of fear.

The first has to do with the basic inwardness of combating fear. Many of us are afraid of the wrong things. I, for one, have trouble distinguishing between real fears,

I'm convinced that most of the things I really need to be afraid of are not out there at all; rather, THEY'RE IN HERE, inside me. That is, outward foes are not as dangerous as inward collapse. We're never going to escape fear entirely. So if you're going to be afraid, don't be afraid of external events; be afraid of internal failure.

I've always liked what a sportswriter said once about former world heavyweight champion Rocky Marciano, "The Brockton Blockbuster." While he didn't possess ballet-like grace in the ring, he was tough as nails. He could absolutely absorb the punishment his opponents dished out. After seeing him come back from what seemed like certain defeat to win a match, a sportswriter once said, "You can hit him, but you can't hurt him." I've always liked that.

He had inner resources that sustained him when the pounding came. The psalmist, too, knew the power of that inner strength. It wouldn't eliminate enemies, but it would give you the resources to cope with them. The real danger is when the inner fiber is lacking.

Do you remember the reasons historian Edward Gibbon gave for the collapse of the Roman Empire? In his monumental book *The Decline and Fall of the Roman Empire*, Gibbon listed five basic reasons why the mighty Imperial Rome was eventually overthrown.

The first reason, he said, was the rapid increase in divorce and the undermining of family. The second reason was increased taxes. The third reason was the craze for pleasure, with sports becoming more and more gaudy and more and more brutal. The fourth reason was the arms race, building gigantic armaments when there was no real need for them. Finally, he said, the fifth reason was the decay of religion, letting faith fade into form until it lost touch with life and could no longer guide it.

He didn't even mention the barbarians out there, slinking around in the forests of Northern Europe. THEY WEREN'T EVEN ON THE LIST.

The real enemy wasn't outside at all. The real enemy was rottenness, a kind of national cancer of inward decay.

Now, I'm not attempting to compare ancient Rome with modern America, necessarily. I do think there's a parallel here with many individual lives—mine included. WHERE THERE'S INNER STRENGTH, THERE'S STRENGTH FOR ANYTHING.

As I'm sure you have, I've known people who have just had it piled on them,
  crisis after crisis,
    tragedy after tragedy,
      one thing after another, yet they bore it all with a kind of radiance that was almost impossible to understand. You wonder how they did it, and maybe they themselves couldn't explain it, but they had resources inside that external events simply were not able to touch.

Personally, I can tell you of one person from my childhood, Dwight Purk. We grew up right around the corner from each other in a small town in Ohio. When seated alphabetically in school, Dwight and I sat together in our classes.

Upon graduation, we went our separate ways—he to the Marine Corps, and I to marriage and a family and ultimately to night classes in an attempt to further my education.

Our lives did not cross paths again until forty-three years later, in the spring of 2011, when I received a handwritten letter whose return address was that of my long-lost childhood friend, Dwight.

In his letter, Dwight inquired if I was the same Dale Perkins who had recently published a book, *Looking at Life Through God-Colored Glasses*, of which he had purchased a copy. I was.

Dwight and I corresponded for a while, reminiscing about old times and talking about where our lives had "diverged in the woods" and the separate paths we had taken. During our conversing, he told me that because of a reaction to Coumadin, he had recently had both his legs amputated at the knee.

After repeating, "I am so very sorry," I committed to Dwight that I would visit him at his home in Ohio. That summer, in 2011, I kept that promise.

I was invited to Dwight's beautiful home in Sidney, Ohio, where I rekindled a dormant friendship with him and started another when I met his lovely wife, Inday, as well as their son, Randy.

As I sat in Dwight and Inday's living room, hearing of all that had happened, all the things that changed in their lives because of this horrible illness, all the different living conditions each family member had to reckon with, where every "step" forward, it seems, was followed by a step and a half backward, I witnessed the most incredible, humbling story of love I had ever heard.

I saw the graphic journaled photos of Dwight's surgeries, the ravaging of his body by the diabetes. But I also witnessed the love of his wife in photos of her lying sleeping, curled in a recliner next to her husband's hospital bed. I listened as their son, Randy, told of all their travels back and forth from home to the hospital, not knowing if his precious father would live or die.

In life, I guess it's necessary to hear and see all the bad things before you can appreciate all the good things. Do you know how Dwight copes when it gets so bad he can hardly take it any longer? He turns all the negatives inward and deals with them as they come, one by one. I have never before experienced such courage as I have seen in my friend Dwight.

"Sure, I get discouraged," he says, "BUT I'M NOT ABOUT TO QUIT. I know the Lord is with me. The Lord is the strength of my life." I think the psalmist is saying that dealing with fear has to start inside . . . within . . . in an openness and a readiness to let God mold your sense of selfhood.

It means TRUSTING Him, being willing to put your full weight down on the validity of His promises. Though it won't keep fears from knocking on the door, it will provide protection against fears breaking it down.

A second perspective that is closely related—the psalmist knew this, too—has to do with the basic impermanence of many of the things we're afraid of, their flawed nature, as far as durability is concerned. Their power to threaten seriously is so limited, compared with what really endures.

I don't understand it entirely, but I'm beginning to learn . . . slowly . . . maybe with age, that fear, while it will take up as much room in our lives as we're willing to let it have, cannot have final jurisdiction when something bigger and more beautiful is there to hold it at bay.

That is, knowing that your life is ultimately in the hands of Another,
        knowing that you belong to God,
         turning the reins of your life over to the truly supreme Being of the universe may not get rid of all fear, but it does undercut its stranglehold on you.

You know that in the ultimate sense, you're safe,
  you're protected,
    you're secure—NOTHING, not even death itself, can finally subdue you, so what is there to be afraid of?

Henri Nouwen, a Roman Catholic priest, a man of enormous spiritual maturity, and one of the authors I like to read more than once, writes on this topic in his book *Gracias: A Latin American Journal*, about his experience living in Latin America.

In one place in that book, he reflects on his fiftieth birthday, which he celebrated in Latin America:

> Within a few years; 5, 10, 20, 30; I will no longer be on this earth. The thought of this does not frighten me, but actually fills me with a kind of quiet peace. I am a small part of life, a human being in the midst of thousands of other human beings. It is good to be young, to grow old, and to die. It is good to live with others and to die with others. God became flesh to share with us in this simple living and dying and thus made it good. I can feel today that it is good to be, and especially to be one of many.
>
> What counts are not the special and unique accomplishments in life that make us different from others, but the basic experiences of sadness and joy, pain and healing which make me a part of humanity. The time is indeed growing short for me, but that knowledge sets me free to prevent mourning from depressing me . . . mourning can . . . deepen my quiet desire for the day when I realize that the many kisses and embraces I received today were simple incarnations of the eternal embrace of the Lord Himself.[1]

"Gracias!" That's what the psalmist is talking about.

When you let yourself be held up by the strong arms of the Lord, when you repose in His everlasting mercy and claim His gracious acceptance, there's no need to be afraid.

Recently, a minister in Oklahoma told his church this story: A young father and his daughter went on a cruise, a "getaway" cruise after the death of his wife, her mother.

Turning to each other to help relieve the pain, they huddled on board the ship.

They cried;

 they talked;

   they tried to understand. On the ship's deck, the little girl asked her father, "Daddy, does God love us as much as Mommy did?"

At first, the father didn't know what to say. But he knew he couldn't sidestep the question. Pointing out across the water to the most distant horizon, he said, "Honey, God's love reaches farther than you can see in that direction." Turning around, he said, "And God's love reaches farther than you can see in that direction, too." Then, the father looked up at the sky and said, "And God's love is higher than the sky, too." Finally, he pointed down to the ocean and said, "And it's deeper than the ocean as well."

It was then that the little girl said the darnedest thing. "Oh, just think, Daddy, we're right here in the middle of it."

And she's right. We're right here in the middle of it all. That's what the psalmist knew.

Will calamity come? It might. Will death come? Someday . . . maybe sooner than we think. Will all fear be eliminated? No.

However, there is One who is with us in the middle of it all, and in our trusting reliance on His sovereign grace, we are ultimately and gloriously secure.

Remember the words of the psalmist: "The LORD is the strength of my life; of whom shall I be afraid?"

Chapter 9

THE FAITHFULNESS
OF GOD

*I proclaim righteousness in the great assembly; I do not seal my lips, as you know,
O Lᴏʀᴅ. I do not hide your righteousness in my heart; I speak of your faithfulness and
salvation.*
Ps. 40:9-10 (see also vv. 1-8, 11)

*Listen to me, you islands; hear this, you distant nations: Before I was born the Lᴏʀᴅ
called me; from my birth he has made mention of my name.*
Isa. 49:1

*He will keep you strong to the end, so that you will be blameless on the day of our Lord
Jesus Christ. God, who has called you into fellowship with his Son Jesus Christ our
Lord, is faithful.*
1 Cor. 1:8-9

Faithfulness . . . the faithfulness of God. That's the common theme of these three passages of
Scripture. The reality, though, is this theme is so prevalent,
$$\text{so ever-present,}$$
$$\text{so ubiquitous,}$$
$$\text{so constant throughout the Scriptures}$$
that no matter where you dip down, you'd be likely to scoop it up. It runs like a thread through
the Bible from beginning to end—the abiding,
$$\text{everlasting,}$$
$$\text{unswerving,}$$
$$\text{persistent}$$
$$\text{and consistent FAITHFULNESS of the Almighty God of the universe.}$$

Each of the three readings touches on it. The psalmist is proclaiming his personal testimony:
"I have spoken of thy faithfulness and thy salvation" (v. 10, RSV). With poetic repetition, in that
verse he adds: "I have not concealed thy steadfast love and thy faithfulness from the great
congregation."

In the Old Testament, in one of Isaiah's magnificent servant songs, God says through the prophet: "Kings shall see and arise; princes, and they shall prostrate themselves; because of the LORD, who is faithful, the Holy One of Israel, who has chosen you" (v. 7, RSV)

And in the epistle reading, in almost the first paragraph of that important letter to the Corinthians, Paul writes, "God is faithful, by whom you were called into the fellowship of his Son, Jesus Christ our Lord" (v. 9, RSV).

FAITHFULNESS, over and over . . . the steady, certain, unchanging, dependable faithfulness of God. No matter what happens, no matter what else may come, or not come, it's something you can count on. It's a word we need to keep in the forefront of our consciousness.

I don't have to tell you that we live in a world where faithfulness is not a bountiful commodity.

What professional baseball player these days remains with one team for his entire career? I don't know of anybody but Cal Ripken. The team members play out their contract and then look for greener pastures, wherever they may be. They sell their talent to the highest bidder with little regard for team or city loyalty.

Of course, it goes both ways. What franchise sticks with a player beyond the point of demonstrated productivity? The franchises' attitude is, *What have you done for us lately?* One bad season, and a player is out of there, sold to a second-division team or sent to the minors.

And this is not only true in sports. Mutual faithfulness, mutual loyalty between employer and employee, in general, is a much more tenuous thing than it used to be. No more gold watches. When the specter of the pink slip is constantly hanging over you, when you know that you, and 16,000 others, may be let go at any moment so the pockets of already fleshy executives may be further lined, it doesn't take long for corporate pep talks about loyalty to come across with a slightly rancid odor.

Indeed, the quality of loyalty is strained—maybe nowhere more so or more painfully than in the realm of marital relationships. I've never wanted to think of myself as a prude. I've always liked to think I was broad-minded and generous in judgment, but the casual way in which not all, but many today seem to take sacred marital vows of fidelity is deeply troubling, even to the extent that it represents a cancer on societal health.

In the wedding ritual of the church, there are some sober words directed to the bride and groom. The presiding minister says to the couple before they make their vows, "I require and charge you both as you stand here in the presence of God and these witnesses to remember that love and loyalty alone will avail as the foundation for a happy and enduring home . . ." Love and loyalty.

Then follow the questions to each one, first to the groom: "Will you live together in the holy estate of matrimony? Will you love her, comfort her, honor her, and keep her, in sickness and in health, and forsaking all others, keep you only unto her, so long as you both shall live?"

Faithfulness in the marriage bond is something more than just a recommendation. Marital fidelity is not just a suggested way of doing things. It's not meant to be just good advice as long as a certain level of emotional titillation is maintained.

FAITHFULNESS WITHIN THE MARRIAGE IS THE BASIS OF FAMILY SOLIDARITY, OF FAMILY INTEGRITY, and the only context in which the fullest expression of meaningful sexual love can be experienced. Take it out of that context, and you inevitably dilute the richness of it because union without communion is dehumanizing. It just is.

God made it that way, and to treat it any other way is to cause something in the very fabric of the universe to go awry. We treat casually the high calling of faithfulness only at our peril.

BUT THAT IS COMMENTARY ON US. Thank God, there is a deeper faithfulness in the universe than our slipshod and tarnished treatment of it.

The biblical conviction, echoed all the way through the Old and New Testaments and pinpointed specifically in these three readings, is that there is a trustworthy consistency about God's character that is unchanging and enduring.

"God . . . is faithful," Paul put it in the letter to the Corinthians. "God . . . is faithful." Maybe we're not, but God always is. He's true to Himself, always and without deviation. You can depend on that. You can count on it. It's the Bible's bottom line.

Really, it's hard to think of a more bedrock, a more foundational biblical conviction. Belief in divine fidelity is the basic premise on which most other Christian beliefs rest.

Our belief in Providence,
    our belief in the ultimate triumph of righteousness,
        our belief in the life everlasting,
            our hope in eternity . . . all these rest on our confidence in the consistent character of God.
The Bible calls it "the abiding faithfulness of God."

Think what it would be like, just imagine the havoc that would result, if the reliability, the faithfulness of nature that we take for granted suddenly exploded.

What if some mornings the sun came up in the West instead of the East?
    What if you planted radish seeds, and eggplants or turnips sprouted?
        What if it took three minutes to boil an egg one day and an hour and a half the next? Can you imagine the consternation it would cause the poultry industry?

One day a man walked into a restaurant and said to the waitress, "Bring me an order of scrambled eggs and some words of good counsel." The waitress came back a little later with his order. She placed the scrambled eggs on the table in front of him. "Okay," said the man, "now, what are the words of good counsel?" The waitress said, "Don't eat them eggs."

What if it were always so? We depend on the consistency of things. We expect, at least in a general sense, to get what we order, to have effect correlated to cause. Take away reliability, and the whole scheme of life would come flying apart.

Remember *Alice's Adventures in Wonderland*, Lewis Carroll's creative masterpiece? In Wonderland, where Alice found herself when she tumbled down the rabbit hole, everything was topsy-turvy, backward, chaotic. In the jury trial, the sentence came before the verdict was pronounced. The queen's memory was about things that were going to happen.

When Alice told her that was impossible, that one can't believe impossible things, the queen retorted: "My dear, your problem is you just haven't had much practice. When I was your age, I always did it for half an hour a day. Why, sometimes I've believed six impossible things before breakfast."[1]

Part of the charm of that whimsical story, where a narrow, relentless logic is depicted in a fanciful setting, is that, precisely, this is *not* the way the world works.

In the real world, there is a consistency and a regularity that we can count on. Because of it, we can do all kinds of things. We can pinpoint exactly when a solar eclipse will occur. We knew, to the minute and almost to the second, when the space shuttle would land at Kennedy Space Center.

We don't have the answers to all the mysteries of science—how genes interrelate, how the brain works, how to control this virus or that, and so on—but we are convinced that there *are* answers, answers that make sense, and that when we discover enough, we'll find that there is a pattern in them that is not simply the result of haphazard chaos.

We may not be able to comprehend the consistency, but the very basis of science, the faith of science, if you will, is that the consistency is there.

Now we need to take a step backward . . . so we can take a step UP. The people of the Book, the ancient biblical writers, didn't know about all that, of course, and didn't care about it; they wouldn't have cared about it. We don't look to them for scientific answers. Science, as we know it, is only a few hundred years old.

But what they do give us is infinitely precious. Those ancient, observant, sensitive, savvy people, watching the regular recurrence of the seasons, the consistent patterns of the starry skies, and the way in which water always seeks its own level, KNEW IN THEIR BONES that there was more behind all that than just ungoverned chaos.

They weren't the only people of the ancient world to come to that realization, of course; others knew it, too, and variously interpreted it.

But those Bible people,
    those Hebrews,
        our spiritual ancestors, in a special way, saw, or were *led* to see—maybe which one depends on how you view revelation—that the dependability, the reliability, the consistency of the created world was itself a reflection of the Creator's consistency. Take that step, and you're in the believer's camp right with them.

The power behind it all, they said, out of their experience . . . the power behind everything is not capricious, not haphazard, not whimsical or fickle.

He had rescued them from slavery, stuck with them even when they disobeyed or ignored Him, maintained His side of the covenant even when they abrogated it.

THIS IS WHOM WE'RE DEALING WITH: the One who is dependable, consistent, faithful. And what is most wondrous of all is they knew they could never have earned or deserved it . . . ONE WHO IS GOOD.

And you see, that's our heritage as Christians. Can you believe it? It's not always easy to believe. The evidence of it is not always plain. Sometimes it seems as if consistency and dependability, especially in the moral order, are so tattered and torn as to be nonexistent.

In the play *The Green Pastures*, written by Marc Connelly for a cast of all black actors, there is a scene in which the archangel Gabriel is sent down to earth by God to check on the havoc the Flood created in the time of Noah. He goes to see and comes back to heaven to make his report. In a deep, back-hills, Southern dialect, he said, "O Lawd, Lawd God, it's awful. There ain't nothin' fastened down there no more. Everything nailed down is a-comin' loose."[2]

It does seem that way sometimes. Can I prove it's *not* so? Can I produce scientifically grounded, irrefutable evidence strong enough to convince the hardest unbeliever that the moral order hasn't come loose,
    that the Ten Commandments haven't budged,
        that the Sermon on the Mount is still solidly in place?

Frankly, no, I can't do that. That's not the basis of our assurance in the faithful steadfastness of God. Our conviction about the abiding faithfulness of God is itself a matter of faith.

But there is something in us, I think, something deep down inside, that resonates with the positive conviction of that old psalmist, and the author of the servant song of Isaiah, and Paul, and all the other witnesses of the biblical testimony IN THEIR RINGING AFFIRMATION THAT GOD IS TRUE TO HIMSELF, that His character can be depended on, and that whatever may happen, HE WILL REMAIN FAITHFUL TO HIS OWN.

We take a stand on that. We hold it, even when disappointment dogs us, even when faiiure strikes. We hold to it when separation visits and when we face the specter of death. We may not have answers to all our questions or solutions to all our problems, but we throw ourselves on the divine trustworthiness, believing that answers and solutions are there . . . kind answers and solutions, loving answers and solutions.

We can't prove it, but we believe it because "God, who has called you into fellowship with his Son Jesus Christ our Lord, is faithful."

In closing, a fitting story comes from the book *The Yearling*, by Marjorie Kinnan Rawlings, a Pulitzer Prize-winning novel about some Florida crackers, largely uneducated, backward people who lived in the Ocala National Forest in north central Florida. The one character who stands out and stays clean amid the hardships of their precarious existence is the father, Penny.

In the story is a pitiful figure, a crippled, half-wit boy named Fodder-wing, whose very existence would seem to some a complaint against the goodness of God. But this child, with a twisted body and twisted mind, had a way with animals, and all the little creatures of the woods became his friends.

Then came the day when Fodder-wing died. His body lay in the rough handmade casket, and the family and a few friends gathered for the funeral. There was no preacher. But as the minds of the people instinctively and inevitably turned to God in the mystery of death, one of them said, "Penny, you've had some Christian raising. We'd be proud did you say something."[3]

So Penny stood there at the head of the open grave, lifting his face to the sunlight while the men took off their hats, and he offered this prayer:

> O Lord. Almighty God. Hit ain't for us ignorant mortals to say what's right and what's wrong. Was ary one of us to be a-doin' it, we'd not a brung this pore boy into the world a cripple, and his mind teched. We'd a brung him in straight and tall like his brothers, fitten to live and work and do.
>
> But in a way a speakin', Lord, you done made it up to him. You give him a way with the wild critters. You give him a sort of wisdom, made him knowin' and gentle. The birds come to him, and the varmints moved free around him, and like as not he could of taken a she-wild cat right in his pore twisted hands.
>
> Now you've done seed fit to take him where bein' crookedy in mind and limb don't matter. But, Lord, hit pleasures us to think now you've done straightened out them legs and that pore bent back and them hands. Hit pleasures us to think on him moving around as easy as ary one of us. And Lord, give him a few red-birds and mebbe a squirrel and a 'coon and a 'possum to keep him company, like he had here.
>
> All of us is somehow lonesome, and we know he not be lonesome, do he have the little wild things around him, if it ain't askin' too much to put a few varmints in heaven.[4]

Well, maybe that's where you have to leave it. But maybe that's enough.

There's a kind of instinctive faith in us, somehow, that however much we can't fathom about God, there is a rightness
    and a justice
        and a goodness there far beyond our notions of goodness, to which He will be true, never failing us.

We can't prove it, but we know it has to be true; it just has to. The Bible calls it "the abiding faithfulness of God." You can depend on it, put your whole trust in it, and count on it . . . forever.

Chapter 10

A RECKLESS COMMITMENT

King Nebuchadnezzar made an image of gold, ninety feet high and nine feet wide, and
set it up on the plain of Dura . . .
Dan. 3:1 (see also vv. 2-25)

I've always been fascinated by hearing Charles Laughton read the Bible. Of course, I realize some readers are too young to remember this eminent English actor, whose notable films include *Mutiny on the Bounty*, in which he is remembered for ordering, "Come here, Mr. Christian."

He wasn't pretty, but he had a rich, powerful, British-accented speaking voice. From time to time, he would read selections from the Bible. He made recordings of Scripture readings, and they are magnificent. It's moving to hear him as the words come tripping off his tongue,
        as he alternates between a whisper and a roar,
                and as he runs the gamut in between to let the words tell the story.

On his lips, they almost seem to sing, or pound, depending on the passage. There's a lyrical quality about them, and a dignity, and a strength that even the casual listener can't help but detect.

The Bible is meant to be read out loud; that's the point of it. It was written that way, to be heard, and the book of Daniel is a prime example. SOMETHING'S LOST WHEN IT'S JUST READ IN SILENCE.

The Hebrew, you see, was always an ear man, if I may put it that way. His religion was primarily a religion of the ear. Yahweh, the Lord God Jehovah, wasn't Someone you looked at, contemplated, gazed at, or even thought about primarily; that was more the Greek approach to religion.

The Hebrew God was Someone you responded to. He spoke, and you had to answer.
                He called, and you had to reply.
                He beckoned,
                    He summoned, and you had to choose.

This is the nature of the biblical record, and its essential nature, too, of the Christian faith—A RELIGION OF THE WORD. The heart of it is encounter,

> dialogue,
> confrontation,
> meeting—man and God, in the private,

personal sanctuary of the human heart.

One of the classic Bible stories that reflects this and that deals with the reckless faith born of such an encounter is the story of those three Hebrew boys found in the third chapter of Daniel. It's part of Mr. Laughton's repertoire; I think it's my favorite of the lot.

You know the background—three Jewish boys in a foreign land, transported to Babylon during the period of the captivity, still faithful to their God even in the midst of pagan idolatry, somehow coming to places of prominence and prestige, yet never compromising their basic loyalty.

AND THEN IT HAPPENS . . . WHAM! . . . just like that. Out of the blue, a decision has to be made. Nebuchadnezzar, the king, sets up an idol, a golden image, probably out there in front of the palace, and out goes the decree, "Hear ye, Hear ye, EVERYBODY COME IN AND BOW DOWN."

That's the way of the tyrant, isn't it? That's always the way, whether it's

> Nebuchadnezzar,
> or Hitler,
> or the ayatollah,
> or the grand dragon,
> or even some little, rinky-dink bully or group.

It's always the same: Do it my way,

> see it the say I see it,
> worship at *my* shrine, or we'll make sure you don't bother us anymore.

A golden image, of course, could represent almost anything, couldn't it? It could represent money,
  prestige,
   popularity,
    success,
     power,
      nationalism . . . It could be almost anything, ANYTHING GIVEN THE STATUS OF ULTIMACY AND SHOVED UP INTO THE PLACE THAT RIGHTLY BELONGS ONLY TO GOD.

So here they are, three young men put in a bind but not able to stomach that kind of affrontery, and not afraid to look the king in the face and say so. There's really a kind of free-wheeling recklessness about it, a kind of almost devil-may-care abandonment about the whole thing.

They gulp, I'm sure;
  they take a deep breath, probably,
   but then they make up their minds. THEY DEFY THE KING, defy him to his face, and refuse categorically to obey the decree, knowing full well the likely consequences of their obstinacy.

"Listen, King, we have no need to answer you in this matter. We believe our God is able to deliver us from this fiery furnace. But even if He doesn't, let it be known to you, O King, we will not serve your gods, and we will not worship the golden image that you have set up."

Maybe it's from this story that Martin Luther got his courage back in 1521, before the Diet of Worms. Remember? When they insisted he take back what he had written in criticism of a corrupt church, Luther said: "I will not take it back. I will not recant. Here I stand. God help me. I can do no other."

It's exactly what these three boys are saying. A man, even if he is a boy, and maybe lots of boys are men—a man has to say NO sometimes in the face of uncompromising evil. He has to say NO because if he doesn't, he'll forfeit something in his soul that will make him less than a man. And right here it is.

So they stand there, in all their youthful vulnerability, looking at the consequence with open-eyed awareness, and then choosing in spite of it all.

You simply can't put yourself in their place without feeling shivers up and down your spine. It's not necessary to dwell on the rest of the story in detail; you know it. The furnace was heated and overheated and then overheated some more. The three were unceremoniously thrown in. It was so hot, those who put them in the fire were themselves consumed by the flames.

They were thrown into the flames and forgotten, for a moment at least, and the twisted reasoning of demonism congratulated itself on its ability to flex physical muscle. BUT LOOK! It didn't last. Something happened. The physical muscle didn't prevail. Deliverance came in the form of another power, another kind of power, a presence, which sustained and protected them, just by its being there.

Don't ask me to explain it because I can't, and I'd be telling you a story if I said I could. I don't know whether the writer intended it to be regarded as history or as poetry, and frankly, what difference does it make?

Truth isn't limited to just literal truth. The important thing is that there's truth here, told in just about as vivid a way as it could be presented.

SOMEONE ELSE, SOMEHOW, WAS THERE WITH THEM, AND HIS PRESENCE SAW THEM THROUGH. Even the king, finally, was moved when he recognized it, this new kind of power unleashed by a reckless commitment.

That's the story as the Hebrew community remembered and recorded it. It became part of their collective religious memory, and they went back to it, time and time again, when other threats faced them. Remembering these three young men and their boundless, reckless audacity helped to strengthen them,
  to steel their nerves for the new fires they had to pass through.

Martin Niemoller, that gallant pastor in Germany during World War II who was imprisoned finally by Hitler because of his opposition to what was happening, wrote after the war:

In Germany they came first for the communists, and I didn't speak up because I wasn't communist.

Then they came for the Jews, and I didn't speak up because I wasn't a Jew.

Then they came for the trade unionists, and I didn't speak up because I wasn't a trade unionist.

Then they came for the Catholics, and I didn't speak up because I was Protestant.

Then they came for me, and by that time there was no one left to speak up.[1]

That hits me; I'm afraid, for its pertinence . . . AND SO DO THESE THREE BOYS. They had no one, humanly speaking, on their side. They were a minority of three, a tiny, feeble minority. Yet in a way, that very fact made their witness all the sharper by contrast.

Through this story in Daniel, it may be true that conditions sometimes don't have to be ideal for a person's witness to have an impact. It's also true that there's no guarantee of victory automatically built into discipleship. GOD DOESN'T ALWAYS DELIVER HIS CHILDREN FROM TROUBLE IN THE PHYSICAL SENSE.

You can't turn the Christian pilgrimage into some kind of Hollywood-type production with the sun slowly sinking in the West. It doesn't always work that way in real life, and it's dangerous to think it does.

God didn't deliver Stephen from the rocks and stones that were flying by the murderous mob that day outside the gates of Jerusalem.
   He didn't deliver Hugh Latimer and Nicholas Ridley from the burning stakes in sixteenth-century England.
      HE DIDN'T EVEN DELIVER HIS OWN SON from the brutal, drawn-out agony of the cross.

No, I don't think physical deliverance is the message of this Old Testament story, and to turn it into that is to misread it. God doesn't call us to be victorious; that's His department. As Dr. Thomas Price Jr. used to say, "We're not in management; we're in SALES."

God doesn't call us to be victorious; He doesn't even call us to be successful. WHAT HE DOES CALL US TO BE IS OBEDIENT. What He does call us to be is FAITHFUL, and He calls us to leave the rest to Him.

Kirsopp Lake, a professor of ecclesiastical history at Harvard Divinity School, in a lecture to a graduating class, put the definition of *faith* this way: "Faith is not belief in spite of evidence. It's life . . . in scorn of consequence."[2] That's the kind of faith these three boys displayed: "life . . . in scorn of consequence."

They didn't know they would win,
   and probably didn't expect to win,
      but they went anyway and took the heat, with a recklessness and an abandonment that sort of puts our puny faith to shame.

I think if we read the New Testament with clarity and honesty, we'll see it doesn't promise anything easier. We're not encouraged there to look for the prize in the package. We're not assured there of any exemption or immunity from life's hardships. We're not promised any cheap triumphs or smooth sailing because of our allegiance.

There is only the call to go
> and care
> and give
> and serve
> and endure
> and trust in His incredible ability to do something worthwhile with our
commitment.

There's not always a guarantee of physical deliverance, of victory over a situation. BUT THERE IS THE STEADFAST REALITY OF GOD'S PRESENCE TO SUSTAIN US THROUGH PERIL AND CRISIS . . . and maybe that's even better.

It's a great story the book of Daniel tells; it just may be one of the greatest in the entire Old Testament. If you find yourself reading it again, or picking up a recording of the book read by Charles Laughton, I urge you to follow it all the way to the end, all the way to the climax of the story:

> Then Nebuchadnezzar the king was astonished, and rose up in haste, and spake, and said unto his counselors, Did not we cast three men bound into the midst of the fire? They answered and said unto the king, True, O king. He answered and said, Lo, I see four men loose, walking in the midst of the fire, and they have no hurt; and the form of the fourth is like the Son of God.
> Dan. 3:24-25 KJV

There,
  there in the shadows,
    there, just offstage in the misty periphery, still keeping watch over His own, is that other
Figure,
  that fourth Man loose,
    that other Reality, whose face we can't quite see, but whose quiet, contagious Spirit pervades our whole existence and refuses, whatever we do, to let us alone.

That's the incredible sustaining power of a reckless commitment.

Chapter 11

WHY DOESN'T IT
GET BETTER SOONER?

O LORD, how long shall I cry for help, and thou wilt not hear?
Hab. 1:2 RSV (see also vv. 1, 3)

As for you, always be steady, endure suffering, do the work of an evangelist, fulfil your ministry.
2 Tim. 4:5 RSV

Hear what the unrighteous judge says. And will not God vindicate his elect, who cry to him day and night? Will he delay long over them?
Luke 18:6 RSV (see also vv. 1-5, 7-8)

Have you ever had the experience of wanting something so badly, honestly believing that it was right and good, knowing in your heart that things would be better and life would be richer if what you wanted could be granted, yet you waited and waited . . . and it wouldn't come?

Have you ever had the experience of praying for something—I don't mean something frivolous or petty, or even something for yourself; I mean praying earnestly for a good, worthy, unselfish cause, something that would benefit people, something you felt confident God Himself would bless—and had your prayer . . . your good prayer . . . seemingly go unanswered?

Have you ever had the experience of lifting someone you loved very dearly up in intercession to God and feeling He didn't even hear you?

Have you ever had the experience of being so empty, so spiritually dry, drained, that even when you offered up a prayer, it seemed to bounce right off the ceiling and hit you square in the face with its ineffectiveness?

The three Scripture passages listed at the start of this chapter come from people who, in one way or another, knew very well those kinds of experiences. How close we are even across centuries.

These three passages are from three different parts of the Bible,
              by three different writers,
                       with three different backgrounds. The settings are different, and
the immediate problems are different, but all three people are wrestling with a common spiritual
predicament . . . one you've had, I bet; I sure have: WHAT DO YOU DO WHEN THE ANSWERS YOU
WANT DON'T COME?

What about those times when your prayers don't get any response? How do you keep going
when nothing comes back . . . but silence? How do you keep your spirits from flagging and your
chin from drooping when things just don't seem to get any better?

These three Scriptures—one from the prophets in the Old Testament, one from the epistles,
and one from the Gospels, in the New Testament—strike a common note. They are dealing with
something *they* had trouble with and that *we*, too, have trouble with: THE SPIRITUAL LIFE IN
THE FACE OF OBSTACLES, when what we want, or believe we want, bumps into trouble, or into
hostility, or maybe worst of all, into the silent void of apparent nothingness . . . when no clear
word from God can be heard at all. We're not the first to experience that.

There's Habakkuk, an Old Testament prophet with a funny name but a sensitive conscience,
pouring out his heart to God,
         audaciously,
              almost desperately chiding the Almighty for being so slow to bring about justice.

What he says could almost have been lifted verbatim from this morning's newspaper. There's
violence,
   contention,
     strife.
       The law becomes slack, and justice never prevails.
         The wicked surround the righteous. "O LORD, how long shall I cry for help, and thou wilt not
hear?"

Talk about a perennially contemporary lament. "What's the matter with You, God?" he's saying,
as you've probably said, as I have said. "What's the matter with You? Don't You see what a
mess things are? You must see it. It can't possibly please You. Why are You waiting so long to do
something about it?"

Good question. Honest question. BUT THIS IS HOW IT OFTEN IS.

And there's Paul, or whoever wrote 2 Timothy. Whoever it was, it was somebody who had respect
and authority in the early church. He was passing the torch to the next generation. I guess we
could call Paul the first member of the Board of Ministry evaluating candidates for ordination. He
knew what those young protégés were going to be up against.

"It's not going to be easy out there," he was saying. "Don't kid yourself. There'll be times when
you'll be tempted to forget your heritage. There'll be people in your 'congregation' with 'itching
ears' who would rather be entertained than hear the truth. There'll be times when the authentic
voice of God may seem far, far away. You'll wonder more than once if things are ever going to get
better. BUT THIS IS HOW IT OFTEN IS."

And there's Jesus of Nazareth, speaking through Luke, speaking through a poor, old widow . . . in an unforgettable story. "Look at her," he was saying of the woman, who had almost no authority, no clout in that society, nobody on her side, and nothing going for her. She's been wronged, apparently, in some way, cheated, aggrieved . . . AND THERE SHE IS, KNOCKING HER HEAD AGAINST A WALL, knowing she has a case, knowing she's right, knowing if she can just get an impartial hearing, she's bound to be vindicated, but unable, despite her best efforts and her constant needling, to get the attention of the one person in a position to assist her. It doesn't seem fair, but . . . THIS IS HOW IT OFTEN IS.

While these three stories are each different, they have a common thread, and all of them are situations to which we can relate.

If we could somehow, on a graph or another way, prove that when we prayed for something— and it was good and worthy, of course—immediately, or at least within a reasonable time frame, say a week or ten days, it was delivered, was DONE . . . IF we could show that it worked that way every time as a natural law works in the physical world, it wouldn't be nearly as hard to practice effective evangelism. Why, we could really rack up in the churches, really draw them in with a card like that.

But of course, it doesn't work that way. Woody Allen, the theologian, seems to have pulled off some shrewd insights along this very line. He at least raises, with both wit and incisiveness, the difficulty of oversimplified certainty. In the movie *Love and Death*, he considers the implications of a universe where God is either deaf or absent completely.

He has Boris, who may well represent Allen, say to Sonja: "Oh, if God would just give me some sign. If He would just speak to me once—anything; one sentence, I'll take two words. If He would just cough." He then stares off into the distance and begins to mutter to himself under his breath, "Nothingness, nonexistence, black emptiness . . . " Sonja says, "What did you say?" and Boris replies despondently, "Oh, I was just planning my future."[1]

The Bible writers themselves . . . THESE Bible writers . . . knew there weren't always simple, *quid-pro-quo* answers. If there is anything they weren't, it is soft-headed and sentimental. SOMETIMES THERE JUST DON'T SEEM TO BE ANY ANSWERS . . . at least no answers in the form we'd like or expect.

So what do you do in the face of the SILENCE, when God appears to be mute, and the things you want and believe ought to happen *don't?* What do these hardheaded spiritual realists give us as their recommended advice?

"KEEP AT IT," they say. That's the first thing. KEEP AT IT. They all say that, right down the line. When no answer comes,
  when nothing seems to improve,
    when your prayer is apparently thwarted . . . KEEP ON PRAYING. KEEP AT IT.

That's the whole point of the parable of the importunate widow. To importune is to press on, to beseech, with urgency. The point of the parable of the importunate widow is *not* that God is like an unjust judge, like someone who has to be nagged and wheedled to be motivated into action. The point is that the woman didn't give up. She hung in there with her petition.

He slammed the door; she kept knocking.
  He zigged; she zagged.
    He retreated; she followed.
      SHE IMPORTUNED relentlessly, mercilessly, unceasingly.

We're not even told that the thing she was asking for was right and honorable, only that she *believed it was.* She was praised and lifted up as an exemplar not for her virtue, but for her doggedness. She didn't give up.

And Luke is saying, or Jesus is saying through Luke, in a sharply etched, vivid way, that if even such an unsavory character as this unscrupulous judge, who by his own admission didn't care a fig about eternal values, is finally touched by a poor woman's persistence, HOW MUCH MORE—there's the key phrase in the story—IS THE TENDER HEART OF GOD TOUCHED BY OUR PASSIONATE CONCERNS?

I think we would all agree that persistence is an indication of intensity. But intensity does not reflect EARNESTNESS because we can intensely want the wrong things, but without that earnestness,
  that hungering and thirsting for the object of our request,
    without that WANTING it, certainly the prayer's effectiveness is diminished.

They say medical missionary David Livingstone used to pray, "God, give me Africa, or I die." THAT'S IMPORTUNING. I don't know how many more of us get that passionately involved. Maybe it's no wonder the power of prayer has such a hard time being released.

You may remember the little boy who was asked one time if he ever prayed. He gave a pretty honest answer and made a profound distinction. He said, "Well, sometimes I pray, but most of the time I just say my prayers." I suspect he speaks for more than himself.

At one time or another, we all taste the dust of a drought-stricken prayer life. At times, we all experience the barrenness of perfunctory conversation with God. There's a world of difference between *saying our prayers* and *experiencing the real power of prayer.*

Real prayer isn't something we do with our lips. It's something we do with our LIVES. Jesus said, "Pray without ceasing" (1 Thess. 5:17, KJV). By that, He did not mean refuse ever to take a break from the act of saying prayers; that would be not only impossible, but totally escapist. Instead, by "pray without ceasing," I think He meant that the constant bent and drift of our being should be toward God. We are to be God-pointed,
                    God-oriented.

Somebody once said of Paul that no matter what you asked him to write about,
                         no matter where he started, He always ended up
dragging Jesus into it. I think that's what "pray without ceasing" means.

In the face of the cavernous "nothing" we sometimes hit when we lift our petitions, when the cold, biting winds of evil blow in our faces with such a relentless force, when right and decency and God seem so far removed, as they will sometimes, we need to hear these seasoned sages of the faith, saying, "SURE, THERE ARE GOING TO BE TIMES OF DRYNESS. WE'VE HAD THEM, TOO.

BUT EVEN WHEN NO IMMEDIATE ANSWERS COME, KEEP ON PRAYING,
ASKING,
IMPORTUNING.
In the very act of persisting, there is blessing, and there is strength.

There's something more in these passages we'll do well to remember when we face what seems like an implacable or an unanswering God. It's the reminder that GOD'S TIMETABLE ISN'T DEPENDENT ON OUR LITTLE CLOCKS. "O LORD, how long . . . ?" cried Habakkuk, his stopwatch in hand. "I don't have all day. Straighten it out . . . NOW. Let's get this show on the road."

But God's word came back to him to BE PATIENT. "There is still a vision for the appointed time . . . If it seems to tarry, wait for it; it will surely come" (Hab. 2:3, NRSV).

Now, I know there's a paradox here, of course, with respect to unanswered prayer in these two bits of biblical counsel. We're told to pray with intense persistence, to pray as if there is no time to spare, yet to remember that we're not the ones who are in charge of the divine schedule. While these seem contradictory, they really go together. Our job is not to advise God on when to act, but simply to report to "central casting," ready to be assigned our role in the play.

Habakkuk learned it. He begins where we so often do, chastening God for His lack of timing, for His slowness to pull up the curtain and get the show moving. But Habakkuk finally comes to see that determining the hour and the day, or even the century and the millennium, is outside his bailiwick of responsibility, and that his job, even while continuing to pray . . . IS TO TRUST.

The bottom line, the place he at last comes to rest, is the line Paul picked up and echoed in the first century, and that became the shaft of light for Martin Luther in the sixteenth century, the pivotal *aha* experience of the Protestant Reformation: "THE JUST SHALL LIVE BY HIS FAITH" (Hab. 2:4, KJV). That is, even if there is no immediate answer forthcoming, and even if the only thing you can see ahead is blackness, TRUST WITH ALL YOUR COMMITMENT THAT THERE IS AN ANSWER and that God's goodness and mercy will prevail in His good time.

AND THEN, LIVE AS IF IT WERE TRUE.

Now, here is the most difficult part for me of the whole answered or unanswered prayer issue. In the face of hostility or silence, when no answer seems to come, in addition to telling us to demonstrate persistence and patience, the paradoxical twins, aren't these writers telling us that when we pray and "nothing" comes back, the "answer" to the prayer, God's answer, may not be what we're asking for at all?

God can't grant a persistent request just because it is persistent, if it's not also in harmony with His good, holy purpose.

While some prayers seem to go unanswered, and we don't know why, and don't need to know why, it also seems some prayers are best unanswered or delayed because God has a better answer than we thought we wanted.

Habakkuk didn't get the answer to the prayer he thought he ought to get. He got a better one, though it took him a long time to realize it.

63

Paul prayed fervently, persistently that his "thorn in the flesh" might be removed, but it wasn't. God didn't answer his prayer that way. Instead He helped Paul see that "My grace is sufficient" to endure his thorn in the flesh (2 Cor. 12:7-8).

I like the story about the little girl who was sent to her room to "think things over" after some irresponsible behavior. Later, she came out all smiles and said, "I thought, and I prayed." "Fine," said her mother, "that'll help you to be good." "Oh, I didn't ask God to help me to be good," said the little girl. "I asked Him to help me put up with you."

More often than we know, it may be that the real answers to our toughest prayers and most heartfelt petitions won't be solutions at all but "answers" designed to help us cope and finally to give in.

Perhaps the most startling example of this is shown in the Garden of Gethsemane, when Jesus was praying just before His arrest. It's where He confronts the problem of unanswered prayer most dramatically. In agony, blood-sweating agony, over the sacrifice God was asking of Him, Jesus prayed, "Is there no other way?"

He interrupted His prayer for a moment to check on His disciples, whom He had asked to watch and wait with Him. To His immense disappointment, they were asleep. After waking them and admonishing them, He went back to His prayer and entreated God with the same supplication: "Is there no other way?"

Again, He interrupted His prayer to go back to the disciples, only to find them sound asleep once more. A third time He returned to them and discovered them, His closest companions, simply unable to keep their eyes open. (See Matthew chapter 26.)

And He realized, maybe at that very moment, that the answer to His unanswered prayer had been there all along. The answer was in those sleeping disciples. Here, even those nearest and dearest to Him, those who knew His message best, were unable in the time of trial to keep the faith. IF THEY FAILED SO MISERABLY, HOW MUCH MORE WOULD THE REST OF HUMANITY FAIL?

Jesus' prayer was answered not as He wanted it and not as He asked for it. His prayer was answered not in a voice from heaven, but in the soft snoring of His sleeping disciples. His prayer was answered not with a crown, but with a cross.

What are we to do when no answer to our prayer is forthcoming?
  What are we to do when we feel overwhelmed by forces arrayed against us?
    What are we to do when the good and the decent and even God Himself seem so far away?

JUST LISTEN. Listen to the wisdom of the ages, through the words of people who have been through it. KEEP ON PRAYING; DON'T GIVE UP.

AND WHEN YOU MAKE YOUR PETITION, BE READY TO HEAR HIS ANSWER, EVEN IF IT MEANS THAT YOUR PETITION MUST CHANGE.

After all, the highway from "O LORD, how long . . . ?" to "Not my will, but thine, be done" (Luke 22:42, KJV) is the highway that leads to LIFE.

Chapter 12

WITH MATTHEW AND THE MASTER

Then Jesus came from Galilee to the Jordan to be baptized by John. But John tried to deter him, saying, "I need to be baptized by you, and do you come to me?"
Matt. 3:13-14 (see also vv. 15-17)

I wish I could have met that Matthew fellow. Maybe someday I'll get to. While no complete picture of him emerges from the sources with which we have to work and the information about him at our disposal is sketchy at best, from his writing, from the way he tells his story, we can pick up enough information to be certain he'd be worth knowing better.

It may be, just as the Record says, that when Jesus saw Matthew sitting at the tax table and said, "Follow Me," he got up straightaway and followed Him. JUST LIKE THAT.

That may be our man. If so, if that was the disciple who later became the Gospel writer, then it's clear there was one thing he didn't leave behind when he walked away from his previous life: HIS PEN. He took it with him and switched from accounting to evangelism, from digits to discipleship. It makes a neat package, an enormously appealing scenario.

Those who argue for the apostolic authorship of the Gospel point to the vivid account of Matthew's call. It's only one verse long, and only Matthew tells it. Could it be a kind of signature insertion into the narrative, they suggest, a subtle way of saying, "I know what I'm talking about in telling the story of this special Man; I was THERE, and here's how I got into it"?

A better clue about the man we call Matthew is in what we can deduce from the Gospel he left, this writing the church has treasured so much it put it first when it collected the books that make up our New Testament.

The Gospel of Matthew, hands down, is the most quoted book in the world. It contains the Sermon on the Mount, at least the most complete version. This book contains the Great Commission, the mandate of the Christian mission enterprise: "Go ye therefore, and teach all nations, baptizing them in the name of the Father, and of the Son, and of the Holy Ghost" (Matt. 28:19, KJV). The book of Matthew contains the cherished and beautiful story of the wise men, who came from far off to worship the Christ Child, the story that inaugurates the season of Epiphany, the season of God's appearing and manifesting Himself to the people.

Matthew was clearly a historian. He had a sense of the broad sweep of things. He portrays Jesus as the culmination of all the Old Testament preparation. Why do you think he begins his Gospel with a genealogy? *How dreadfully dull*, we think. So-and-so begat so-and-so . . . and on and on. Who can even wade through it? BUT A GENEALOGY IS ONLY DULL WHEN IT'S NOT *YOUR* GENEALOGY. If it's *your* family tree being charted, your ears will perk up.

That's what Matthew's trying to say with his acute sense of history: "Look, folks, Jesus didn't just hop into history through a plate-glass window. See, He has roots, and they're Old Testament roots. They're *our* roots. God has been planning this thing all through the generations. There's a pattern here, a design and purpose."

For Matthew, Jesus is the new Moses. If you look closely, you can see the parallels between the Moses of Exodus and the Jesus of Matthew. In both cases, the wicked king tries to kill the child, and both came out of Egypt. Moses gets the Law from the mountain; Jesus proclaims the new Law from the mountain—the Sermon on the Mount. The books of Moses are five in number, the Pentateuch; the book of Matthew also has five parts. The similarities are remarkable. MATTHEW WAS A HISTORIAN.

He was also, plainly, a teacher. (I should know; I'm married to one.) His Gospel is well-organized. It has structure and development, far more than Mark's. Matthew was doing more than telling a story; HE WAS TEACHING A LESSON, with students in mind. Matthew's Gospel is easy to memorize. Could that be accidental? The very form of it lends itself to easy remembering:

"Blessed are the poor in spirit . . ." (Matt. 5:3).
  "Blessed are the meek . . ." (Matt. 5:5).
    "Blessed are the pure in heart . . ." (Matt. 5:8).
      "Ye have heard that it was said . . . of old . . . . But I say unto you . . ." (Matt. 5:21, KJV). Indeed, the man who put this book together had obvious teaching qualities.

What's more, he was a CHURCHMAN. He loved the church, supported the church, and believed in building up the church. The word "church," *ecclesia*, is found only twice in the Gospels—lots of times in Paul, but only twice in the four Gospels, and both are in Matthew. The main reference is at Caesarea Philippi: "Upon this rock I will build my church," Matthew quotes Jesus saying to Simon Peter, "and the gates of hell shall not prevail against it" (Matt. 16:18, KJV).

Here was a man who believed that the main business of Christianity was disciple-making, and he believed the church was the principal matrix in which Christian character could be forged. He says a lot about tithing, about service, about self-denial, about obedience. He says Jesus thought those things were important. It wouldn't be far off to call the Gospel of Matthew a handbook in Christian discipleship. He wrote it as a manual of First-Century Church membership . . . DO YOU WANT TO BE A FOLLOWER OF THIS MAN, THIS INCOMPARABLE PERSON? Here's who He is, and here's how you do it.

It's a small wonder that when the church compiled its Book, gathered its early writings together to form its New Testament, it made Matthew's account the lead-off entry.

Matthew had trouble with the baptism of Jesus, as did the early church. That it happened, that it took place was too well established to deny.

Luke says He was baptized when He was about thirty years old. That much seems clear. The question was *why* was He baptized? *Why* did Jesus submit to baptism at all, and especially to John's baptism? John's baptism was a baptism of repentance. "Repent and be baptized," John proclaimed. He was saying, "Change your ways. Turn your life around." People came from all over to respond, people who knew their lives needed to be turned around. HOW DOES THAT APPLY TO JESUS? Of what did He need to repent? Wasn't He without sin, completely unblemished in character and deed? That's what the early church claimed.

Matthew, along with much of the church, wrestled with how all this could fit together without contradiction. In his account, Mark doesn't deal with it. Mark, who wrote earlier than Matthew, just ignores the problem. He says Jesus was baptized by John in the Jordan . . . PERIOD, and goes on to the next thing. He gives no elaboration whatsoever. He states it but doesn't explain it. He declares it but doesn't interpret it. By the time Matthew wrote, some explanation, some interpretation had to be given. To new members coming into the church, to beginning Christians, there was the danger of giving the impression that since John baptized Jesus, John was more important than Jesus. Some of John's disciples were actually saying that. (Yes, John the Baptizer had disciples.)

Matthew makes it clear that he's aware of the ambiguity this lack of clarification causes. Why was Jesus, the sinless One, baptized? Matthew says JESUS CHOSE to be baptized. It was His decision. He went to the Jordan "to be baptized by John" (Matt. 3:13). That is, Jesus went deliberately, voluntarily, intentionally. He wasn't simply caught up in the excitement of the moment; He wasn't swept up in the emotion of the setting or the preaching. HE WENT ON PURPOSE, with the specific intent of being baptized.

In addition, John himself recognized the uniqueness of the situation, the ticklishness of the relationship. John himself, Matthew says, was nervous about the request and protested when Jesus came to him, saying, "I need to be baptized by *you*, not vice versa." He clearly subordinates himself to the superiority of his cousin.

AND THEN, Matthew tells us, Jesus gives John upfront His rationale for being baptized: "Let it be so now; it is proper for us to do this to fulfill all righteousness" (Matt. 3:15).

I think what He's saying is, "I am doing this now because it's what God wills. I am doing it as an act of conscious fidelity, as an act of faithfulness to the commands of the heavenly Father."

WHAT AN EXCITING THING! It's no wonder Matthew had to get it all down. JESUS DIDN'T *NEED* TO BE BAPTIZED; HE *CHOSE* TO BE BAPTIZED as a means of identifying with those who *do* need to be baptized. It was for Him, Matthew is saying; it was an act of commitment, an act of dedication, not on account of His own need, but on account of people and their need. It was the opening moment of self-giving on behalf of a hurting and needy world. From that time on, from that very moment on, Jesus would, as it were, be one with humanity.

It's not the virgin birth that makes Jesus one of us. Matthew tells that, too. That's the other side of the picture, a way of saying Jesus was more than just human, that He somehow was different and special. Matthew believed that about Him. But he's saying that as special as Jesus is, He also was totally immersed in the fullness and complexity of real human life, just like the rest of us. He's not up there, remote from reality, insulated from the dust and grime of daily living. Though personally sinless, He identified with humankind in its sin and did so as a conscious act of obedience to the Father's bidding.

What's the significance, if any, for you and me? Isn't it that Matthew is saying to us that our Savior, our Redeemer, this One we follow and look to as Lord, is not so far off and removed from the realities of life that He doesn't understand the mess life can sometimes be? He was baptized for *us;* He elected to join *us;* He jumped into life with *us* . . . all the way. He knows, because He, too, has been through it, what it is to feel pressure to produce and what it is to have people misunderstand your motives and your intentions. He knows what it is to experience disappointment and letdown, what it is to have friends who say one thing and do another, and what it is to experience the ache of separation and isolation and grief. HE'S BEEN THERE in *all* of it.

He was baptized into life. When trials and pressures and hardships come our way, when we have to face the consequences of our own sin, the searing pain of remorse that comes from our recognition of wrongdoing, we can know that Someone before us, Someone infinitely greater— though sinless Himself—understands, out of being there, too, and still sticks with us.

HE CHOSE TO BE BAPTIZED IN IDENTIFICATION WITH GOD'S PEOPLE.

The baptism of Jesus—as exemplified by His willingness to submit to it out of obedience to the Father's will and as a reflection of the Father's heart, two things that always go together—is, in part, His pledge that no matter what happens, we are not alone. Hang on to that, Matthew is saying to us.

Also interesting about Matthew's account of the baptism is he gives almost no emphasis to the baptism itself, the actual laying on of hands, the ritual act of baptism. We can assume it was done by immersion—it says He came up out of the water—and that should make all the Baptists happy—but the report of the baptism itself is relegated to a relative clause.

Matthew's emphasis is not on the *mode* of baptism but on the declaration of God with respect to what was happening.

In Matthew, there is not a word offered about how Jesus felt about the baptism experience; there is nothing in the account to suggest that He was elated or ecstatic or moved . . . or anything. There is no mention of His emotional condition. No, we can't tell from Matthew's report what was going on inside of Jesus at the baptism. What Matthew focuses on is what *God* announced at the baptism. As at any baptism, GOD IS THE CHIEF ACTOR. This is an "epiphany" story. *Epiphany* means appearing, manifesting; making known. Light, brightness, clarity, and revelation are all epiphany motifs.

With graphic epiphany language, Matthew shows us the glory. The heavens themselves were opened, a symbol of divine revelation, and the Spirit descended on Jesus to bestow empowerment. AND MATTHEW SAYS THE VERY VOICE OF THE LORD GOD ALMIGHTY WAS HEARD, SAYING, "This is my beloved Son, in whom I am well pleased" (Matt. 3:17, KJV).

Luke's and Mark's versions of the same scene are subtly different. Luke and Mark tell this story, too, but in those Gospels, the voice of God says, "YOU are my Son . . ." (Mark 1:11; Luke 3:22, emphasis added). It's a word spoken to Jesus directly. For Luke and Mark, the declaration is a matter of personal experience, for Jesus alone. But in Matthew, it's a public announcement. It's for everybody: "THIS is my beloved Son" (emphasis added). It's a message for the world to hear, and Matthew tells his story for that very reason.

It's as if he were saying, "Listen up, nations, peoples, everybody. Hear this! God has declared something ineffably magnificent: HIS SON, IN WHOM DWELLS ALL OF THE FULLNESS OF THE GODHEAD BODILY, HAS COME, AND IN HIM THERE IS REDEMPTION."

I would've liked to have met that Matthew fellow, wouldn't you? He was no mean evangelist.

Matthew was a Jew, a good Jew, a devout, pious Jew, saturated in the Hebrew Scriptures, where he would have recognized the two parts of the public declaration attributed to God. Matthew's Jewish readers would have recognized them.

The first part of the phrase, "This is my beloved Son," comes from Psalm 2:7, part of a coronation psalm, a psalm that was read when a new king was crowned. The king was considered GOD'S son. After David, this took on Messianic connotations. Someday a new King will come, even more powerful and more splendid than David.

The other part of the phrase, "in whom I am well pleased," comes from one of the suffering Servant passages of Isaiah, Isaih 42:1. Here, unexpectedly, they are put together:

A Messianic statement—a suffering Servant statement.
  A statement about a King—a statement about a Victim.
    A statement about a Power—a statement about weakness.
      A statement about One who would be victorious—a statement about One who would be submissive.
        A statement about One who would triumph—a statement about One who would voluntarily give Himself up.

The connotations are poles apart . . . except in the case of God. A Messiah who suffered was a contradistinction in terms . . . BEFORE THIS.

Before this, messiahs did not suffer; rather, messiahs made others suffer. Here begins the hallmark of Jesus' ministry, one precisely of winning by losing,
                    overcoming by surrendering,
                        achieving triumph by laying one's life squarely on the
line. The implication of this baptismal formula *points straight to the cross.*

"This is my beloved Son, in whom I am well pleased." To anyone immersed in the Hebrew Bible, here is a statement so bold as to leave a hearer gasping in its presence. IT STILL DOES. You see, in the divine economy, sovereignty is tied to sacrifice.
                    Honor is linked to humility.
                    Leadership is joined to service.
                    Greatness is affixed to sharing.

Glory is found in giving.
Life is achieved through death.

It is God's announcement of His values, Matthew is saying, and Jesus leads the way. In Matthew, it is surely no surprise that immediately on the heels of the baptism is the temptation experience. How else could the weight of this commission be worked through? Now Jesus must wrestle with the implications of what He has heard.

The Father has called. The Son has started. But thank God, He never looked back.

I would've liked to have met that Matthew fellow, wouldn't you? I've got a lot of questions. Maybe lunch one day. I'll bring the lox and bagels.

Chapter 13

THE WILD ONE

And when he was come out of the ship, immediately there met him out of the tombs a man with an unclean spirit . . .
Mark 5:2 KJV (see also vv. 1, 3-20)

Even out of the torment of crazed bedlam came sanity, purpose, and a new beginning. WHAT A STORY! Could it really have happened? Could it happen still? Is there no limit to this Carpenter's magic?

Do you know this old story? I've never written on it before. I've honestly tried to before but have been frightened away. Recently, I've been trying to wrestle with it again, and I can't seem to turn it loose . . . or maybe it's the other way around.

It's an eerie kind of story, isn't it? It's a weird, improbable, unnatural kind of story . . . from another time,
  another place,
    and almost another world.

It's a story with caves,
               tombs,
              fog,
                anger,
                fear,
                   desperation,
                    chains that clatter,
                      screams in the night,
                      demons that speak,
                         pigs that are possessed, squealing and racing into the sea . . .
WHAT KIND OF STUFF IS THIS? Is it the Bible, or is it voodoo?

It's the kind of story that belongs on a rainy night with the wind howling. If you were making a film of it, you'd want to shoot it in black and white. It's an unsettling story . . . yet it's somehow morbidly intriguing.

It does finally end satisfactorily, but it leaves so many questions.
  It unnerves you, even as it grabs you by its intensity and drama.

It both repels and attracts, like a gold-covered spider or something.

I know why I've never tackled it before; I didn't know what to do with it. YET I CAN'T GET AWAY FROM IT. There's something very moving and suggestive here.

This story, twenty verses in Mark, is the longest and most detailed of any of the healing stories of Jesus. Matthew and Luke both tell it, but shorten it. Mark is undoubtedly the original source. Most scholars point out that it contains elements of folkloric accretion that, for whatever reason, have become attached to it as it was told and retold through the years. But the essential plot hangs together.

The point of the story, I think, the reason Mark includes it and spends so much time on it is to stress the calm confidence and courage with which Jesus faced and helped this poor, twisted demoniac.

I like that word, *demoniac*. I don't like the thing, but I like the word *demoniac*, one who is full of demons. This man was the toughest case Jesus ever had to handle. It took Him longer to cure him than any other case He ever had to handle. If He could heal him, I think Mark is saying, if He could bring this wild one back to normal, or better, if He could bring wholeness out of his battered personality, what do you think He could do for you? WOW!

There's more here than we can possibly deal with in one chapter. One sermon from the pulpit couldn't do it justice. This story is an unfolding panorama.

Jesus comes ashore from across the lake and disembarks in the country of the Gerasenes. That's in the region of the Decapolis, the ten cities. *Decapolis* is a Greek word, and this was a Greek area, not Jewish at all. Jesus is in foreign territory. This is Gentile, pagan country, from a Jewish perspective.

If Mark's chronology can be trusted, they land at night. In fact, it was already evening when they set out from the other side of the lake, and it was a good five to seven miles across. That makes it all the more eerie . . . dark, misty, with every sound magnified. The eastern shore of Lake Tiberias, or the Sea of Galilee, is rough country; it's grim, forbidding landscape. Along the shoreline are limestone caves, used in those days as tombs for burial. Sometimes, though, the living—especially outcasts, lepers, and the demented—resorted to using them as well.

In that dark, harsh, God-forsaken setting, there was a WILD MAN who was strong, undisciplined, running loose, out of his mind, and demon-possessed. Mark describes him as a "demoniac."

I don't know what that means literally in terms of modern experience. I know what they thought it meant in that day: Something from the outside,
>   something not of man,
>   something evil and foreign,
>   something alien to the man's true self had gotten hold of
him and turned him into a monster. They called that something a demon. It was real to them, and it was vicious. It changed people and made them someone other than who they really were supposed to be.

We don't think of it in those literal terms anymore. We're modern and better educated. We use modern terms. We speak of psychoses, neuroses, mental aberrations, and the like. We've progressed. BUT WHO DO WE THINK WE ARE KIDDING? Why does this wild man look so strangely familiar?

Don't we, too, know perfectly well what it is to be possessed, to be captured by forces that control us, instead of the other way around?

Is *possessed* too strong a word to describe the alcoholic who refuses to admit he has a problem? Is it too strong a word to describe the insatiable lust that burns in those suffering from a Don Juan syndrome? What about the incorrigible child abuser, the compulsive gambler, or the hooked addict? What about the woman blinded by jealousy?

Extreme, perhaps, in its characteristics, but I suspect we've all known moments at least when we were in the grips of obsession,
     or a compulsion,
         or a drive . . . something not really of us that pushed us beyond the brink of control.

This is not just ancient myth. Read the story of Roskolnikov in Dostoyevsky's *Crime and Punishment*. Read Golding's *Lord of the Flies*, and see the power of the demon.

Call it something else if you prefer. You can change labels all day long and not change the inner reality. I see this wild man as being closer kin to us than we might want to admit.

What *does* control us, anyway?

Our values are shaped by television's values.
  Our ethics are molded by Madison Avenue's ethics.
    The bottom line is king.
      The ends determine the means. What kind of sanity is that?

William Butler Yeats saw it developing and said it almost seventy years ago in "The Second Coming":

> Things fall apart; the centre cannot hold;
> Mere anarchy is loosed upon the world . . .
> The best lack all conviction, while the worst
> Are full of passionate intensity.

It hits right at home. A wild man? Yeah! I think I've seen him around.

Mark's demoniac can be seen,
                ought to be seen, as more than just one lone person suffering from mental imbalance. Of course, that would be enough for Jesus, but there's something even more here. In a way, he represents a picture of all of us, individually, collectively, thrashing around in desperation and confusion when we're separated from the one Force, the one Power that can bring our dissipated energies into useful focus. This is about more than just an individual; this is the human situation.

Now enters Jesus. What happened when that encounter took place, the meeting of these two, the healing? WHAT HAPPENED? I don't know. How's that for a cop-out? I simply do not know. I'm sorry. If you're looking for a medical explanation of this cure, this radical transformation, I can't give it.

We don't even know how the man knew who JESUS is. He recognized Him somehow, but there are so many unanswered questions. Sometimes in the dialogue, it is the man who speaks; sometimes it is the demons. "My name is Legion," he says when Jesus asks his name. "My name is Legion . . . for we are many" (Mark 5:9). A Roman legion contains up to six thousand soldiers . . . six thousand forces, pressures, pulling in every direction.

This man had six thousand soldiers fighting in his skull. He both wanted to be cured and feared it,
    both sought healing and dreaded it,
        both desired freedom and clung to his bondage.

"Don't torment me," he said to Jesus, YET HE WORSHIPED HIM. "Stay away from me . . . please; don't leave me." He felt the pull of torment.

No one who ever lived saw into the depths of the human mind with the perceptiveness of Jesus of Nazareth. Put Him down in any age of human history, and He would have been a brilliant psychologist.

Somehow, maybe—knowing that *perceived* reality is as real to a person as reality itself, perhaps even more real; knowing that logic simply doesn't prevail where emotion runs high; and knowing the depth of obsession this man had with the thought of his legion of demons—HE REALIZED THAT NOTHING ON EARTH WOULD EVER CONVINCE HIM THAT THEY WERE GONE EXCEPT WHAT HE HIMSELF WOULD REGARD AS VISIBLE DEMONSTRATION THAT THEY WERE GONE.

There were pigs nearby, a herd of swine. Remember, this is not Jewish country. Mark tells us the man felt the demons asking to be sent into them. The perception *is* the reality. There was noise and commotion, the man's moans and shouts. The pigs were spooked. They broke, terrified, and raced down the slope into the sea.

"Look," said Jesus, "your demons are gone."

I DON'T KNOW THAT IT HAPPENED THAT WAY. Maybe you'd rather write a different scenario. I only know it had been a long time since this demoniac had been the recipient of some personal, caring interest. That's when miracles happen.

Jesus came to him totally without fear, even though this was a wild man. Think of the physical courage it took. He came to him without any sense of repulsion. There was no one else in that whole region who would have done it. He didn't hold his nose. He didn't gag.

Remember the account of the woman who went to Calcutta and visited the hospital of the Sisters of Mercy?

There was Mother Teresa, scrubbing the floor in a ward of men who were covered with putrid, running sores. "Oh," said the woman, "I wouldn't do that for a thousand dollars." Quietly, as she continued scrubbing, Mother Teresa said, "Neither would I."

Without fear, without repulsion, and maybe most beautifully of all, Jesus came to know the man without any sense of superiority. He didn't say, "Man, what's wrong with you? Snap out of it." He didn't scold him or reprimand him. He didn't look down his nose at him—that would have been easy.

Instead, with infinite compassion and unprecedented tenderness, He treated him as a person, entering into his frame of mind to deal with where he was. I suspect there are miracles today, right around us, waiting for exactly that kind of approach.

Almost always, the beginning of healing is compassion. Most doctors know it well. In order to cure, you start by being kind. It happened here; it happens over and over.

The response of the community to Jesus' healing? What a funny, funny thing. Not funny as in ha-ha, unfortunately, but funny as in peculiar . . . and sad.

Word spread like wildfire: "Have you heard? Jesus of Nazareth, that Carpenter from across the lake, has healed the crazy man down by the rocks. Come on. Let's go see."

Mark says when the people of the district arrived on the scene, they found the man clothed and in his right mind. They heard the story—of a miracle, a transformation.

The next sentence OUGHT to say, "They glorified God for all He had done and begged Jesus to stay with them." Shouldn't it? Instead, it says, "Then the people began to plead with Jesus to leave their region" (Mark 5:17). They wanted Him to get out of there. They didn't want Him.

Did the pigs prompt that negative response, the loss of that important income-producing animal husbandry product? I'm sure that was part of it. Anything that touches the pocketbook touches the emotions. Hit a man's wallet, and you hit his disposition, typically not for the better.

Paul and Silas ran into the same thing in Philippi when they cured that poor, demented girl whom unscrupulous men were using as a fortune-teller. TO THEM, SHE MEANT MONEY. Of course, they were furious when that source of income dwindled.

In Jesus' case, they begged Him to leave the region. He was bad for the economy. However, I wonder if there was even more involved in this negative reaction. Mark says when they saw the man sitting there, clothed and in his right mind, they were AFRAID. That's a different emotion from anger. They were afraid.

Apparently, they feared sanity more than insanity.
They feared coherence more than confusion.
They feared logic more than lunacy. Strange . . . or is it? A SANE MIND CAN BE A TERRIFYING APPARITION.

The last thing in the world members of a hate group, a Ku Klux Klan, or a narrow, single-interest group want is a sane man, a clear-eyed, rational man, in their midst.

This story of a human being's transformation, which should have brought joy and celebration to the community, instead brought anger, fear, and disquietude. Apparently, religion sometimes has to bring disruption before it can bring wholeness and peace.

But what about the demoniac . . . or the ex-demoniac? Here's a great moment . . . the bubbling up and overflowing of gratitude for deliverance. This is what spiritual experience is all about.

Everybody else may have wanted Jesus to be gone . . . BUT NOT THIS MAN. "What have you to do with me?" he had said just a few hours earlier. Now he's saying, "What can I do for you?"

Mark says the cured man begged Jesus to let him go with Him because he wanted to stay with this Man who had cleared his head and set him free. After all, this is the normal, natural, human response of a person who has had something big and life-changing happen to him. If you've ever been there, you know.

Despite the man's request, with what must have been extraordinary tact and uncommon kindness (don't you wish you could have been there to see it?), Jesus explained to the man that his assignment *now* was to stay where he was and bear witness.

Jesus tells him, "Go home to your family and tell them how much the Lord has done for you, and how he has had mercy on you" (Mark 5:19). Jesus wants the man to go back to the people who knew him at his worst and let that be his place of ministry.

Boy, that's tough. It's one of the hardest lessons a person who genuinely wants to be a Christian witness ever has to learn, but it's also one of the most important.

As Christians, it's not our primary duty to look for someplace where it's easier to be a Christian, but to be Christians where we are.

"Go home; go home," He said to the man . . . and to *us*. "That's where I need you. Go to your classroom, to your office, to your bridge club, to the country club, and maybe even to the Sunday school class."

No place is more appropriate for your witness to be made than precisely where you are known best. What it lacks in glamour it more than makes up for in timeliness and relevance, AND HE WILL BE WITH YOU AS YOU GO.

So the man did go home, Mark tells us, and he "began to proclaim in the [Decapolis] how much Jesus had done for him" (Mark 5:20, RSV). Then Mark adds this concluding note: "All men marveled" (v. 20).

It's more than idle commentary. Later in Mark's Gospel, in the seventh chapter, we find Jesus coming back to Decapolis. On that return trip, He heals a deaf man, taking him away from the crowd because of the press of people around him. Even so, even though it was done completely without ostentation, the word gets out. Mark says, "They were astonished beyond measure" (Mark 7:37, RSV). And then they say of Him, in a beautiful expression of admiration and respect, "He has done all things well." WHAT A SWITCH.

How do you explain the change in attitude? Where did those people come from, in the very region where earlier they had begged Him to go away?

Is it so hard to believe? I like to think at least some of them were brought by this wild man, this ex-demoniac whom Jesus had so wonderfully healed.

The cycle was complete. From possessed to proclaimer,
    from shackled to sharer,
     from babbler to bringer,
        from wild man to God's man, he had found his purpose and found himself.

why did Mark begin his writing @ Jesus baptism? (Roman)
1. gave comfort to early Christians
2. audience was the guns new life

1.6.13 lesson

······················· **Chapter 14** ·······················

THE INCARNATION
ACCORDING TO MARK *AD 69*

he is in Rome.
Nero was king
Christians were persecuted

In those days Jesus came from Nazareth of Galilee and was baptized by John in the Jordan.

Mark 1:9 RSV

Take heed, watch; for you do not know when the time will come.

Mark 13:33 RSV (see also 1:1-3; 13:34-37)

I wasn't raised in the church. In fact, the only time I recall being in a church with my mother was at my wedding. My father and I never once saw the inside of a church together, even at his wife's, my mother's, funeral.

They both knew the Bible and quoted verses from Scripture quite often, mostly in anger, to their five children. My mother often spoke of her own religion-filled childhood, those family members who attended the local church, and she even spoke of her Sunday school memories. Also, one of her brothers, Tom, became an ordained Baptist minister. To this day, I'm uncertain why the tradition of church attendance wasn't carried on with their children.

Just down the street from where I was raised in St. Paris, Ohio, was a Church of the Nazarene. I often would walk by it, on Lynn Street, on my way to school, thinking that one day I would be able to buy a suit so I could attend this church. At that time, I did not know that formal attire isn't a prerequisite for attendance.

At Christmastime each year, the Church of the Nazarene always displayed the manger scene on its front lawn, and I was aware of the old-fashioned Christmas pageant that was taking place inside on a designated night, as some of my classmates participated in it.

I can still imagine them there, bedecked in outrageous sheets, which covered practically nothing yet managed to impede all forward motion. On their heads were draped, more or less artistically, Cannon towels, probably obtained as gifts, anchored by rope and some borrowed diaper pins. And on their feet were a pair of rubber thongs, invariably about eight sizes too small.

Someone had spent all afternoon decorating the chancel area of the church with a liberal sprinkling of evergreen branches. The rickety old shed, covered with the local flora, was overarching a wooden manger, all of it in front of the old ten-ton pulpit, which had been shoved back from its usual perch to make room for the extravaganza. At last, the stage was set.

Outside in subfreezing weather, they all stood, anxiously waiting for their cue with all the other shepherds, angels, or whatever you happened to be in the pageant.

Now, I share this nostalgic memory with you for a reason. Although I never participated in any of these Christmas pageants as a child, I was aware of the *how* and the *why* of them, derived either from stories told by my parents or from Christmas TV programs. I imagine most of us learned most of what we know about the Christmas story from watching, hearing, or participating in pageants like that.

It probably isn't a bad way to learn. In fact, as I have learned as an adult, pageants such as these were used as a method of teaching at different times throughout history. Their roots go all the way back to the old medieval morality plays.

Even now, there is a tendency among us to think of the Christmas story as simply a kind of pageant. Our idea of the way it was is drawn from all the Gospel sources lumped together in our minds to form a kind of religious collage.

Have you ever read the beginning portions of each of the Gospels comparatively? If you do, you may be very surprised at what you uncover. Here's a sampling of what I found.

There is no place where the shepherd and the wise men, for example, were ever together at the same time. The shepherds appear only in the book of Luke. The wise men appear only in the book of Matthew; they're different. Only Luke has the angelic chorus singing. Only Matthew has the star; they're not the same. Matthew tells the story from the point of view of Joseph, the father; Luke tells the story from the point of view of Mary, the mother. There is variation.

We've put it all together in our mental recreation of the story to make a composite picture, and it's this collage, this composite picture, that our pageants always depict.

If you wanted to do an in-depth analysis of the four Gospels, comparatively speaking, you would have to begin with Mark because Mark really is the first Gospel,
the oldest Gospel,
the earliest Gospel to be written.

But what you will notice quickly when you begin your investigation, your comparison, beginning with Mark because it was written first, is that MARK IS THE ONLY GOSPEL THAT DOESN'T HAVE ANY CHRISTMAS STORY AT ALL . . . none whatsoever.

Isn't that strange? If what we knew about Christmas depended on the information we could glean from the oldest account, we'd know nothing. Bethlehem,
shepherds,
the star,
angels—all would be missing.

Mark just doesn't have a Christmas story.

But look out! There is significance even in that conspicuous absence. If Mark doesn't speak specifically of Christmas, he does speak of something even more fundamental. What is his Christmas story? IT HAS TO DO WITH THE BASIC, FUNDAMENTAL FACT OF THE INCARNATION, the belief on which the Christmas story rests.

Incarnation literally means "the enfleshing," the Christian conviction that somehow, in some special, unique way, God has visited His world in the flesh, in the historic personality of a particular Man, Jesus of Nazareth. Belief in Christmas is dependent on belief in the Incarnation, not vice versa, and that's the basic axiom that underlies all Mark has to say.

Now, some quick background material is called for here. We'll not dwell on it too long, but it is important. First of all, we need to remember that the Gospels were not written principally to serve as historical biographies of Jesus. Of course, they do contain historical material. In fact, they're the only source of material we have of His life and teachings.

But the Gospel writers were not writing primarily as historians. THEY WERE WRITING AS PREACHERS.

They were not principally record-keepers, or chroniclers; they were evangelists,
witnesses,
believers,
testifiers,
and proclaimers of a
message. For the most part, they were writing to specific people, just as Paul had done earlier, and they were writing to meet specific problems and opportunities.

I've often felt that to really understand the Gospels, the New Testament, we must first understand the Old Testament. The Old Testament always points forward toward the New, and the New Testament always points backward toward the Old. Each continually speaks about the other. They tie each other together.

I imagine these old PREACHERS were trying to write a sermon to be used on Sunday mornings, given to a congregation. As they sat down with quill in hand, questions would abound:

How do I go about it?
  Where do I start?
    What do I feel I just *have* to include?
      And what would I leave out? I think those same questions cross the minds of present-day pastors who prepare for a sermon to be delivered to their respective congregation every single Sunday.

Mark, the first Gospel writer, opens his account with Jesus being baptized in the Jordan by John, WHEN JESUS WAS ALREADY A FULL-GROWN MAN. Mark starts his story in the middle . . . in fact, almost at the end. Nearly half of Mark's Gospel deals with the final week of Jesus' earthly life. There's nothing about the birth, or the growth, or the early manhood of Jesus, and only a limited amount about the early ministry.

Why? Why should the beginning of the story be cut short? The reason is found in the circumstances that prompted him to write. He was not writing a biography; he was writing a SERMON.

And he was writing to some hard-pressed, beleaguered Christians who were shivering together in fright in the catacombs of Rome.

The year was A.D. 65, and the emperor, the Caesar, was that cynical, sensual, egomaniac whose name was Nero. Remember this from your history books? He was the one, it was said, who fiddled while Rome burned. Many historians think he was the one who set the fire . . . maybe just for diversion, maybe just for kicks. That's the kind of man he was. But it's sort of grisly when you think about it—music to burn cities by.

When it was over and most of Rome was reduced to cinders, he needed someone to put the blame on; he needed a scapegoat, so he turned to the Christians.

Why not? They were atheists, weren't they? Everybody said that. It's an exquisite irony. Christians were called atheists because they didn't believe in the gods . . . the *Roman* gods.

Furthermore, they were treasonable. They were subversive. They had a higher loyalty than to the state. THEY WERE PERFECT SCAPEGOATS.

So out went the decree from Nero to round up the Christians. And Peter was put to death— crucified upside down, tradition says, because he didn't think he was worthy to die in the same fashion as his Lord. In addition, Paul was put to death—beheaded, says the legend, and it may well be true.

Even at that, they were luckier than some of the others. It's not a very pretty picture. Others were covered with skins of animals and thrown to the dogs. They were covered with pitch and used as human torches to light the garden parties of Nero.

HOW LONG WOULD YOUR FAITH HAVE LASTED UNDER THOSE CONDITIONS?

Mark is saying to the Roman Christians: "I know you're going through fear
                                                            and torture
                                                    and persecution. I
know this is a tough time to be alive. BUT LOOK AT JESUS, the Lord Himself. He didn't have it so easy, either. LOOK AT HIM. He faced opposition,
    misunderstanding,
      forsaking,
        betrayal,
          humiliation,
            beating,
              and DEATH. Look at Him; that's what He had to go through."

At this time, Mark is not concerned too much about the teachings of Jesus. He wrote very little about the words of Jesus, the parables of Jesus. What he needed to lift up was the MODEL of Jesus, the EXAMPLE of Jesus. That's what his readers needed most. To face courageously and victoriously the very real possibility of martyrdom, at any minute, they needed to have confirmed that Jesus deliberately *chose* the way of the cross . . . for them, and that He did so under the guidance and direction of God.

"Look at Him," says Mark. "Look at Him, as he hangs there at Calvary." He's not the helpless victim of circumstance.
He's not the "galley slave, scourged in his dungeon"—don't you see?
He's the PRINCE OF GLORY, being obedient, even unto death, death on a cross.

What about the Incarnation in Mark? He doesn't talk about it.
He doesn't elaborate on it.
He just takes it for granted. God was in Christ, and the proof is not in a miraculous birth; it's not in the presence of angels,
or shepherds,
or wise men, reverent and
beautiful as those stories are. THE PROOF IS IN THE DIFFERENCE HE MAKES IN THE LIVES OF THE PEOPLE WHO FOLLOW HIM.

One of the greatest things about the Christian faith is that we don't have to understand all about Jesus before we can love Him and worship Him and serve Him. Listen to Harry Webb Farrington's hymn:

> I know not how that Bethlehem's Babe could in the Godhead be;
> I only know the manger Child has brought God's love to me.
> I know not how that Calvary's cross a world from sin could free;
> I only know its matchless love has brought God's love to me.

Mark is saying something those early Christians needed to know—AND WE NEED TO KNOW: The FACT of Christ, the REALITY of Christ, is more important than the EXPLANATION of Christ.

I've heard people in my Disciple class, people who have sat in their respective, designated pew for years, say, "Oh, if only I could just understand this. If I could just figure this out. If I could just understand the Trinity or the Resurrection or why there's evil. Then . . . *then* maybe I could give myself to Him
and serve Him
and REALLY join His church." Come to think of it, *I've* said something like that myself.

Well, Mark is saying it isn't necessary to have all the answers in pocket before you begin. IN FACT, IT ISN'T EVEN *POSSIBLE* TO HAVE ALL THE ANSWERS IN POCKET BEFORE YOU BEGIN. You don't have to have that formal suit before you can enter.

Real knowledge here, as in most areas of life, doesn't precede commitment; it follows it. If you insist on knowing before you begin, you'll never begin.

Commit yourself to as much of Christ as you can understand. Commit yourself to as much of Him as you can believe in, and then see if your understanding isn't stretched and stretched as He leads you farther and farther along the road.

More than 100 years ago, Albert Schweitzer wrote in his monumental classic *The Quest of the Historical Jesus* these haunting, probing words about Jesus, which may tell us something of the motivation of his own remarkable life:

> He comes to us as One unknown, without a name, as of old by the lakeside.
> He came to those men who knew Him not. He speaks to us the same words: "Follow Me."
> And set to the tasks why He has to fulfill for our time. He commands. And to those
> Who obey Him, whether they be wise or simple, He will reveal Himself in the toils, conflict,
> The sufferings which they shall pass through in His fellowship, and, as an ineffable
> Mystery, they shall learn in their own experience, WHO HE IS.[1]

As Farrington's hymn says:

> I know not how that Bethlehem's Babe could in the Godhead be;
> I only know the manger Child has brought God's love to me.

The Incarnation, God in Christ, this complex miracle that stands at the center of the Christian story—who can ever claim to understand it?

Of course, the disciples didn't. BUT THEY KNEW SOMEHOW THAT IN THIS CARPENTER, GOD WAS WITH THEM . . . to sustain them,
>   to undergird them,
>   to give them hope. AND THAT WAS ENOUGH.

Sara and I have always loved the ocean. At one time, we even owned a condo on New Smyrna Beach, Florida. I often have sat on the sand, looking out across the vast ocean at the fishing boats heading out to ply their trade.

These fishermen will go out during the daylight hours and fish until nightfall and somehow find their way home almost blindfolded. They can tell changes in the weather by sniffing the air. They can navigate, almost infallibly, by the stars, and even, some tell me, by the clouds. They know the sea perhaps better than they know the backs of their own hands. Of course, they don't know the whole sea. Maybe they've never sailed through the Straits of Magellan. Maybe they've never endured a storm on the north Atlantic or a Pacific typhoon. Wide areas of the sea may be unknown to them.

BUT THEY KNOW THE SEA. They know the essence of it. Because the sea has a near end, they've been raised on it. They've seen its tides come in and go out. They've seen its waves slap the bows of their fishing boats. They've felt the raging power of it when it was angry, and they've been lulled to sleep by the music of it when it was calm.

They know the essence of the sea, by years and years of study and experience, and I would suggest to you that maybe this is a kind of true analogy of our understanding of God.

Of course, there is a lot about Him that we don't understand. His greatness,
>   His vastness,
>   His size and power are
leagues beyond our comprehension.

But like the sea, God has a near end, and Mark says we call it Jesus. It's part of our faith—in fact, the very core of it, as Mark saw so clearly and expressed so eloquently—that in Jesus of Nazareth, God Himself has come very near so never again will people have to wonder about the nature of the integrity of the hope of ultimate reality.

When we know Jesus, we know God, for God was in Christ, reconciling the world unto Himself.

This is the Incarnation.
 This is the tingling anticipation of Advent, of the Christmas pageant.
  This is the hope and assurance, not only of history, but of eternity.

Remember the words of Farrington:

 I know not how that Bethlehem's Babe could in the Godhead be.
 I only know the manger Child has brought God's love to me.

The FACT of Christ is more important that the *explanation* of Christ. This is the Incarnation, according to Mark, given to a young, unchurched boy from St. Paris, Ohio. I have those formal clothes now. And I'm ready and eager to get caught up on all that I have missed.

what is meant by — "the reality of Christ is more important than the explanation of Christ?"

what credential are we considered Christians?

what key will I most reflect on from this chapter?

Chapter 15

THE HOUR OF TRIAL

In those days Jesus came from Nazareth of Galilee and was baptized by John in the Jordan. . . . The Spirit immediately drove him out into the wilderness. And he was in the wilderness forty days, being tempted by Satan. And . . . the angels were ministering to him.

Mark 1:9, 12-13 ESV (see also vv. 10-11, 14-15)

In this passage, the most glaring word peering out at us is *tempted*. Temptation is the alluring, deceptive, ubiquitous antagonist of the moral life.

If you've been around at all, you've known it.
 If you've lived at all, you've faced it.
  If you've grown at all, you've fought it, AS DID JESUS HIMSELF THROUGHOUT HIS LIFE ON EARTH. It would be hard to think of a theme more perennially pertinent or more probingly personal than TEMPTATION.

Mark is not sequentially listed in the Bible as the first of the four Gospels, but his Gospel was written first and in a sense is the fundamental Gospel, the essential one. The other Gospel writers, at least Matthew and Luke, had copies of Mark before them when they wrote. We know that for certain, for sequence and even specific wording show this. You can see that dependence when you compare them.

Matthew and Luke frequently elaborated on what Mark had written, expanded it, corrected it when correction of detail may have been called for, and smoothed it over to make it more fluid. But they were hard-pressed to improve his vivid,
                 hard-hitting,
                    no-nonsense style. It has been said of Mark that he is the Ernest Hemingway of Gospel writers . . . using pungent, direct prose. If you want flowery, baroque writing, go somewhere besides the Gospel of Mark.

As we read this book, we find there's that breathless character about Mark. It almost wears you out to read it through at one sitting, which you can do in about an hour and a half. It's an extremely worthwhile exercise. I guess you could call it spiritually aerobic.

His favorite word seems to be *immediately*—the King James Version says "straightaway"—"Jesus did this . . . and then He did that . . . and immediately He went over there. . ." By the time you read a few chapters, you're huffing and puffing with exhaustion.

If *poetry*, according to William Wordsworth's definition, is "emotion recollected in tranquility," I guess you could call the Gospel of Mark "emotion blurted out in impetuosity." He's written an action book, one that moves. It's as if he could hardly wait to pour the story out . . . AND I SUSPECT THAT'S EXACTLY THE CASE.

It only takes him six verses to describe the baptism,
the temptation,
and the beginning stages of Jesus'
preaching ministry . . . two verses apiece. Talk about conciseness and brevity, wonderful preaching characteristics. I would imagine preachers take these lessons to heart—well, maybe at least the conciseness part.

In Mark's condensed, packed version of Jesus' temptation in the wilderness, found in the middle two verses of this passage, he gives us fewer details than either Matthew or Luke. Mark doesn't tell us, as Matthew and Luke do, anything about the specific nature of the temptation. Turning stones into bread and feeding the people, leaping from the Temple and dazzling the people, bowing down before Satan and coercing the people—NONE OF THAT IS FOUND IN MARK.

The temptation for anyone wishing to use Mark for a devotional would soon find little treasure for homiletical exploitation. BUT OL' MARK WILL FOOL YOU. You've got to keep your eyes on that boy.

This is biblical concentrate, as it were. There's some good, practical stuff here, ungilded, to be sure, but undiluted, solid grist for the mill, and it deals with something contemporary, on the cutting edge of the timely, because it's . . . TIMELESS. IS THERE ANY HUMAN EXPERIENCE MORE UNIVERSAL, MORE PERVASIVE THAN THE EXPERIENCE OF BEING TEMPTED?

Be honest. Are you called upon daily to wrestle with some form of temptation?

Now, of course, the details of this temptation will vary from person to person. Also, the temptations of childhood are different from the temptations of maturity. I remember the story of the little boy whose mother strictly charged him to keep his hand out of the cookie jar. "Do not touch those cookies," she explained, "on penalty of permanent disfigurement." Indeed, she was a tough mom.

When she checked back a while later, she found one small cookie remaining out of the plentiful supply she had deposited. "Johnny," she erupted, "there's only one cookie left in here. How do you explain that?" He said, "Gosh, Mama, I don't know. I must have missed it."

What tempts you may not be what tempts me. I confess I can identify with that little boy. I, too, have some difficulty, some abiding struggle with caloric temptation. Those of you who know me would be surprised at that confession, given the svelte nature of my waistline.

But alas, unfortunately, it's true. I sometimes dream at night of being chased around town by legions of Krispy Kreme pistachio doughnuts. They lurk behind mounds of whipped cream and leap out at me, screaming to be devoured. It's awful. It's, it's . . . wonderful. But I'm happy to report that I'm doing better lately. Now I eat in excess only on the days that end in *Y*.

Indeed, we're not tempted by the same things. But I submit that we are *all* tempted, in some way,
  in some fashion,
    constantly,
      over and over, by lures that come,
        by experiences,
          by opportunities that present themselves.

Sometimes the temptations are so big, so compelling as to be virtually overwhelming. The alcoholic faces a constant, unending struggle with temptation. Representatives from Alcoholics Anonymous say if an alcoholic struggling to recover gives in to it just one time, just once, he or she is trapped again.

The same goes for the compulsive gambler, the obsessive Don Juan, and other addicts. Most of us don't have to fight that kind of thoroughgoing compulsion—and you can thank God if you don't—but that doesn't exempt any of us from the destructive power of temptation. WE ALL FACE THE STRUGGLE OF TEMPTATION EVERY DAY.

Maybe it's the struggle not to surrender to the feelings we know are unworthy,
  the struggle not to take shortcuts in our work,
    the struggle not to take advantage of somebody we know is defenseless,
      or the struggle not to succumb to a gradual lowering of standards. The possibilities are
endless.

Maybe these kinds of temptations are even more insidious than the grosser, bodily ones. They're certainly subtler. AND SUBTLETY IS WHAT GIVES TEMPTATION ITS DECEPTIVE ENTICEMENT.

At a superficial glance, most real temptations look pretty good. They seem to offer something worthwhile: escape from the grind,
                        from responsibility,
                          from the awful boredom of routine. They seem to offer a recess, a reprieve, or a quicker way to get what we want. WHAT'S WRONG WITH THAT?

After all, you tell yourself, you've worked hard, and you deserve a break. What harm can it possibly do? If only the tempter always were required to appear with visible horns and an obviously identifiable long, pointed tail, he or she sure would be a lot easier to deal with.

Is it surprising to you that most satanic portrayals are not the image of someone like Count Dracula or the Wicked Witch of the West—where would the appeal be in that? The image is more likely to be someone like Jack Nicholson or Al Pacino as the archetypical, smooth-talking evil one. THERE HAS TO BE SOME APPEAL, OR THERE'S NO CONTEST.

In Christopher Marlowe's famous play *Dr. Faustus*, Mephistopheles appeared in the garb of a Franciscan monk—not only good drama, but astute, incisive theology. THAT'S THE WAY IT WORKS.

The insidious nature of temptation is exactly that it often looks so good and seems so plausible. With just minimal effort, you can convince yourself that it's a positive thing, and before you know it . . . GOTCHA!

The truth only emerges later when the mask comes off. It's subtle, pervasive, ubiquitous, and demonic. What we're dealing with is a formidable foe.

I think Mark is saying temptation is a part of life. No one is immune. What a COMFORT, then, what a RELIEF to realize Jesus Himself wasn't immune to temptation, either. He, too, had to deal with it, and somehow that gives us something to cling to in our fight with the same foe.

To me, one of the strengths of Mark's version of the temptation comes out of the very forcefulness of the description. "The Spirit immediately drove him out into the wilderness . . . " The same Spirit had just descended on Him at the baptism, and then IMMEDIATELY—there's that word again, that typical Markan word—the Spirit drove Him out for testing.

Jesus was tempted, which in Greek means "put through trials." The adversary is none other than Satan himself, and His fortifying comes through angels who minister to Him . . . *not* after the experience, but during it. Mark is saying this thing wasn't some kind of charade,
some kind of game,
a shadow-boxing experience.

It was a real,
>soul-searching,
>>intense,
>>>agonizing struggle, with real issues at stake, and a different outcome was perfectly possible.

Mark is insisting JESUS FACED THE SAME KIND OF STRUGGLE WITH CHOICES YOU AND I FACE. While the stakes were higher with Him, the nature of the struggle is the same. I think that's good news. He knows firsthand what it's all about.

I have read accounts from some Christian writers who, in an attempt to exalt the divinity of Jesus—what makes Him different from us—would suggest that because He was special, He was somehow above having to deal with the human battles the rest of us have to fight.

It's as if some Christians want to shield Jesus from trials, temptations, and other difficulties common to the human lot for fear that conviction about His uniqueness will somehow be eroded by those experiences.

In going through all these things, He was just setting us an example, they say. He was above all that. He was too pure, too holy to be lured into real struggle with temptation.

In a sermon, Dr. Thomas Price Jr. of First United Methodist Church in Winter Park, Florida, would call that understanding as being PURE HERESY THROUGHOUT CHRISTIAN HISTORY:

> It cuts the very heart out of any concept of Incarnation. Anyone just playing a role . . . just walking through experiences that are not personally engaging, just to set an example is

absolutely *not* setting an example.

Sincere or not, such interpretations rob Jesus, rob the Scriptures, rob the Gospel, and rob life of any semblance of reality. AN UNTEMPTED SAVIOR IS NO SAVIOR AT ALL.

It would be a contradiction in terms. If He, too, did not have to wrestle with choices, to make decisions about conduct and behavior, to choose whether to do this or that, go here or there, if there were never really any options open to Him except the ideal, and He was programmed for that automatically, then He really is only a MODEL, a paradigm, an unblemished pattern, an unapproachable example, not a Rescuer, not a Redeemer at all, and what good would that do us?

Dr. Price is saying that if this were the case, Jesus would just be something that, by its very perfection, would only drive us further away from reconciliation with the Father. If it weren't a fight for Him, too, it would only underscore for us how hopelessly separated from God we are. But His temptation was real. FURTHERMORE, IT WAS ONGOING, not just limited to His forty-day period in the wilderness. In Luke's account, at the end of the temptation story, when Jesus has successfully resisted the various ploys of Satan, when He has beaten him back those three times, we are told that the devil departed from Him FOR A SEASON.

How instructive is *that? FOR A SEASON*—that is, not for all time; in fact, not for long, but simply until the next available opportunity to tempt. It was a constant struggle all His life . . . all the way to the end.

That agonizing period of prayer in the Garden of Gethsemane that night before the Crucifixion, when sweat and blood commingled on the ground, says to us that He was tempted to not go to the cross. Of course, that was a real temptation. It makes the hair stand up on the back of your neck. We don't dare turn it into a charade. Running away,
                      or compromising,
                           or begging off were live options. He could have given in to one of them and, on one level of His being, no doubt wanted to.

The point of Nikos Kazantzakis' controversial novel *The Last Temptation of Christ*, which was later made into a movie directed by Martin Scorsese, is that Jesus physically was lured, at least briefly, to consider abandoning the Messiah's mantle in order to assume a "normal" life, with marriage and family.

Whether Kazantzakis was right about that particular point is, of course, highly debatable, but that Jesus faced tough choices, hard choices, real choices, choices between different levels of good I don't think *is* debatable. Take that out of the story, and you remove what aligns Him, what identifies Him with the human experience.

The struggle Jesus had—TO BE WHAT HE WAS TO BE and TO DO WHAT HE WAS TO DO—was awesome and relentless. We can only remove our hats and stand in reverence before it. It was not in immunity from temptation but IN THE WAY HE HANDLED IT that the true scope of nobility of the Savior is seen. And nowhere is the reality and the seriousness of the battle more vividly portrayed than at Gethsemane, to which the experience in the wilderness is prelude. Gethsemane is a garden, but for a part of one long, harrowing night, it, too, was a WILDERNESS.

The next time we find ourselves in our own personal "wilderness," whatever it is—some obsession,

some panic urge to break away,

some choice between a greater good and a lesser one, WHATEVER—we need to remember that Jesus Himself has been there, too, with even greater issues at stake than ours.

But where do we lay our hands on real and sustaining resources to help us cope with temptation when we finally identify it and want to keep it at bay?

AREN'T WE GIVEN A CLUE IN THE PASSAGE ITSELF? The Bible is always its own best interpreter. THE SPIRIT and the ANGELS, remember? Isn't that the clue? Mark says the Spirit drove Him into the wilderness, the Spirit that was there before at the baptism and afterward when He began His ministry of preaching.

The Spirit was there *with* Him in His hour of trial. Mark describes it with the simple, graphic phrase so typically Markan in its directness: "And . . . the angels were ministering to him."

THAT'S HOW HE MADE IT.

Sure, it's picture language, as much Bible language is, but isn't Mark saying that throughout this massive struggle, throughout this time of wrestling with how He was to respond to God's laying His hand on His life, throughout this period of soul-searching, HE WAS SUSTAINED AND STRENGTHENED TO DO BATTLE WITH LESSER POSSIBILITIES BY THE AWARENESS OF GOD'S PRESENCE TO UNDERGIRD HIM?

"The angels were ministering to him." THAT'S HOW HE MADE IT. Now, throughout the Bible, we find that God, in His infinite grace, is terribly reticent about imposing Himself on His creation. It's part of His incomparable charm. He never forces His guidance on us, even when He must surely have to bite His tongue to hold back.

We must ask for His direction and counsel.

We must seek His strengthening.

We must invite the angels to minister to us. It's why the church has always stressed the importance of regular worship habits and the Christian's devotional life. I DON'T THINK IT'S ABOUT THE NUMBERS GAME, BUT BECAUSE WE KNOW WE CAN'T KEEP THE LINES OF COMMUNICATION OPEN ANY OTHER WAY.

Resisting temptation,

struggling against evil,

and preparing ourselves to meet human need can't be left to mere will power or psychic strategies. It simply won't work.

But a real power—

the power of the Spirit,

the ministry of the angels, as Mark calls it—is available to those willing to meet the conditions of its coming. With the asking, God will strengthen us to resist the lures of the tempter and to leave the wilderness unscathed.

No, it's not being tempted that is crucial; IT'S WHAT WE DO WITH IT.

A church or an individual, armed with the Spirit, open and responsive to the ministry of angels, will not be overcome by evil, but will overcome evil with good. AND WE DON'T HAVE TO BATTLE IT ALONE.

Chapter 16

LET IT GO

This is what the kingdom of God is like. A man scatters seed on the ground . . .
Mark 4:26 (see also vv. 27-29)

It may be that the hardest thing in the world to do is WAIT. To *have* to wait doesn't sit very well with us, does it? We Americans are not made that way. We're not inclined that way. We're activists,
  doers,
    producers,
      movers and shakers. This is how we're constituted. We're people who solve problems by rolling up our sleeves,
  by tackling issues,
    by getting in there and stirrin' the puddin'.

Our history is replete with examples of the "take charge" guy, or woman, or group, for whom sitting down and waiting for almost anything would have been worse than death. For the most part, American heroes are *not* the patient, long-suffering, stoic types.

Instead, American heroes are vigilantes. The Minuteman, Sergeant York, John Wayne—these are the people with whom we identify, the DOERS, who precisely don't wait but roll into action to change things.

So with this programming so consistently built into us, it's not always easy to appreciate the strong emphasis Jesus placed on the importance and wisdom of waiting.

Now, I don't mean He was a passive non-doer. He was *not*. You can never read the Gospels carefully and miss the fervor, the intensity of Jesus' ministry. He absolutely said some of the most scathing things ever uttered by human lips. The righteous anger of Jesus could curl your hair.

And chasing the money-changers out of the Temple that day was like something out of *Die Hard 2* . . . it could have happened in Dodge City.

But here's what's so striking. There's a balance about it. Jesus always knew when to act and when to wait for God to act. He knew when to move ahead and when to hold back, when to lunge and when to linger, when to tackle and when to trust. And one of the surest evidences, I think, of His sanity is that He kept the two polarities in proper tension.

Try to contrast two Gospel scenes in your mind. One is Gethsemane, where Jesus is actively praying while the disciples over in the corner of the garden have stretched out on the ground and gone to sleep.

The other scene is in the middle of the Sea of Galilee during a storm. Remember? *This* time, while the disciples are awake and frantic with fear at the plight they're in, there is Jesus, stretched out comfortably in the back of the boat, napping.

WHAT A CONTRAST! Isn't that intriguing?
  Jesus is awake; the disciples are asleep.
   The disciples are awake; Jesus is asleep. It clearly suggests something about Him they hadn't learned yet: There was a time to be awake and a time to sleep,
   a time to be up and a time to lie down,
    a time to do and a time to trust,
                        a time for activity and a time for acquiescence,
                        a time to go and a time . . . TO LET GO.

There is a time to get in there with all the energy you possess, but there is also a time when you must simply step back and let God in His wisdom take charge and do His thing in His own way.

I think this is what this little parable, the brief story Mark has placed in his book for us to find, is all about. This is the meaning, the lesson of the silently growing seed. THERE COMES A TIME WHEN YOU MUST LET IT GO AND TURN IT OVER TO GOD.

Mark is the only one of the Gospels to tell this particular story. You don't find it in the other Synoptic Gospels. That's a little surprising since Mark contains such a minimum of "teaching." It's Matthew and Luke who tell us most of the parables.

But Mark tells this one. It is important to him to include it. Knowing as we do that his Gospel was written during the persecution of the early church by Nero, this little vignette must have spoken with comforting directness to Christians who couldn't see much evidence right then that God's work was going on.

"What's happening?" I'm sure they were saying. "Why is God allowing this? What does it mean? The whole enterprise is coming down around our heads."

"WAIT," Mark says Jesus says. "JUST WAIT. That's our job right now. This is not the time to do. This is not a time to charge around. NOW IS A TIME TO TRUST."

The seed is not visible; you can't see it growing. But that doesn't mean nothing is happening. Planting has occurred, and watering has taken place. NOW LET IT GO. Just turn God loose, and trust in His ability to work His good purpose. You can count on Him. HE WILL NOT LET YOU DOWN. As Mark 4:28 says, "First the blade, then the ear, after that the full corn in the ear" (KJV).

The positive assurance of the kingdom's triumph in spite of anything that might happen is the theme of the parable.

To bring it down into our day, make it current, take this fundamental principle,
this theme,
this faithful willingness to
wait for God, and try it on for size.

Being both a parent and now a grandparent, I think this parable is a marvelous illustration. Raising children is a tough assignment, maybe tougher today than it has ever been. In saying that, I know I'm not divulging a surprising new insight. Nothing about it is a snap, but maybe the hardest part of all is learning how and when to release them . . . stage by stage.

At what point do you stop fretting yourself unmercifully with planting and watering, and commit them into the hands of a higher power?

Of course, it's not a once-and-for-all thing, and in a sense, you never stop being a parent. You always worry about your children and fret over them.

If there is anything worse than a parent who abandons his child to the weeds and neglect, maybe it's the parent who stifles his child so much that he can never breathe the air of independence.

Apron strings, I guess, are to growing youngsters sort of what fertilizer is to growing plants—too little, and there is no rootage; too much, and the individuality is burned out.

As with the farmer in the parable, there comes a time when the wise and loving parent has to say: "All right, I have done what I could. I have planted and watered the best I knew how. I have tried by both precept and example to say to my child, 'THESE THINGS ARE IMPORTANT;
THESE THNGS ARE PRECIOUS
AND VALUABLE
AND GOOD.
I WANT YOU TO BELIEVE IN THEM, TOO.

'My prayer for you is that, in time, you will come to accept them for yourself and live by them, but I cannot arbitrarily impose my standards and values on your life. So now I go to sleep, turning you over to God and trusting that in His gracious, dependable providence, He will take what has been sown and bring it to glorious fruition.'"

Somewhere along the line, the wise parent has to do that. It's a prerequisite for the child to obtain maturity.

However, it can never be used as a shortcut.
It can never be a substitute for early nurture.
It can never take the place of fair, consistent, disciplined training in the formative years. The planting and watering stage is necessary, but YOU CAN'T KEEP A CHILD THERE FOREVER.

The purpose of growth is for the individual to reach a stage where he or she is a full-blown, ripe, complete person, and for the goal to be reached, that means the reins must be slackened sometimes.
There comes a time when we must trust,

when we must yield,
when we must relax,
when we must wait and allow God's inspired influence to do the work. As parents, we will be driven up the wall if we can't do that.

In the parable, the farmer planted,
then watered,
then LET GO. Jesus commended him for it. He did what he could, and then he went trustingly to sleep. God did the rest, even through the night, while the man was not aware of it.

I'm told that in the ancient biblical town of Shechem, the town in which Jacob settled en route to Egypt during the famine, now called Nablus, north of Jerusalem in Israel, streams run beneath the streets. During the day, you can't hear them, when the bazaars are open
and the merchants are shouting
and the goats and camels are wandering through the alleyways. You'd never know they were there; there's simply too much noise.

But after sundown, when the city has settled down for the night and all is quiet for a while, if you listen carefully, you can begin to make them out, gently flowing underground. It's the comforting sound of life-giving water to nourish a parched, dry land.

Call it a parable, if you like . . . OUR OWN NOISE AND CONFUSION, OUR OWN RATTLING,
CLANGING,
and SELF-RELIANCE sometimes keep us from experiencing the nourishment that is right around us.

We must work.
We must labor.
We must plan.
We must organize, but then we must LET GO, and allow God to move through our organization.

It is God who gives the growth.
It is He who produces the change.
It is He who sustains when we stop our hectic frenzy and simply let Him . . . BE.

We can learn from what Paul Scherer writes of being present at the final concert Toscanini ever conducted. He was over eighty, and they had built a slender railing around the podium to support him. He touched it lightly with the frail fingers of one hand. The he raised the baton. Says Scherer:

Something physical seemed to happen to the orchestra. The performers moved into the music of the great symphony as ONE PERSON.

And as they progressed, each player, one after another, violin, viola, cello, bass . . ., lifted his eyes from the notes and fastened them on the maestro there, with the wistful little smile on his face.

98

They knew him, they loved him, they trusted him . . . and all the music that was in them swept up toward that face.[1]

Plant,
 water,
 and then sleep in trust, for the great Maestro has not yet retired.

Chapter 17

THE MAN BY THE SIDE OF THE ROAD

Jesus stopped and said, "Call him."
Mark 10:49 (see also vv. 46-48, 50-52)

In a way, this healing story from Mark about blind Bartimaeus is such a simple story. There is nothing special about it, nothing all that unusual or distinctive. Stories just like it are scattered throughout the Gospels.

According to the Record, Jesus was always healing people . . . men, women, children, the lame, and the blind. Once he healed a man with a withered arm. And once He healed ten lepers from the terrible disease leprosy. HE WAS ALWAYS DOING THINGS LIKE THAT. It was so typical of Him, so normal, so in character.

Yet it seems this particular story, which, incidentally, is paralleled in both Matthew and Luke, has an especially unaffected and natural quality about it, an ingenuous, matter-of-fact quality about it . . . almost as if the physical healing was not intended by the author to be the most important thing to be remembered.

It *is* a simple story; it has no complex plot,
no sudden twists and turns,
no highly developed personality characterizations,
and very little dialogue. It's a simple story. Even a child can understand it
as it flows from the page.

Yet there is something here so profound and so . . . searching, so timeless and so wonderful that we could spend days on it and not exhaust the material.

The setting is Jericho, the city of palms—in Jesus' day, a tourist city, a resort city, a good place for beggars, located down in the valley, near the banks of the Jordan, about fifteen miles from Jerusalem on the road that leads to Transjordan.

A blind man named Bartimaeus lived there, with no means of support except to beg. We don't know how he became blind. Maybe he was that way from birth.

Maybe his blindness resulted from an accident
or maybe from a disease. Even today the Middle East has a
shockingly high percentage of blind people. It's one of the first things you notice when you travel
there. The accounts just don't tell us that information.

This man was forced, apparently, to eke out a precarious existence the best he could by playing
on the sympathy of others.

Don't you wonder what he might have thought on this day as he went out to his station along the
highway? Don't you wonder if he had any premonition of what it might bring? Do you suppose he
went out that day resigned or optimistic?

After all, it was the Passover season, a good time of the year for beggars. It was sort of like
Christmas, when our hearts are tenderer than usual and human compassion is more easily
aroused. Could he have had an inkling of what was to come?

At any rate, suddenly, it happened—a parade, an entourage. Bartimaeus couldn't see, but he
could feel,
    sense,
    hear, "Jesus of Nazareth is passing by."

This is parenthetical, but if you could put yourself down any place, if you could transport yourself
across distance, if you could pick yourself up and move across time, as in a time capsule, so that
you could be an eyewitness to a Gospel event, any one, which would you choose?

Would you be present at Calvary? I'm not sure I could take that. I don't know if my stomach
would hold it. Would you want to witness the glory of the Transfiguration or His baptism, or
maybe be present to kneel with others at the manger in Bethlehem? Wouldn't that be something?
If I could pick any one, I'm not sure what event I would choose, but maybe it would be enough
just to stand in a crowd like this one . . . and feel the tingle,
                                        the excitement,
                                        the electricity
of expectancy that would *have* to be there as people looked up the road and saw Him coming.
"Jesus of Nazareth is passing by." Thinking about it literally sends chills up and down my spine.

Because he was blind, Bartimaeus couldn't see any of it. BUT HE KNEW; HE UNDERSTOOD. THIS
WAS IT. IT WAS NOW OR NEVER. AND HE RESPONDED.

Yelling louder than anybody else in the crowd, he shouted, "Jesus, Son of David, have mercy on
me!" (Mark 10:47). He knew it was his chance, the best opportunity he would ever have. If he
could just get a response from the Man, it would be a lot bigger than a couple of coins clanging
in a cup.

Now, you can say what you want to about Bartimaeus. This may seem brash to us, or even crass.
It obviously did to the crowd.

But you have to say this for him: He may not have had manners, but he sure had motivation.
                    He may not have had finesse, but he sure had fervor.

What he lacked in etiquette, he more than made up for in earnestness.
Give him an "F" in the social graces, if you like, but you've got to give him an "A" in persistence.

The more the crowd tried to shush him, the louder he shouted, "Son of David, have mercy on me!"

And this is the part I like best. Mark says; Can you see it in your mind's eye—the crowded street scene, the noise, the tumult, the parade winding its way along, the man on the side of the road, shouting out his plea? Mark says, so simply, with not a word with more than one syllable: "Jesus stopped and said, 'Call him.'" There it is. THE CROWD BUZZED.

And Bartimaeus—the words are almost alive in Mark; they almost move on the page in front of you—sprang to his feet. This is a blind man, a man who can't see a thing. Bartimaeus sprang to his feet, and throwing aside his garment—that's got to be an eyewitness touch—he ran out on the road where Jesus was. FORGET MODESTY AT A TIME LIKE THIS. There are more important issues at stake.

Isn't that a vivid image, the two of them standing together there on the highway?

There was the Man who is the Creator of everything . . . and the man who has nothing,
  the Man who could do *anything* . . . and the man who couldn't even pay his own way,
    the Man who could see into the very depths of the human soul . . . and the man who couldn't see his own hand in front of his face,
      the Man of abundant life . . . and the man of miserable existence. What a contrast!

And, ironically, the One was on His way to die, and the other was on the threshold of a whole new dimension of life. *He knew, still took the time.*

It was incredible that even at that point, even near the end, Jesus continues to give. In a sense, the whole Gospel is encapsulated here. The whole grand "Good News," in all its mystery and gracious fullness, is symbolized, in a way, in the meeting of these two men on the road.

Jesus asks, "What do you want me to do for you?" And Bartimaeus grabs the offer while it's hot. "Rabbi, I want to see" (Mark 10:51).

I tell you, if we don't feel the poignancy, the voltage, of that, then I'm afraid we're blinder than Bartimaeus himself.

Well, it moves quickly from that point in the story on. Of course, Jesus heals him. Right there. Don't ask me how. I don't know. The New Testament doesn't explain it and isn't even interested in the mechanics of it, the kinds of questions we most naturally would want to ask.

Since Jesus was an extraordinary Man, it follows that He would do extraordinary things; that's the New Testament assumption, and that's where Mark leaves it.

Knowing as we do today the close, intimate relationship among mental, spiritual, and physical health, the close bond of that interrelatedness might make us suspect that Jesus was aware of

Ruth—See Christ as 103 *he is coming down the road.*

some physical healing principles still beyond our present-day knowledge. Maybe someday we'll discover that. In this case, faith seems to have played a part, but it doesn't always in the New Testament accounts of healing.

Mark would be astonished that we'd even wonder. He wasn't writing a medical document; he was writing a spiritual document. Jesus asked Bartimaeus what he wanted most. Bartimaeus told him, and JESUS GAVE IT TO HIM. It was a compassionate response to a need.

"Immediately," Mark says, "he received his sight" (v. 52). Then, he concludes his account with this beautiful touch: "he . . . followed Jesus in the way." It's more than a miracle of vision; it's a miracle of deliverance. He *saw* in more ways than one.

Now, that's the story as Mark sets it down. It's a good story, a simple story, but with Mark, it's never a complete story that he's trying to tell. Mark is saying to us that THERE IS MORE THAN ONE KIND OF BLINDNESS.

Bartimaeus had one kind, the most obvious kind. Call it blindness of the outer eye.

I was about sixteen years old when I received my first pair of glasses. Up until then, I had never had any trouble seeing. I never even thought about it much. I took it for granted. The stitches on a curve ball,
  signs at a distance,
    small print . . . I could see it all.

Never had a problem. But all at once, or what seemed like all at once, there was a change. My perceptions were altered. I noticed deterioration in the quality of newsprint. I thought it was a conspiracy, a plot or something. People's faces were sometimes blurry. *What's happening to them?* I wondered. People were pointing out details I couldn't even see. I DIDN'T KNOW WHAT I WAS MISSING.

Remember the story of the woman who was taking a shower at home one day when the doorbell rang? She called out, "Who is it?" And the man at the door answered, "Blind man." *Well*, she said to herself, *blind man. I guess it doesn't matter whether I'm dressed or not.* So she answered the door *au naturel.* The man said, "Where do you want me to put these venetian blinds, lady?"

IF YOU CAN'T SEE, YOU CAN MISS A LOT.

That was Bartimaeus—physically blind, cut off from experiencing certain things. That's one kind of blindness.

But there's another kind of blindness, and it may be more crippling than his kind. Call it blindness of the INNER eye. It's when you're not *willing* to see.

In this story, it's represented by those other people in the crowd, those townspeople and neighbors, the people of Jericho who were so annoyed with Bartimaeus.

They may have had twenty-twenty vision, but they saw him only as a stereotype, as a nuisance, not as a person. See how Mark puts it when Bartimaeus was calling for help: "Many rebuked him and told him to be quiet" (v. 48).

Well, no wonder; I can understand that. He was embarrassing them—all that noise, all that commotion, for heaven's sake.

They were probably thinking, *What's wrong with you, man? Don't you know how to act in public? Cool it.* They could tolerate him, as long as he stayed in his place, as long as he behaved . . . on the fringe. But assert himself? COME ON. They wanted him to be quiet, stay out of their hair, not bother them.

They never saw him as a human being. They were blind to what was really going on. In our own day, is it all that different? I don't say this with criticism or to harp, but where do we see the Bartimaeuses today? Or do we ever wish to *see* them at all? They're there, you know. *homeless, mentally ill, elderly* They are the ones with whom Jesus principally identified. That's sort of hard for us. In fact, they're the ones He seems to have liked best. People who didn't approve of Jesus' associates gave the harshest criticism of Him found on the pages of the New Testament. "Look at Him," they sneered. "He associates with harlots and publicans and sinners."

AND HE WORE IT, THAT CRITICISM, AS A BADGE OF HONOR.

"Thank God," somebody has said, "Jesus never lost His taste for bad company."

Maybe one of the tragedies of our time is that the more secure we become, the less sensitive we become to those who have no security at all, and the more fortunate we are, the less likely we are to *see* those who are less fortunate in the world.

Who are the blind? Are they those who can't see, or those who won't look? Are they those with detached retinas, or those with a detached heart?

Maybe the blindest people of all are those who are so wrapped up in their own comfort
                                                          and security
                                                               and protection against
annoyance that they've trained themselves not to notice the hurt around them.

Maybe the true meaning of this story is that Bartimaeus isn't the only blind person. Certainly, it raises the question as to which kind of blindness is harder to cure . . . or which kind of recovery represents THE NEED FOR THE GREATER MIRACLE.

Another observation in Mark's story is that there are miracles that will never take place until SOMEONE IS WILLING TO . . . STOP, as Jesus did. It's so eloquent . . . in its very simplicity. It's eloquent the way Mark just says, "Jesus stopped and said, 'Call him.'"

In commenting on this passage in The Interpreter's Bible, the late Hal Luccock says:

> The art of stopping is a high art. We have a schedule, and as an acute observer noted, we often spell that word 'skedaddle'. So we 'skedaddle' from here to there, to arrive breathless at the exact moment of the appointment. It's not easy to stop. It takes humility and it takes

reverence for personality. But stopping is a prelude for any real work for healing. Jesus never healed anybody on the run. And the disciple is not above the Master. He must learn to stand still and to stand at attention before his brother and sister in Christ.[1]

There are situations in life that are never going to be cured, that are never going to be remedied, until we have learned and practiced . . . the art of stopping.

If we are not willing to stop, then the very people who need it most—little children at a formative stage,
    older people along the sidelines,
     the hurt,
      the bleeding,
      the disillusioned,
all those who can't demand it for themselves—will fail to receive the ministry God wants them to have.

"Jesus stopped and said, 'Call him.'" It's one of the most gracious things about Him I know. It became right there a one-on-one situation.

With that great heart of compassion for a fellow human being, He focused His entire attention on that man's personal need. I think that's what authentic ministry is all about.

Malcolm Muggeridge, a maybe eccentric but brilliant English journalist and writer who became a Christian a few years ago, says Mother Teresa was chiefly responsible for leading him to the faith. He has written a book about her, titled *Something Beautiful for God*.

The whole world knew Mother Teresa. She wasn't a beautiful woman externally, not by any stretch of the imagination. Instead, her beauty was on the inside; she had an inner radiance that was winsome and contagious.

The first time Muggeridge came in contact with her, he says, was years ago on a visit to Calcutta in India. He saw such misery there, such deprivation and poverty and filth that it made him physically sick. It was too much. "I went back to my comfortable hotel room," he writes. "I went back to my room and had a stiff whiskey and soda to expiate Bengal's wretched misery. I ran away and stayed away. Mother Teresa *moved in and stayed,* and that's the difference."[2]

Exactly! That's the difference. There are miracles that will never happen until someone is willing to *move in and stay*. Jesus stopped and said to bring the man to Him. That's when the healing and the transformation took place.

On the other side of the story, while Bartimaeus waited a long time, when his chance came, he LEAPED . . . literally. He wasn't qualified.
 He wasn't trained.
  He didn't have any gifts or graces of significance.

As Dr. William Barclay points out, Bartimaeus even had a woefully inadequate Christology. Twice he called Jesus "Son of David," which was a strictly Messianic title with heavy military and political overtones, the very implications from which Jesus most wanted to stay away. Of course,

Bartimaeus didn't understand. BUT HE ACTED ON WHAT HE DID KNOW.

And, you see, that's the wonder and that's the miracle of the Gospel. That's the REAL miracle. YOU DON'T HAVE TO BE A FINISHED PRODUCT TO COME TO JESUS AND ACCEPT HIS ACCEPTANCE. We can come as we are, and He will receive us—not on the basis of our worth, but on the basis of our desire to come.

Why, it's like being blind . . . and suddenly, miraculously, being able to see.

The Good News is that there is Someone who hears us when we cry out to Him,
who sees us even when we're sightless,
who finds us even when we're lost in the crowd.

He calls to us, and when we respond, darkness turns into light and even the night becomes as day.

If we quickly gloss over this beautiful story,
  if we miss the poignancy of it,
    then we are quite possibly blinder than Bartimaeus ever was.

what key will I most reflect on from this chapter? Response to the blind (inwardly) at their greatest need. Do not postpone, the opportunity may not be available again

My qualification is desperation.
what 2 do see but do not see — visibility
spiritually
which one needs the greater cure? Visible or spiritual?

Give boy a chance
Give the church a chance
Give the steps a chance
Give a sponsor a chance
Give the Big Book a chance

Give the 1st & 12th 1
Chance
Give the promises a chance.

2.17.13   God,
I am a child of
a loving and being,
creative human being.

Chapter 18

12.12.12
2.17.13

IT'S REALLY HARD
TO FIGURE, ISN'T IT?

Ye shall find the babe wrapped in swaddling clothes, lying in a manger.
Luke 2:12 KJV (see also vv. 13-15)

. . . And every common bush afire with God;
But only he who sees, takes off his shoes—
The rest sit round it and pluck blackberries.
Elizabeth Barrett Browning,
nineteenth-century English poet

Each and every December, we almost stand on our tiptoes, looking ahead in anticipation. There it is up ahead, just over that hill, around that corner. CHRISTMAS IS COMING. Admittedly, our first thoughts about THE SEASON, about Christmas, are not entirely on Incarnation.

Incarnation is the word that stands for God in our midst,
the Lord God of the universe being with us,
divine downward mobility—not for God's sake, but for
ours, a theme so daring and so generous it makes your head swim even to think about it.

We're all aware of the place of the Incarnation—"in Bethlehem in Judea," of all places (Matt. 2:1)—and when it happened; Paul said it happened "when the fullness of time had come," at exactly the right moment, or as soon as conditions were ready for it to work (Gal. 4:4).

Each and every December, we stand in awe before the event itself and attempt to catch our breath. For although we know the story by heart and could probably recite it verbatim from memory, it still draws us up short.

It's really hard to figure, isn't it? Is it as hard for you as it is for me? After all the buildup—after all that laying of the foundation
over all those centuries,
after all that Old Testament preparation leading up to something new and dramatic, the birth of God's Son—when it finally comes, it is so LAID BACK, almost CASUAL.

109

It's really hard to figure, isn't it? Here is the biggest event of history, for crying out loud, the *hinge* of history, theologian Carl Michalson called it, the crossroads happening of the human panorama, and it's almost done under a bushel, to use Jesus' phrase. You almost have to go looking for it.

"Ye shall find the babe wrapped in swaddling clothes, lying in a manger." My gracious! Talk about an unobtrusive entrance.
  Talk about unpretentiousness.
    Talk about slipping in virtually undetected.
      Talk about a covert operation. James Bond, 007, couldn't have done it so well.

If you want to make an impact on the world, if you want to IDENTIFY—presumably that's the point of the Incarnation—why would you do it that way? Why would you do it so surreptitiously? Why would you almost go out of your way to hide what was happening from prying eyes and inquiring minds? It's *really* hard to figure, isn't it?

What is *with* God, anyway? Doesn't He have a strategy board?
                    Doesn't He have a council of economic advisers?
                    Doesn't He understand that if He'd just get a good P.R. man, if He'd just turn His account over to an energetic agency, if He'd just get Madison Avenue to work on His case, He could double His sales overnight?

It does seem strange, doesn't it, that after all that time of getting ready,
  through prophets
    and seers
    and visionaries
      and dreamers, God handled the Christmas scenario as He did?

Look at it. What kind of business operates through a peasant couple in a remote, obscure village miles off the beaten track? What kind of business lets the main event take place in a smelly, primitive cow barn so far from civilization that authorities didn't even know something unusual was up? What kind of business lets the first word be released not to the press but to a scruffy band of wandering shepherds, way out in a distant pasture, and sends them back home by a different route with explicit instructions to keep the story under their turbans? WHAT KIND OF BUSINESS IS THAT?

Is this any way to peddle a product? Is that how *you* would have handled it if you had been in charge of production? What do you suppose got into God? It's *really* hard to figure, isn't it?

Of course, the power of the birth story is in its simplicity and in its restraint. We can see it now, of course. It touches us so deeply not because it's overstated, but precisely because it's *not*. In fact, understatement often can create a greater effect than pulling out all the stops can.

For example, a teacher who suddenly drops her voice to a whisper may grab the class's attention when a strident yell wouldn't make a shred of difference. My wife, Sara, a teacher, does this to me in any disagreement we have. She knows how to disarm me . . . quickly.

It was not the florid rhetoric of the then-famous orator Edward Everett that everybody remembers from the dedication service of the battlefield of Gettysburg. He spoke for more than an hour on that cold day in 1864, and all that elaborate oratory scarcely made a ripple in anybody's mind. But the brief, simple, mostly one-syllable, dignified words of Abraham Lincoln, sketched out on a scrap piece of paper on the train en route to the dedication, are now forever etched in the public consciousness—which shows the power of simplicity and restraint.

It's the very thing we see in the Christmas story. Maybe that's the most astonishing thing about the whole business—the controlled, understated, always downplayed restraint of it. Nothing in the story is more beautiful, or maybe, in the long run, more powerful. *Allah?*

THE GOD OF JESUS CHRIST DOESN'T KNOCK YOU DOWN AND DRAG YOU OFF INTO HIS CORNER. Isn't that what it suggests? He could, of course. Of course, He could . . . if He wanted to. He could in a second, easy as pie. That's what omnipotence means. God clearly has that latent power.

If He decided to, He could perfectly well DEMAND allegiance, COERCE cooperation, by the snapping of His fingers. If He decided to, He could MAKE us be His simply by dazzling us with His might, simply by overwhelming us with His power. But He doesn't. It *really* is hard to figure, isn't it?

Bethlehem could have been the Normandy beachhead. But it wasn't. And it's beginning to look like the restraint was entirely intentional. Maybe nothing offers us a clearer hint of the divine working.

Don't we see Jesus Himself operating in the same pattern? Talk about a chip off the old block. How are we to understand the Temptation experience that marked the beginning of His ministry? Doesn't Jesus have to wrestle there with essentially what God had to wrestle with before Bethlehem—the temptation to take a shortcut,
                    the temptation to dazzle,
                    the temptation to unleash His power directly . . . all of those
temptations to overwhelm people, to MAKE them disciples instead of winning them?

BUT HE REFUSED. There's the bigness of it. Jesus rejected that approach categorically and instead chose the longer, harder, more personal way. He chose God's way even though it ultimately meant humiliation and death on a cross. *in the fullness of Time*

God and Jesus showed divine restraint, power on a leash. Oh, there are times, to be sure, when the full, unrestricted might of God is turned loose in the Bible . . . against old Pharaoh in Egypt— "Let my people go," He says (Exod. 9:1); and against the Canaanites at Jericho—He just blew the walls away. He unleashed explosive, raw power when it took that to blast out implacable opposition.

However, those incidents are rare. When God is dealing with His own, it's astonishing how subtle and restrained His revelation is. When He has business with Moses, He calls him through a little fire burning in a bush out there on the mountainside. When He has business with Jeremiah, He speaks to him through a potter turning an earthen jar on a wheel. When He has business with Mary, He whispers in her ear.

Typically, the whisper of God is His authentic voice—not the loud,
                                        clanging,

irresistible force that bowls you over and slams you into a slot, but the quiet, persistent whisper that respects your integrity even as it makes its appeal.

Don't you think that's why the shepherds came so quickly to the manger? "Let us now go even unto Bethlehem," they said when they heard the announcement (Luke 2:15, KJV). Sophistication hadn't ruined their capacity to take in a revealed truth. They wanted to believe. They were better theologians than their uptown cousins with twice the education. Yet maybe it's also why the Wise Men were able to find Him when Herod couldn't.

Herod . . . what a real stinker,
            what a goof-head,
                        what a farce. He wouldn't have known what he was looking at if he had gotten there. If he had come to the manger, he wouldn't have seen anything miraculous . . . just a baby, a mother, and a dirty stable. He would have thought, *THIS IS IT? BIG DEAL!* Births took place every day in his kingdom.

HE WOULDN'T HAVE KNOWN WHAT HE WAS LOOKING AT IF HE HAD SEEN IT.

The Wise Men found Him because they were LOOKING for Him. They wanted to find Him, and with eyes of faith and longing, they saw, even in a primitive setting, grandeur and beauty that transcended material limitation.

God won't mow us down with His power; that's the Christmas story, or part of it. He whispers gently. With polished tact and impeccable manners, He places before us hints and promptings, invitations and overtures, but we must pick them up and respond to them for them to come alive with meaning.

Remember how Browning put it in her poem about Moses' burning bush experience?

> Earth's crammed with heaven,
> And every common bush afire with God;
> But only he who sees, takes off his shoes—
> The rest sit round it and pluck blackberries.

She's saying, "TAKE OFF YOUR SHOES!" It's right here. You've arrived. That for which your heart is really hungry is right here, as the old story says:

In the manger,
 in the unpretentious place,
  in the hurting place,
   in the needy place,
    in the ugly place . . . that's where you find the Savior.

IT'S WHERE HE'S BEEN SINCE HE CAME. IT'S REALLY HARD TO FIGURE, ISN'T IT?

While it wasn't really meant to tie into Christmas at all when he wrote it, in a sense, Francis Thompson possibly wrote one of the most characteristic Christmas verses of all:

I fled Him, down the nights and down the days;
I fled Him, down the arches of the years;
I fled Him, down the labyrinthine ways of my own mind;
And in the midst of tears I hid from Him...
From those strong Feet that followed, followed after...

—"The Hound of Heaven"

That's whom we're dealing with—THE HOUND OF HEAVEN, the God of Jesus Christ, who never gives up pursuing us in undiscourageable love . . . until, after we finally quit clawing and scratching and fighting, we surrender.

He'll beckon.
  He'll point.
    He'll plead.
      He'll whisper. And in the nick of time, He descended the stairway of heaven with a Baby in His arms, garbed in utter helplessness and innocence to show us that real power doesn't coerce; it stimulates. Greater love hath no God than this, that He withholds His power for His people.

In the book of Revelation, we are given the graphic image of the risen Christ standing before a closed door, and the text reads, "Behold, I stand at the door, and knock" (Rev. 3:20, KJV). What an astounding image. The very angels of heaven must be breathless at the restraint of it.

But then, is it really necessary to figure it out? All we have to do . . . is accept it. "Do not be afraid. I bring you good news of great joy that will be for all the people. Today in the town of David a Savior has been born to you; he is Christ the Lord. This will be a sign to you: You will find a baby wrapped in cloths and lying in a manger."

What unrestrained love this is from God, who "so loved the world that he gave his one and only Son, that whoever believes in him shall not perish but have eternal life" (John 3:16).

IS IT REALLY THAT HARD TO FIGURE, AFTER ALL?

What key will I reflect on from this chapter?

Galatians 4:4? Who is the fullness of time

Power on a leash.
Wise men found Him because they were looking for Him.
Donkey vs horse. (humility)
Peter repented, Judas did not.

Chapter 19

THE COMMENDED AND COMMENDABLE CROOK

What is this I hear about you? Give an account of your management, because you cannot be manager any longer.
Luke 16:2 (see also vv. 1, 3-9)

My gosh; what kind of a story is this, anyway? Is it from Jesus, or is it from O. Henry? I know it's in the Bible, but somehow it just doesn't sound like the Bible . . . where morality is supposed to prevail and virtue is supposed to be rewarded. That's not what happens here. It sounds more like a plot from a Martin Scorsese movie or an episode of *L.A. Law.*

You think, *Maybe the ending was chopped off or something.* It just sort of stops. Did this guy ever get what was coming to him, his just desserts? Did he ever get retribution for what he did? WHAT HAPPENS NEXT? You think, *Surely there's more than this.*

Remember the sequence of events: A "steward," he's called in the King James Version, an employee given a good bit of responsibility, a foreman, an estate manager for a wealthy man, was fired after he mismanaged the boss's property. The Record says he "was accused of wasting" the goods (v. 1). The New Revised Standard Version says he "was squandering his property". . . maybe on lottery tickets
　　　　　　　　or savings-and-loan stock,
　　　　　　　　　　　or maybe he bought season tickets to the Chicago Cubs games
. . . that would certainly constitute squandering.

At any rate, they caught him, nabbed him red-handed, with his fist firmly planted in the cookie jar. HE WAS HAD! There was no question about his complicity,
　　　　　　　　　　　　no doubt about his guilt. It was an airtight case. All that remained to do was to settle up, straighten the books, clean out his desk . . . and GO. There was no way he was asking for a reference.

What could he do? What was he supposed to do now? Go back and be a day laborer and wear one of those green hard hats? Get a job at Burger King? At his age? Working once more at a minimum wage was beneath him. What about resorting to begging? NO WAY. He had lost his job, but he hadn't lost his pride.

So he schemed. He thought fast. He finagled. HE ACTED. He called together the boss's principal debtors, those who owed him the most. "He asked the first, 'How much do you owe my master?'" (v. 5). I'm not sure why he didn't know already. Maybe it's a rhetorical question. "'Eight hundred gallons of olive oil,' he replied."

"Eight hundred gallons of olive oil." That's enough to cook eighty bazillion matzah balls.

The manager said, "Take your bill, sit down quickly, and make it four hundred" (v. 6). The manager told the debtor that for fifty cents on the dollar, they'd close the account. DONE DEAL.

To the next debtor he asked the same question: "How much do you owe?" "'A thousand bushels of wheat,' he replied." "Take your bill and make it eight hundred" (v. 7). (That's a 20 percent discount. What happened to the 50 percent discount?) Maybe the sheer prodigality of the initial transaction chilled his nerve. No telling what rate he was offering down the line.

By sacrificing his "commission," as it were, he secured his future and kept a roof over his head. Even though the boss took a loss, he didn't lose everything, and he took a shine to the chutzpa of his steward. He was impressed with the man's prudence,
> his ingenuity,
>> his shrewdness under pressure. No Burger King for this boy.

And Jesus, who tells the story, also praised the man to His disciples. Jesus commended him, saying, "The people of this world are more shrewd in dealing with their own kind than are the people of the light."

But, as with most parables, we need to HEAR IT THE RIGHT WAY. It's not the steward's dishonesty Jesus commends in the parable. It's not his spirit of larceny. It's certainly not his motivation. Let's face it. THE GUY WAS A CROOK. Jesus pulls no punches about it. The man was an opportunist who got caught and then wiggled every way he could to extricate himself from embarrassment and financial ruin.

There is absolutely nothing in this man's character that we can point to for edification. BUT THAT'S IRRELEVANT. This is not a story about character. We're talking parable here, not moral object lesson. A parable, by definition, is a little story with one point, one thrust, one major idea to get across. Like a good joke, you have to see it from the right perspective to get it. It either hits you, or it doesn't.

Jesus told parables like that. He picked the people for His stories from real life to illustrate what He wanted to say. He selected His characters with a sweeping, sovereign sense of freedom, and He didn't bother to sanitize them first.

Jesus' commending here is not for the steward's morals
> or his motivation
> or his manners—all reprehensible. Instead,

what He's commending is his RESOURCEFULNESS,
> his ingenuity,
> his street smarts,
>> his competence in accomplishing what he feels has to be

done. The steward is not a Christian. He's not a disciple, not a believer at all. He's completely in the *other* camp, without so much as a glimmer of life's spiritual dimension.

But Jesus is saying there's something the disciples can learn from the steward. He's basically saying, "If only the children of light, My followers, the people of God would be as resourceful about kingdom business as secular people are about secular business." Oh, my.

It's a lament, this parable. Jesus told it, I suspect, with a crack in His voice. Maybe He dug His fingernails into His palm as He spoke. IF ONLY our side would work as imaginatively and creatively at the business of ministry as some people work at making money,

or building a career,

or getting ahead, JUST

THINK WHAT A DIFFERENCE IT MIGHT MAKE.

Don't each of us have the same twenty-four hours in a day? The same 86,400 seconds? What did you do with all the wealth God gave you today?

Some people go to church having made no more preparation for an encounter with the living God than they would make for an appointment with the hairdresser . . . maybe even less. How strange that we can make such exacting, careful preparation for our immediate lives and be so flippant and nonchalant about . . . *forever.*

Through this parable that Luke gives us from across the centuries, you can almost hear Jesus saying, "If only my disciples would be as excited about the business of heaven as they are about the business of earth."

I think Jesus is telling us to not be satisfied with mediocrity or with only good will in ministry. That's a beginning, but is it enough? We should be at least as committed to spiritual excellence as our secular friends are to temporal excellence. I have a close friend, a dear friend, a brother who told me once, "This life is temporary . . . a mere journey on our way to a new life. . . . Eternity is forever." I will always remember Wayne's words and the manner and tone in which he said them. HE WAS SINCERE! AND HE WAS RIGHT!

I don't want to sound fussy when I say, if you're not currently an active participant in some sort of Christian education experience—Sunday school, Disciple, or Alpha, for example—then maybe your absence needs to be justified.

If you don't know as much as you should about the Bible—God's Word—there's a place for you to learn. If you know plenty already, there's a place for you to teach. A literate, learning people, competent and committed, is the most potent human resource a church can have.

And I believe with all my heart that THE CHRISTIAN HAS A MORAL OBLIGATION TO BE AS INTELLIGENT AND AS WELL-TRAINED AS HE OR SHE CAN BE, JUST AS SURELY AS THE CHRISTIAN HAS AN OBLIGATION TO BE AS GOOD AS HE OR SHE CAN BE.

So, although the steward was a rascal and a commendable crook, we don't need to make him our patron saint, but we can certainly learn from him. WHAT HE DID WASN'T GOOD, BUT HE WAS GOOD AT WHAT HE DID.

Resourcefulness - God uses it.

Spiritual excellence - eternal

Temporal excellence - brief

Life lasts - If you were given $4,600
every day to do with as you wish, what
would you do with it?
Each day has 84,600 seconds. If wasted,
never can get it back.

" Seems that behind me to
Be careful of your words. stand on their shoulders."

Chapter 20

FAITH FOUNDATIONS: FORGIVENESS

Father, forgive them, for they do not know what they are doing.
Luke 23:34

Forgive. It's not the longest word in the New Testament, nor is it the most frequently used word. I did some quick spot-checking, and simple words like "heathen," "ointment," and "pillar" appear more frequently in the Bible than "FORGIVE." Isn't that interesting?

While "forgive" is neither the longest nor the most frequently used word, FORGIVENESS must be the most powerful,
  the most liberating,
    the most radical,
      and the MOST NEEDED experience the human heart can know. FORGIVENESS, blessed FORGIVENESS—where do we see it placarded with greater intensity than in the suffering and death of Jesus on the cross?

We see it more around the season of Lent, the event that stands at the very heart of our faith. Why is forgiveness there? Why was that brutal cross event necessary? Because there was no other way, God being God and humanity being estranged through insidious corruption, for there to be reconciliation with integrity. It was all done for us. If anything can be said to be universal, it's the need for forgiveness. After all, WHO IS THERE AMONG US WHO DOESN'T NEED FORGIVENESS?

"Father, forgive them," He said, "for they do not know what they are doing." Whom was He talking about, anyway? To whom was He referring when He said that? "Father, forgive them . . . ." Forgive *whom?*

You know the setting. We all do. Every year, we hear it again. And it never gets any easier to take. They had just nailed Him up, just finished the job, brutally, methodically hammered His flesh to the rough timber, and then, not gently, raised the whole apparatus to let it plop into the slot.

That was the worst part, they say . . . excruciating pain, literally. "Excruciating," etymologically, means "cross-like" pain. If you dwell too long on it, you get sick to your stomach. There He hung, the Son of God, the Creator of all that is.

119

the first and the last meaning only

And the first words He uttered, the very first words He spoke when it must have been hell to say anything, to push His body upward to catch a breath against the very nails that penetrated His feet, were these words, which are the last words you would have expected . . . unless you knew Him: "Father, forgive them, for they do not know what they are doing." *did they, know*

WHOM WAS HE TALKING ABOUT, ANYWAY? *Who they were crucifying*

Could it have been the soldiers? Maybe that's whom He meant. After all, they were the closest by. Theirs were the hands that lashed Him to the timber,
> that did the pounding,
> > that raised the beam into the air and let it slam down.

It can be a dirty job, this soldiering business. There are veterans in our everyday walk of life who can attest to that. You get hardened after a while. You get immune after a while. You no longer feel after a while. It becomes a job, and you just do it; you go through the motions. After a while, the soul itself becomes numb.

Those soldiers had seen death before. They'd had crucifixion duty before . . . and they'd have it again. Maybe they didn't like it, but they didn't have to like it. They were soldiers. This was their assignment. The best thing was to get through the job as quickly as possible and get back to the barracks. Then they could check one more day off the calendar, meaning one less day until leave. They don't think about it, don't ask questions, and don't get involved. Therefore, it would have made sense for Jesus to utter about them, "Father, forgive them, for they do not know what they are doing."

If not the soldiers, could He have been thinking about the Jewish leaders, the Sanhedrin crowd? Maybe that's whom He meant. They, the very people to whom He'd been sent, had been stubborn from day one. AND WITH UTTER SINCERITY, that was the tragic part. He'd seen it coming, seen it building up. He knew exactly what they were thinking: *Have you noticed how lax He is on the Sabbath observance? Don't get me wrong; I'm as broad-minded as anybody, but look at the kinds of people He hangs around with. A disreputable lot they are! Why, He puts people, human need, ahead of the laws of Moses. What kind of priority is that? And He has this crazy idea that God takes an equal interest in everybody, even Samaritans and tax collectors. The very idea!*

It was almost humorous at first, but then it started getting ugly.
  When He said, "Narrow is the way . . .," they got nervous.
    When He said, "Woe unto you, hypocrites," they got defensive.
      When He said, "You shall not turn God's house of prayer into a den of thieves," they got mad.
It was the moneychanger who finally iced it.

Former presiding bishop of the Episcopal Church John Hines once said: "They did not crucify Jesus for saying, 'Behold the lilies of the field, how they grow.' They crucified Jesus for saying, 'Behold the thieves in the temple, and how they steal.'"

That's what did it. He called them what they were, and it wasn't pretty—organized religion,
> organized business,

organized politics. He cut across their vested interests with devastating logic. It stung, cut right to the quick, and there was no way they were going to let Him get away with it. So they needled and wheedled; they wiggled and finagled until they got the Romans to do the job for them. Perhaps it was them Jesus was thinking about when He said, "Father, forgive them, for they do not know what they are doing."

Or, could He have been thinking about somebody else when He spoke? Maybe it wasn't the soldiers. Maybe it wasn't the ecclesiastical leaders. When He said, "Father, forgive them," maybe He was thinking about the CROWD.

It's been pointed out over and over that essentially the same multitude, the same crowd, the same people who yelled, "Crucify him, crucify him" (Luke 23:21) on Friday had just as loudly screamed "Hosanna" only five days earlier. On Sunday, they thought He was coming into town to set up His kingdom, to reestablish in glory the old Davidic empire . . . FINALLY. The palms were a way of saying: "We're tired of being kicked around. We're fed up with being picked on. We're hungry to be on top again, to strut our stuff again. Here's our dream; here's our agenda. Come and fulfill it for us. You look like the Man who can do it." Judas thought so. That's why he attempted to push Him into action that night in the garden. "We've been told for centuries of Your coming to reclaim Your kingdom, to overthrow all the oppression, the opposition. It's been foretold over and over again. NOW it's time to get on with it. There they are, right in front of you. GET 'EM!"

Well, they were right, and so was Judas . . . partly. They missed a big chunk of it. They were right about the triumph but dead wrong about the way to it. They were right about the outcome but wrong about the process. It wasn't Rome He was out to conquer; it was what Paul called "principalities and powers." He didn't come to Jerusalem to sidestep death but to meet it head-on. He would win . . . by losing,

> conquer . . . by suffering,
> triumph . . . by dying,
> win over His enemies . . . by forgiving them. My God, what a plan!

No wonder the crowd misunderstood. It's hard to be the cause of someone else's disillusionment. When the person is expecting one thing and you know you can't deliver on that basis, it's tough. PEOPLE DON'T UNDERSTAND THAT KIND OF THING EASILY. People don't tend to be tolerant of that kind of thing. Who is despised more than the one who fails to live up to expectations, even misguided expectations? AND THEIR DISAPPOINTMENT SHOVES THEM TOWARD GETTING BACK AT THAT PERSON. Their being let down makes them determined to get even. "Get rid of Him; we'll look for somebody else," they say. Jesus could be referring to them when he said, "Father, forgive them, for they do not know what they are doing.'" *He lined up to no ones expetitions*

Or, in yet another direction, maybe it was the DISCIPLES He was talking about when He said, "Father, forgive them." These were His closest friends,

> His nearest and dearest companions,
> His most ardent supporters, whose ardor wasn't

burning as He'd hoped it would be. All their braggadocio,

> their air of confidence about their allegiance,
> all their brash talk about drinking the cup and sitting at the

right hand and never denying Him turned into so much froth. When the going got tough, the tough . . . SPLIT THE SCENE. Not one stayed through to the end.

Soldiers, leaders, Romans, Disciples / defied their expetitions

121

Judas was already dead—maybe more shattered in heart than body. Peter the wolf was cowering like a beaten puppy. The rest had fled out of town or were trying to get away. HOW BADLY JESUS MUST HAVE WANTED THEM THERE. How desolate and abandoned He must have felt.

There are spiritual resources that strengthen and uplift—thank God for that—but sometimes simply the comfort and support of a friend when you're hurting are among the greatest blessings the human heart can know.

Jesus must have wanted human support in His time of agony. After all, He was human. Every human craves that kind of undergirding. If He hadn't coveted that, He wouldn't have invited those three to go with Him to the garden to pray. And now, in His moment of greatest need, they are absent, gone. They have left Him. He suffers alone, with no human hand to reach out in sympathy.

When He said, "FATHER, FORGIVE THEM, FOR THEY DO NOT KNOW WHAT THEY ARE DOING," was He talking about the disciples?

WHO WAS HE TALKING ABOUT? To whom was He referring in that agonized utterance? Are you kidding? The soldiers,
> the Jewish leaders,
> > the crowd,
> > > the disciples. . .stretch it on out; stretch it *way* on out. Just be sure you make it inclusive enough.

He was talking about ME. He was talking about YOU. He was talking about EVERYBODY. The old spiritual asks, "Were you there?" and the answer is, YOU BET YOUR LIFE YOU WERE. We're ALL standing out there on that rough-hewn hill.

There is no one who doesn't need forgiveness. That's precisely the human predicament. Between the strict justice of God, utterly pure in its holiness, and the painful reality of the human situation in stark contrast before it, there is a gaping chasm, a gigantic pit yawning, the distance across it so wide we could never make it from one side to the other unaided.

But LOOK, LOOK! There is a way across the pit, not from our side to God's, but from God's side to ours. There is a bridge with which God in His infinite grace has spanned the chasm, and that bridge is called FORGIVENESS. The cross is where we see Him constructing the bridge.

God freely forgives us, freely restores the relationship that has been severed by our callousness,
> our indifference,
> > our selfishness,
> > > our resentment,
> > > > our grasping for our own way and our own agenda. His forgiveness is a gift, unearned, unmerited, undeserved, but it's that forgiveness that both illuminates the blackness of our experienced separation and provides the basis for our restored relationship.

We don't "get right" and then receive forgiveness. In fact, it's the other way around. God forgives us, and in receiving His forgiveness, we are empowered to "get right." THIS IS THE GOSPEL.

When we believe in His verdict, we can believe in ourselves and be free. ✓

The great missionary E. Stanley Jones tells one of the most heart-compelling stories I've ever heard about the cost of forgiveness. He tells of the conversion of a man who was a government official in India. His work caused him to travel away from home frequently. He was tempted. He wrestled with it awhile, but then he succumbed and fell into dishonesty and shame. He lived with it for a number of weeks, but the weight of his guilt tormented him.

One day he called his wife into the room and began unfolding the whole sordid story. As the meaning of his words dawned on her, she turned as pale as a ghost, grabbed her chest in agony, and staggered against the wall, with tears flooding down her cheeks, as if she'd been struck by a whip. "In that moment," he said afterward, "I saw the meaning of the cross. I saw love crucified by sin. MY SIN."

In time, his wife forgave him, and their relationship, though scarred, was restored. FORGIVENESS DOESN'T COST ANYTHING? Are you kidding? It's the costliest thing in the world. God's forgiveness may be free to you and me, but that doesn't make it inexpensive.

But there is also the beauty,
        the charm,
         the graciousness,
          the joy,
           the ebullience of forgiveness. Maybe you can't describe it; maybe you have to experience it to know it. It's having a heavy load lifted from your shoulders. Never does the Bible sing with greater ecstasy than when it sings about the rapture of being forgiven. "This my son was dead, and is alive . . ." (Luke 15:24, KJV). "There will be more rejoicing in heaven over one sinner who repents . . ." (Luke 15:7). You can almost see the confetti being thrown and hear the kazoos buzzing.

You don't have to understand it to receive it. You don't have to comprehend it to know it. There's no way you can understand it totally. It's too big for that. At bottom, you can only CLAIM IT, with a childlike trusting heart.

James Stewart, in his classic book *A Faith to Proclaim*, tells a story about a soldier who, as a boy, had gone from bad to worse. He had engaged in almost every kind of sin before he was grown, had somehow been allowed to enlist in the service, and quickly became the most incorrigible member of his regiment. He was about to be drummed out of the army entirely.

But one of the officers, as a last, daring experiment, took one final chance with him. He made him his orderly and treated him with kindness, respect, and dignity. Then, an almost magical transformation began. His unit was sent to the front, and in the battle that came, this reprobate soldier threw his life away with gallantry for the man whose trust had changed him.

As darkness descended on the battlefield after the enemy attack and his life was ebbing away, by some strange quirk of memory, the words came to him of an old childhood prayer his mother had taught him in those days before his life of reckless sin.

Gasping for breath, he began to repeat them. The stretcher bearer heard him and said he was

123

like a tired child at the close of day:

The day is done;
O God the Son,
Look down upon
Thy little one!

O Light of Light,
Keep me this night,
And shed round me
Thy presence bright.

Garden Life — Ideal for God!

Be in sales, not management!

And on the scarred face of the man no one loved was a light like the radiance of heaven. Then, brokenly, the last words came:

I need not fear
If Thou art near;
Thou art my Savior
Kind and dear.

So he crossed the river. Dr. Stewart adds, "AND WHO DOUBTS THAT JESUS WAS THERE TO MEET HIM ON THE OTHER SIDE?"

You don't have to understand this Gospel of forgiveness to receive it. That's the wonder, the glory.

When He said, "Father, forgive them," to whom was He referring? I think you already know.

What key will I most reflect on from this chapter? It is through Christ I am forgiven and gain the power to forgive others for they do not know what they are doing.

What did the Jews expect of Jesus?
1. They wanted a King
2. they wanted a Warrior

free will?
The dichotomy of human beings -
I Never Knew I Had a Choice -

Chapter 21

12.27.18

LITTLE BROTHER

The next day John was there again with two of his disciples. When he saw Jesus passing by, he said, "Look, the Lamb of God!" . . . Andrew, Simon Peter's brother, was one of the two who heard what John had said and who had followed Jesus.

John 1:35, 40 (see also vv. 36-39)

In some ways, he's a lesser character in the vast New Testament panorama, part of the supporting cast. His role is a minor one in the story. He was a disciple, one of the twelve Jesus selected to be with Him for special training. That gave him a certain automatic status, but though he was among the first to be chosen, maybe *the* first, he never quite made it into the inner circle.

He's like famed baseball player Jim Bunning—so close to election into the Baseball Hall of Fame each year, but just a few votes shy of the number needed for induction.

Other disciples with more talent,
          more native ability,
               and more pizazz constantly overshadowed him, especially his brother, who quickly moved in and took over. It wasn't a sneaky thing; it was a natural thing. His brother was a leader, and he naturally assumed that position within the group and in the center of the stage.

Our man never played that role and never coveted it. He was never a center-stage person. He had an appealing, winsome personality. Unfortunately, infrequently, as he slips into the story, he quietly plays his part and then moves on.

Who is he? You've probably guessed already. I'm thinking of the disciple Andrew, the younger brother of Simon Peter who in his lifetime successfully managed to escape notoriety and seemed to prefer it that way.

Even now, after two thousand years, I doubt if he'd want me to drag him on stage. I'm sure he'd be embarrassed. He'd probably throw up his hands and say, "You've got the wrong man," but that's the very reason I know I've got the right man. There's a good story here, an important story. I would like to present to you at this time Andrew, a sterling, shining example of evangelism at its best.

Unfortunately, today there are certain evangelists who give evangelism a bad name. That's sad, but it's true. By their extremes,

> their techniques,
> their inappropriate pressures,

and sometimes their improprieties, they have tarred, blackened, a whole segment of Christian motivation.

Evangelism is simply helping people find Christ. That's it. You can't have Christianity without it. Evangelism is simply pointing the way toward ultimate reality—which we believe, and it's a breathtaking thing, has become incarnate in Jesus Christ.

That's the Good News. That's the evangel. Evangelism is publicizing it. The evangelist is not the end . . . EVER. The evangelist is the means,
> the instrument,
> the channel,
> the conduit that leads to the end.

I like D. T. Niles' classic definition of *evangelism*. A third-world Christian, a native of Sri Lanka, formerly Ceylon, he has said evangelism is nothing more or less than one beggar telling another beggar where he has found bread. Evangelism is just a simple sharing, in love and compassion, of some wonderfully good news about . . . nourishment.

Andrew was that kind of evangelist. Our details are sketchy, admittedly; we have minimal concrete evidence to go on. But there's enough in the Gospel Record to form the basis for a picture. And it's a very attractive picture, one that has something extremely important to say to the church today, especially about our role as modern-day disciples in it.

Most of the evidence is from the Gospel of John. Except for a couple of instances where just his name is listed, Andrew shows up in the Gospels only three times.

He was not among those who accompanied Jesus to the mountaintop for the experience we call the Transfiguration. He was not among those who were invited to go with Jesus to the garden to pray before the betrayal.

Most frequently, in most of the stories, he remains in the background. There are just these three quickly etched vignettes in which he appears that the Gospel writers have given to us. But a common thread runs through all three, and that thread enables us to see a winsome character in focus.

The first is the account of his own call, told briefly in John. He became a disciple of Jesus' through the ministry of John the Baptist. Then, the account says, the next thing he did was find his brother and tell him the good news. "We have found the Messiah," he blurted out, little brother to big brother . . . one beggar telling another where he has found bread (John 1:41, RSV).

"We have found the Messiah." And the Record adds, with unadorned, eloquent simplicity, "He brought him to Jesus."

The second glimpse of Andrew is in that exquisite story of the feeding of the five thousand. It's the one story all the Gospels tell. In John's version, the multitude followed Jesus some distance out into the hills one day to hear what He had to say. Later in the day, they were hungry, yet most of the people hadn't brought anything. No food was available; they had no supplies. They couldn't even stop by a local 7-Eleven for a quick Big Gulp.

But Andrew found a little boy who had a sack lunch. Jesus fed five thousand people through one little boy with one little brown bag. Preposterous. BUT HE BROUGHT THE LITTLE BOY TO JESUS. "There is a lad here," he said (John 6:9, RSV). And you know the rest of the story.

Only once more do we hear about Andrew. Later in the public ministry, certain Greeks, Gentiles, people with no Old Testament background, began expressing an interest in this strange Carpenter.

The word had spread about Him; people started to talk. That's what happens when something worthwhile, something good, something important is going on.

Those outsiders, those Greeks, were intrigued. They had heard a little and wanted to know more. They came first to Philip, who had a Greek name. Philip knew the lay of the land. He knew how best to handle this new development, this new breakthrough. Philip took them to Andrew. It was Andrew, then, who brought them to Jesus and made the introduction.

So there you have it—three stories with a common thread. It's all we have, but they're all linked; they're all variations of the same theme. The common thread? He brought someone to Jesus. Though we only see Andrew three times, each time, every glimpse we catch, even when quick and fleeting, shows us a man bringing someone to the Master. Who knows how many more we don't know about?

More than with any other disciple, even the more lavishly chronicled ones, the image of Andrew as bringer is the one that consistently emerges. That's evangelism.

He brings someone within his own family—which is perhaps the toughest kind of witness of all. He brings a little child. He brings strangers from a totally different culture. The variety is astonishing. Wrapped in a spirit of what seems to be an engaging humility, an absence of pretentiousness, not worried for a minute that his role is the role of a second fiddle, he is constantly directing people, not toward himself, but away from himself toward the Source of his faith. He represents one beggar telling another where he found bread.

Andrew shines from the pages of the New Testament with a lustrous clarity as the introducer. That's evangelism, and I think I'd even go so far as to call it the highest accolade a disciple can have.

Wouldn't it be wonderful,
 wouldn't it be exciting to have someone like Andrew in your congregation? You do, you know. You have people just like him, people with the same kind of spirit
                                          and motivation
                                          and attitude that this splendid disciple
displayed two thousand years ago halfway around the world. Only the setting has changed.

What he did is still being accomplished in the same way he did it. Indeed, Andrew-type evangelism, the best kind of evangelism, is going on right now among us. What's more, I'm convinced that more of us can learn how to be *introducers*.

Now, what made Andrew so effective? What about him made his life and witness, admittedly not flashy, have such a positive impact?

It's partly speculation, of course; it has to be with the limited biblical references we have. But I don't think I'm playing fast and loose with the evidence. I've witnessed enough people like Andrew—bringers, introducers—to know that they all have something in common. They all look a lot alike, and he fits the pattern.

The primary reason for his evangelistic success was simply the quality of the life he lived. That has to be the primary reason. It always is. There's something radiant about him,
                              something warm and appealing,
                              something that lacked a judgmental
spirit. There was something in his bearing, in his demeanor, in the way he conducted himself that gave off an aura of goodness and integrity.

He didn't parade it, and may not even have been consciously aware of it, but people, even little children, noticed it and were attracted to it. They saw something in him that they wanted to have in their own lives.

That's how it always starts in this evangelism business. That's how he was able to become the introducer. It was easy to believe in Andrew's Christ because it was easy to believe in . . . Andrew.

Nowhere in the Record is there any evidence of his speech-making ability. As far as we know, Andrew never preached a sermon,
        never gave a testimony,
            never stood before a throng of people and regaled them with oratorical eloquence.
He wasn't that kind of person.

BUT HE WAS AN EVANGELIST. He brought people to Jesus, and he was able to do it primarily by living before them a quality of life that was noble
                    and kind
                    and interested
                    and sympathetic
                    and open
                    and good.

He displayed a moral tone that was exalted without being obtrusive, that was lofty without being obnoxious. He showed by example that it is possible to have principles without being a prude, that you can stand for something without beating people over the head with it.

Quietly and effectively, he drew out the best in people, until they wanted what he had, and it was a simple matter then to introduce them to the Christ who was responsible for it. That's the story of Andrew.

THAT'S WHERE IT STARTS WITH NEARLY ALL OF US, even when we're children—some fleeting glimpse of God's glory, resplendent on a face or speaking through a life.

Paul saw it in Stephen's face while he was holding the coats of the men who were stoning him out there by the gate . . . and it haunted him until he finally gave in to it.

Augustine saw it in his mother and in the courageous career of Ambrose, a bishop of Milan—a sense of purpose and wholeness. He knew he didn't have it, and it kept eating away at him until at last he surrendered.

Remember what Stanley said after his journey into the heart of Africa to find Dr. Livingstone? "I went to Africa," he wrote, "as prejudiced as the biggest atheist in London. But there came for me a long time for reflection. I saw the solitary old man there, working patiently among those poor people, and I said to myself, 'How on earth does he stay here? Is he cracked, or what?' But little by little, his sympathy became infectious. Seeing his gentleness, his pity, his earnestness, I was converted by him, though he didn't try to do it at all."[1]

And there it is. That's where it starts. That's the beginning of the beautiful, world-changing process of bringing people to Christ.

It's Andrew-style evangelism, one beggar showing another where to find bread.

Bringing
Introducing

vs

Teaching (lecturing)
The (only) way.

Chapter 22

HALLOWED HUNGER

I am the living bread which came down from heaven: if any man eat of this bread, he
shall live for ever: and the bread that I will give is my flesh, which I will give for the life
of the world.
John 6:51 KJV (see also vv. 52-58)

There is hunger . . . and there is *hunger.* There is the biological, gnawing ache for physical food, and there is the internal, restless yearning for spiritual food. That John, or whoever wrote the fourth Gospel, is aware of and is speaking to this duality of drives becomes clearer and clearer as the sixth chapter unfolds.

Hunger is not something with which we largely overweight North Americans are intimate. To most of us, hunger means the discomfort of postponing supper for an hour or so. It means not having in the refrigerator what we want to snack on before we go to bed. Not many of us are truly conversant with what it means to be without food entirely, over an extended period of time.

Most of us are not familiar with what it means to feel the tightening of the stomach muscles due to deprivation. I have read that as long as the feeling of hunger is present, there is hope for a person who is starving. There comes a time when the hunger pangs themselves go away, and that's when life becomes in jeopardy.

A prayer has been recorded from one of the African tribes struggling through a long drought: "O Lord, make us hungry again." We don't know that kind of experience. We see images on television of emaciated, stick-like bodies in Somalia and Zaire, and we look at pictures of Holocaust victims barely human any longer, and it's all so foreign and seems almost unbelievable.

But hunger,
 real hunger,
  undiluted physical hunger, is not just a bad dream or an illusion that disappears when you turn off your television. It's a reality for millions of people. Being without food—proper, nourishing food in sufficient quantities to sustain life—is a specter that haunts many parts of the world. And it haunts you and me.

The Bible knows about it. It's known about it all along. In fact, hunger is a major biblical theme. When you begin to count the Scripture references that in some way relate to hunger—references to eating, drinking, and food—the number is staggering. Drop down almost anywhere, and there they are.

Hunger plays a role in the account of the original divine-human estrangement. Right at the start, in the first part of Genesis, the first book of the Bible, there is that disturbing, troubling scene concerning the consumption of a piece of forbidden fruit. Hunger brought on disaster. How modern it all sounds. Eat the wrong things, and you get into trouble. Well, maybe it's a little bigger than that. Disobedience to the built-in laws of life inevitably wreaks havoc.

Hunger is used as a symbol of that. It's how the whole sad saga begins. And it ends with a reference to hunger, the alleviation of it. At the conclusion of the book of Revelation, the last book of the Bible, is a vision of the coming reign of God, in which there is the promise, among other things, that the people of God "shall hunger no more" (Rev. 7:16, KJV).

That is a magnificent statement of faith in both the capacity and the willingness of God to satisfy. Hunger as an image both begins and ends the story . . . our story.

And think of all the references in between: Abraham prepares a feast for three hungry strangers as an act of hospitality, not knowing that he is entertaining angelic representatives from the Lord. It is hunger that gives Jacob the advantage over his famished brother, Esau. That changes the line of blessing and alters the story. It's famine as the result of drought that drives the Hebrews down into Egypt in the time of Joseph. And it's hunger and thirst that almost form a rebellion during those long wilderness years. The people survive only because God sends manna to fill their empty bellies.

The theme of hunger plays a prominent role in the book of Ruth. The psalmist writes about a God who "preparest a table before me in the presence of mine enemies" (Ps. 23:5, KJV). In a passage that depicts the hell of war when Jerusalem is under siege by the Babylonians, Jeremiah cries out to the people, "Lift up your hands to him for the lives of your children, who faint from hunger at the head of every street" (Lam. 2:19).

How well the Bible knows the horror of the empty stomach. And while it's true that the enemies of Jesus in derision once referred to Him as "gluttonous, and a winebibber" (Matt. 11:19, KJV), there is ample evidence to show that He was not unaware of the effects of food deprivation.

In the temptation experience, we are told that He fasted out in the desert for forty days. Matthew's cryptic comment on it is, "Afterwards he was famished" (Matt. 4:2, NRSV). Indeed, He knew about hunger.

The reason Jesus cursed the fig tree for not bearing fruit that day in what appears to be an out-of-character response may be found in the verse that immediately precedes the incident. Mark says, "When they came (into town) from Bethany, he was hungry" (Mark 11:12, NRSV). Maybe that sheds light on it. Hunger, if it goes on long enough, can drive even the most serene of spirits to irritability.

Sure, He knew what hunger was all about. His language is filled with references to it:

"Which of you, if his son asks for bread, will give him a stone?" (Matt. 7:9).
  "I was hungry and you gave me something to eat" (Matt. 25:35).
    "Blessed are those who hunger and thirst for righteousness" (Matt. 5:6).

In fact, He likened the kingdom itself to a great banquet where there would be an unlimited supply of food. And when He wanted to choose a symbol for Himself, something to represent His very life, an intimate, personal symbol that His followers could have with them to remember Him by when He was gone from them physically, HE CHOSE THAT SIMPLE, earthly, commonplace, everyday element that is a staple of life all over the world and an antidote to hunger—the symbol of BREAD. "This is my body, which is broken for you" (1 Cor. 11:24, KJV).

Everybody knows what bread is. Everybody knows what bread does. It nourishes. It sustains. It tastes good; that is, it provides flavor to the palate while also filling the stomach. It's a wonderfully rich symbol, even for people who need to go on a diet, even to the wealthy and overweight, because it has a connotation that goes beyond the simply physical.

And that's the sense the author of this passage in John is seeking to impart. There's a preacher at work here with extraordinary skill and insight. He takes a story right out of the life of Jesus—a good, straightforward, meaningful, touching story about a little boy and the compassionate Jesus, who knew about people's being hungry because He's been there, too—and uses it to say something more,
  something on another level,
    something additional about Jesus,
      something in his preacher's heart he wanted the world to know: *Jesus, who met the physical hunger of people that day on the lakeside by giving them bread, is Himself the Bread of Life.* He is the One who can supply the satisfaction for our human and spiritual hunger.

How interesting that the story of the feeding of the five thousand is the only story out of the public ministry of Jesus that is common to all four Gospels. It's the single incident before the events of Holy Week that is found across the board. Matthew, Mark, Luke, and John all tell it. No other happening in His ministry is better authenticated.

But look at the difference. When Matthew, Mark, and Luke tell it, they do so to emphasize Jesus' magnificent sense of caring for people, especially people who are suffering. They were hungry; He saw that they got something to eat.

But John's emphasis is on something else, or something MORE, not to take away from that, but to add to that. He seems to want his readers—*us*—to see not just what Jesus *did,* but who Jesus *is*. Here is the One who can feed you, in every inclusive,
                              broad,
                                glorious sense of the word.

He fed people physical bread to stave off physical hunger, and that's great. But the even bigger news about Him never ends; it never gets old. A living relationship with Him fills and overflows the very depths of your soul.

"I am the living bread that came down from heaven," Jesus says, according to John (John 6:51). He puts the words on the lips of Jesus Himself because that's how he's come to experience it himself. "I am the living bread that came down from heaven. If anyone eats of this bread, he will live forever" (vv. 51-52).

And here is where this story grabs us, it seems to me, where it ceases to be just something back there and becomes something right HERE, about where we are right now. You and I may not know a great deal personally about physical hunger, but I'll bet there aren't many who don't know what it is like in some sense to long for,

> to yearn for,
> to crave,
> to ache for,
>   to hunger for a more abiding sense of fulfillment.

Why is it that we seem to feel empty much of the time? What's missing? Why is it, even when our tables almost buckle under the weight of pans of lasagna, casseroles, cheeseburgers, and fries, that we still can't get rid of that persistent, deeper hunger?

To take it even further, deeper, why do we go to church? What's the point? Why bother? Well, some people don't, of course, and maybe some sitting in the pews each Sunday wish they hadn't gone. The beach or the golf course, or that lavish breakfast waiting at home, or the prospect of perusing the Sunday morning newspaper in peace may offer a much more compelling appeal. A lot of other things we could do maybe on several levels would be more fun.

But most of us, I suspect, are in church, and we go regularly because we get hungry. That's the simplest and best answer I can think of. We get hungry, hungry to be in touch with a Reality none of those other experiences provide.

If hunger isn't the perfect metaphor, it certainly comes close. Something gnawing inside of us, akin to physical hunger, churns away annoyingly until we feed it. You almost suspect it's something God has put there to let us know He's around.

Years ago in one of his most famous statements, Augustine wrote: "Thou hast made us for Thyself, O Lord, and our hearts are restless until they find their rest in Thee."

We all know that restlessness, don't we? We busy, driving, well-fed Americans know that hunger that no amount of food, activity, or acquisition can totally satisfy. We know so well the incompleteness of "having it all," the vacuum that someone has described as a "God-shaped blank" down inside of us.

That's why we come, and why we come back, and why we keep coming back. We know if we don't, we'll starve. We'll slowly waste away to nothing. "O Lord, make us hungry again" for the Bread that truly nourishes.

What John is saying to everybody within earshot,
> to everybody who'll listen,
> to everybody everywhere who can identify with that inner emptiness
is, THE PERSON OF JESUS CHRIST, GOD'S SON, CAN FILL THE VOID YOU HAVE INSIDE and can give you, when you receive Him into your life, when you welcome Him into your being, the soul equivalent of a full and contented stomach.

He can replace your drive to have to keep proving yourself with an acceptance that undercuts the need for that. He can replace your obsessive compulsion to drink, to gamble, to lust, to grasp after things as sources of satisfaction with a new and charitable orientation, one that is outward-turning instead of inward-clutching.

"I am the living bread that came down from heaven," John says Jesus says. *What kind of language is that?* Well, of course, it's Sacrament language. It's Eucharist language. It's Holy Communion language. "Those who eat my flesh and drink my blood abide in me, and I in them" (John 6:56, NRSV).

If we weren't so familiar with it,
  if we hadn't taken Communion so many times across the years,
    if those words hadn't been drummed in our ears so often, it would be almost too much to stomach. I mean that literally. Eat His flesh and drink His blood? No wonder the Jews who heard it had their hackles raised. It's almost an "in your face," or should I say "in your mouth," way of expressing it.

But here is intimacy,
          oneness,
                identification just about stretched to the ultimate limit. Yet how else could John express it and begin to do justice to the sheer audacity of it? Using the language of food, John says He does it when we receive Him, when we take Him into our very bodies, into our lives, when we ingest Him and let Him be one with us. When we do that, He abides in us, John says. The deeper gnawing hunger goes away, and we are made over.

The New Testament uses a number of graphic images to express the intimate relationship between Christ and those who believe in Him. For example, Paul uses an anatomical image: Christ is the head, and we are the body. John elsewhere uses the image of the shepherd and the sheep, and the vine and the branches. All these images depict closeness and indissolubility.

Now here's the shocker, the surprising thing about all this, which is astonishing, really, when you think about it: This is clearly Lord's Supper talk, yet there is no account of the institution of the Lord's Supper in the Gospel of John.

In the upper room in John's Gospel, Jesus washes the feet of the twelve disciples, but there is nothing about the Sacrament.

He doesn't tell us that Jesus broke bread and gave it to the disciples, saying, "Take and eat; this is My body." He doesn't inform us that after the meal, He took a cup of wine and passed it among them, saying, "Drink from this, all of you. It represents My blood." We see none of that in John.

We get that information from the other Gospels and from Paul, who describes it in the first letter to Corinth. John, no doubt, knew that tradition. His language reflects his familiarity with it. Yet for John, who also doesn't tell us about the baptism of Jesus, Sacrament—which is a channel to grace, a conduit, if you will, a pipeline of the unquenchable and unbounded love of God for people, "an outward and visible sign of an inward and spiritual grace," God's breakthrough into human life—may take place anywhere,
                anytime,

under almost any circumstance,

whenever God's presence is recognized and received.

This sustaining reality of Christ as Bread isn't restricted to an ecclesiastical environment and a liturgically correct worship service.

Isn't that refreshing? Isn't that wonderful?

It may have frightening vocational implications for preachers and other professional religionists, but isn't that a glorious, liberating, expansive concept?

As here in this passage, John is telling us any meal—any experience in which the spiritual presence of Christ is looked for,

sought,

expected anticipatively—may be a moment of life-filling

nourishment as He comes in to bestow the Bread that is Himself. That's big.

What a poor thing Christianity would be if it were confined to churches. John is telling us that we can find Christ anywhere in a Christ-filled world.

It's not a belittlement of Sacrament. It's an expansion of Sacrament. We meet Christ at the table, and ingest Him, and then we go out and meet Him out where men and women work and struggle and cope.

A number of years ago, a fire ravaged a church in England, burned it to the ground. During the blaze, one person raced inside to try to save whatever could be salvaged. He managed to drag out a life-sized statue of Christ standing with arms outstretched.

The statue was propped up on the sidewalk beside the smoldering ruins. A short time later, someone passing by, seeing it there, said, "Well, finally, they got Jesus out of the building and into the street."

In heaven, John must have smiled. The great and glorious Good News that he wrote about with such verve and insight is that Christ is out on the street with arms and hands outstretched, offering bread, the Bread of His own nourishing life, to feed the hunger in our empty souls.

Hungry?

Chapter 23

LOOKING THROUGH
THE EYES OF JOHN

*And as Jesus passed by, he saw a man which was blind from his birth. And his
disciples asked him, saying, Master, who did sin, this man, or his parents, that he was
born blind?*

John 9:1-2 KJV (see also vv. 3-41)

Our "sight" toward Jesus may not come all at once, and it may or may not come cataclysmically.
But let Him go to work on you, and it will come—as you give up having to control your own
agenda, as you begin to practice putting your faith in the faithfulness of the One who already
accepts you as His. A film is lifted from your eyes, and you see, as if moving from night to day,
the radiant glory of His redeeming grace.

This story of the blind man in the ninth chapter of John is about a man who comes to see
more than just with his eyes, moving from blindness to physical sight and to spiritual sight in
progressive stages of illumination. AND HIS STORY IS NOT THE ONLY STORY IN THE STORY. John
also is telling us the story of people who, while physically able to see, are really tragically blind.
And he's telling us the story of a Christ who brings light
and dignity
and purpose to those who let Him do it.

But first let me lay some groundwork about the writer, John. With John, a story is never *just* a
story. It's always a vehicle for expressing a bigger story, some important aspect of the evangel,
the Good News that John has discovered and wants to share.

He talks about Nicodemus to say even the best people need Christ. He talks about the Samaritan
woman to say even the worst people are not beyond the reach of His redemption. And here we
have a story about a blind man who comes to see with more than just his eyes. As we make our
way through his story, he grows right before us.

John was a preacher, you see. That's the thing, I guess, we need to remember when we read his
book. Of course, the other Gospel writers were, too, but maybe none more so than John, or at
least none more undisguised.

If you hang around long enough, John always will bring Jesus into the story. And this story of the blind man is a perfect example of it. It starts with a healing, but the healing is not the climax of the story. IT'S THE INTRODUCTION TO THE STORY.

Jesus and the twelve are *passing by*, in no particular setting, somewhere on the streets of Jerusalem, a crowded city, presumably sometime around the Feast of Tabernacles. They are passing by when they see a blind man. Nowhere in the story is he given a name; he's just referred to as a blind man, who was blind from birth, one like thousands you still see in the Middle East. Back then, blindness was a punishment, they believed . . . kismet, fate. You got what you deserved, and you deserved what you got. It was as simple as that, all neat and wrapped up like a package.

Of course, this man deserved to be blind. If he didn't deserve to be, he wouldn't be. The only question was, Who was to blame for this handicap?

The situation prompts a theological debate as they journey along the street. It's almost casual. "Hey, look there," one of them says. It might have been Nathaniel, who was probably something of an intellectual dilettante, anyway. Or it might have been Thomas, a professional doubter. "Hey, look at that. Who sinned? The man himself, or the parents of the man?" There's no hint at all that there may be some other possible explanation . . . or none.

Jesus will have no part of it. For Him, it's not a riddle; it's a person. It's not a problem to be solved; it's a need to be addressed,
>> an opportunity to be seized,
>>> a chance to show the power and compassion of a powerful and compassionate God.

Quickly, He concocts a little paste of mud and saliva and smears it over the man's dead eye sockets. The man never even asked to be healed; he never said a word about wanting to see. That's nowhere in the story. The whole thing is done on Jesus' own initiative.

Jesus anoints the man, sends him off to the pool—the same pool, incidentally, from which water for the temple services was drawn—tells him to wash the paste off in the pool, and then leaves to reappear only at the end of John's play.

Surprisingly, the man goes and follows the instructions exactly, maybe half believing that he's the victim of a cruel hoax, maybe half hoping against hope that this Stranger knows what He's doing.

Can you imagine how he must have felt when, for the first time in his life, color
>>> and form
>>> and shape
>>>> and faces began to emerge?

Can you imagine what it must be like to receive a new sense? Imagine the thoughts that must have been swirling in the man's brain. I'm sure he was grateful. I'm certain he was confused and curious, and I wouldn't be surprised if he was frightened by all that had happened so quickly.

He is healed now, but there is something unnerving about it. His change . . . *brings more changes*. His friends are nervous. He gets it from every side. The neighbors are disturbed that he's no longer blind. They're not sure how to deal with it, so they bombard him with questions: "Can you really see?" "Who did this thing?" "How did He do it?" "Where is He now?" It's kind of a tragic and comic jumble. Arguments break out. They all get into it. Some raise their voices. The man discovers a hard truth that many other followers through the years could echo: Good news frequently makes enemies.

Sometimes there is no joy,
                          no gladness,
                          no praise,
                          no encouragement,
                          no thanking God for His deliverance. Change sometimes produces that effect. BUT SOMETHING WAS GROWING IN THE MAN.

Still learning to use his new eyes, the man is hauled before the religious authorities. They don't want answers; they want blood. They don't want truth; they want justification for their already formed opinion. "Let's see now, this alleged happening, I notice, was done on the Sabbath. Hmm . . . don't you know, my dear brother, you're not allowed to heal on the Sabbath? Anyone who does that must be punished. It's the Law. Surely you don't want to find yourself in the position of opposing the Law."

But even *they* can't agree among themselves. Among the judges, there is dissension. SO THEY PUT THE MAN ON THE STAND TO TESTIFY. Once more, he tells his story, with simple, straightforward reporting: "He put clay on my eyes, and I washed, and I see."

The very unpretentiousness of it boggles their minds. A plain-spoken testimony from somebody who has been there will do it every time. THEY CAN'T PIGEONHOLE IT. They can't fit it into any ready-made slot. There's nothing in the manual about this. There are no precedents in the book for this unorthodoxy, so they don't know how to handle it.

I think this is the first example of non-directive counseling in the New Testament. They ask the man himself—I mean, they're desperate, "Well, what do you think?" And look at what he says. He replies with the highest accolade he can think of at that moment in his growing experience: "He is a prophet."

Okay. We're getting nowhere fast. It's time to bring in the big guns . . . bring in poor, aging Mom and Dad. They have taken care of this blind baby, then boy, then grown man all his life. Now they have to face the grilling.

"Is this your son? Explain this business." In spite of their love for their son, the old folks simply fold under the pressure of intimidation. To me, this is the saddest part of the story. It's the best way out, they decide. It's better to just not get involved at all.

With his parents gone, they bring the man back in for a second interrogation before the authorities. By now, interest has mounted, and some reporters show up; it's almost as if Lindsay Lohan or Charlie Sheen has been spotted. CBS sends in a camera crew. Pressures build, and tempers flare. BUT THE MAN IS MORE POSITIVE NOW. "One thing I do know. I was blind but now I see!" (John 9:25). What's more, *his* faith is forming now. "Do you want to become his disciples, too?" he asks (v. 27). Where did that "too" come from? He never would have used that word at

139

an earlier stage.

And it infuriates the authorities. It sends them straight up the wall. He has put them in a bind. Either they must admit that he has been healed, and it's God who has done it, or they must stand on the Law and reject everything, categorically.

And it doesn't take them long. In a collision between institutional defensiveness and individual non-conformity, you can guess who usually gets bruised. The man is excommunicated; he didn't even know he was Catholic, but was summarily kicked out of the church.

Jesus finds the man, the Record says, and comforts and strengthens him. And in the beautiful flowering of one man's spiritual pilgrimage comes this dialogue: "Do you believe in the Son of Man?" "Lord, I believe" (vv. 35, 38). And the next part of the sentence reads: ". . . he worshiped him."

The Bible itself gives us no record of subsequent development. But through John's story, we've seen a man grow; we've seen him sprout and blossom from total incapacity and helplessness to physical sight,
    to defense of Jesus,
        to recognition of Jesus as a prophet,
            to unspoken commitment, to public confession of faith and discipleship. We've seen him enter a totally new life, not simply because he could see—that was just the beginning—but because he came into a vital relationship with Jesus Christ, the Son of God.

EVEN IF HE HAD LOST HIS SIGHT AGAIN THE NEXT DAY, HE NEVER WOULD HAVE GONE BACK TO WHERE HE WAS BEFORE. He was a new man.

The change may not come all at once, and it may or may not come cataclysmically . . . but let Him go to work on you, and it will come.

An old legend from early church history, though I can't vouch for the historical accuracy of it, says this blind man, still nameless, after this encounter with Jesus became one of the Master's ardent followers. Some say he was the man, the unknown friend, who later provided the donkey Jesus rode when He entered Jerusalem on Palm Sunday, and that he was in the crowd in the Upper Room on Pentecost, where he saw with the others who were there the tongues of fire descending and heard the mighty rush of wind that filled the room. It is said that he went then as a part of that turned-on, fired-up band of believers we call the church to proclaim to a blinded world not only what God in Christ has done, but what He could do to anyone willing to give Him a chance.

Some say he went down into Africa and started a Christian community there, a community that later produced such eminent church fathers as Clement of Alexandria, Philo, and the great Origen. And they say that when the blind man died, they placed his body in the eternal sands of Egypt, with this final epitaph, words from his own lips, his own emerging statement of faith from that memorable day he was hauled before the authorities: "One thing I do know. I was blind but now I see!"

This was a man brought from darkness to sight,
            from sight to vision,
                and from vision to useful, radiating service through Jesus Christ, our Lord.

Chapter 24

....

GOD'S EVERLASTINGNESS

On the evening of that day, the first day of the week, the doors being shut where the disciples were, for fear of the Jews, Jesus came and stood among them and said to them, "Peace be with you." When he had said this, he showed them his hands and his side.
John 20:19-20 RSV (see also vv. 1-18)

What in the world is happening here, anyway? What on earth is going on? It's the greatest story that ever took place, and he tells it almost as if it were a travelogue. It's the biggest event of all time, the highest point on the human horizon, and John describes it almost as if he were reporting on a Sunday afternoon outing.

THIS IS BIG STUFF WE'RE TALKING ABOUT HERE.

This is cataclysmic stuff,
       revolutionary,
          earthshaking stuff, big enough to break history in half. Yet when he talks about it, you're hardly aware of a change of inflection.

What's striking and surprising about John's version of the Resurrection story is how matter-of-factly he presents it. With a story of this magnitude, you'd expect more fanfare, more marching bands, more hoopla. You'd expect multitudes of the heavenly host
                 and peals of thunder
                    and cascading fireworks . . . wouldn't you? Wouldn't you at least expect bass drums or the Mormon Tabernacle Choir?

Instead, what do you get? A couple of off-duty angels who don't even hang around very long; two sweaty disciples; and a woman so distraught she can't see straight. What *is* going on here, anyway?

Would you have told it that way,
            that plainly,
              that mundanely if you had been telling about the supreme event of human experience?

Make no mistake about it. THIS IS BIG STUFF. This event is the heart and core of our faith. It's the bedrock of our belief, the foundation of our hope and confidence, the central hinge of the history of the world.

Christianity is built on a belief in an *event,* on a belief in something God has done—the Resurrection of Jesus Christ from the dead—and it's that event that infuses meaning into everything else.

Bethlehem, Nazareth, Bethany, the mountain of Transfiguration, Gethsemane, even Calvary—all these have their place. They're all important. They all inspire and lift us. But not one of them would even be remembered today if it hadn't been for the empty tomb.

And, of course, the central figure of the New Testament, the Star of the book, is not the earthly Jesus, but the risen and glorious Christ of eternal life.

The writers presuppose that a wondrous phenomenon has occurred, something breathtaking, and they tell the story in that light. Nothing in the New Testament was written—not one line, not one sentence, not one word—apart from the conviction, passionately believed, that the One about whom these things were being told had conquered death and was alive forevermore.

As Emil Brunner put it, "It is the Jesus who proved Himself to be the Christ in the Resurrection whose life and words are to be narrated."

Easter is where you start if you want to read the New Testament on its own terms. The Resurrection is not just an epilogue. Nothing could be further from the truth. It's not just an appendix, tacked on for good measure. It's not just a "happy ending" pasted there in retrospect to mitigate the harshness of the story. IT *IS* THE STORY. All the way down the line. It is the awesome, unexpected, undeserved miracle around which everything else revolves.

How much power do you think there would be in the New Testament if it had been written in memoriam, if the last thing you had to point to was the figure of a broken, crushed idealist, hanging limp upon a Roman cross?

Nobody is more aware of, and more impressed with, the power and splendor of the risen, transcendent Christ than the author of the fourth Gospel. When John writes about Him, about His earthly life, His pre-Resurrection life, he makes no attempt to present Him as He was, cloaked in historical fact. He presents Him as Christian experience has found Him to be, as John himself has found Him to be—radiant and glorious,
                                        majestic and soaring—even in His carpenter's tunic, even hiking the dusty trails of Galilee, even hanging on the cruel cross. He's already the Christ of the ages. The Resurrection is the prism through which we see Him in John.

In spite of all that, when John gets to the part of the story that *is* the prism, that is the key,
                                        the hinge,
                                            the perspective
that gives the rest its meaning, he becomes surprisingly subdued.

Where you would most expect flourish, there is reticence.

Where you would most anticipate hyperbole, there is reserve.

Instead of letting it all out, he almost holds it in.

Instead of shouting, he whispers.

Instead of pouring it on with all the bombast at his command, he simply relates in plain narrative form what happened to the principals . . . and doesn't even try to adorn it. HE JUST TELLS THE STORY.

Why did he take that approach? *The story . . . the Resurrection of Jesus Christ . . .* my God! It's too big, that's all. It's too big! You stand before it and look up at it . . . and anything you say or anything you *try to think to say* simply pales.

I think that's the way John must have felt, too. It's too enormous, too gigantic to get your hands around or to find adequate words for. You'll never explain it; you'll never even understand it entirely. Marching bands or exaggeration won't help. Better just tell it, just tell what happened to the people who were there. Let the story itself do the job, and hope some get it, as the first witnesses did.

It all began early one Sunday morning, even before daybreak. It was as soon after the ending of the Sabbath as they could get there. Mary wants to anoint the body, to perfume the corpse. It is all she has left, and she feels it is the least she can do. He had blessed her in life; maybe she could at least do this for Him in death.

Of course, she has no idea how she is going to get into the tomb. It was sealed; she knew that. She decides she'll worry about that when she gets there.

But when she gets there, it isn't sealed. It isn't closed at all. The stone, the heavy, circular stone used to cover the entrance to the tomb, had been rolled away somehow, and there is an opening big enough to walk in through . . . or to walk out of.

Mary isn't sure what it means, so she runs for help. She goes to Peter and John . . . who else? She finds them and probably wakes them up. While they yawn and rub their eyes, she blurts out her discovery. "Come quickly. Something's not right. Something's happened. It's not like we left it. I think they've stolen the Lord's body and moved it somewhere."

Quick as a flash, the two men are off. At this point, they don't know what it means. It is not an Easter urn yet. It's not a race of exhilaration; it's a race of consternation. They've been robbed of their leader. They saw Him die, and now they don't even have His remains to mourn over.

They wonder, *Who did this to us? Pilate, Caiaphas, some penny ante grave robber? WHO?*

The younger disciple, and we presume it's John—the disciple Jesus loved, he's called—arrives first at the tomb but doesn't enter right away. Peter, always the leader, especially in a crisis, goes in first and sees . . . nothing.

No body is there. He finds only the strips of linen, the graveclothes, the death shrouds, lying in place. Then John goes inside and notices something else—the napkin. It's the burial napkin, used quickly on Friday to swaddle the head.

There had been so little time that day. The sun was going down. They had to finish the job before the Sabbath began. The Sabbath began when three stars were visible. They did all they could, as fast as they could, wrapping the body with the grave wrappings but applying *that* linen cloth with special care and tenderness. They placed it over the face and around the brow, where the thorns had left their mark.

Here now was that cloth, maybe blood-stained, but neatly, even meticulously, folded and set aside, in a place apart from the other garments, as if placed there on purpose for someone to find.

John says that's what did it. It was when the disciple saw that cloth that he believed. That's when the scope of what was going on first hit him. You see, in Jesus' time, when the master of the house would sit down for his meal, it was customary for the servant to stand by at a distance, waiting for the master to be finished, and the servant would clean up. If the master left the meal and was finished, he would wad the napkin up in a ball and place it on the plate, signifying that he would not return. If the napkin was folded and placed to the side of the plate, it signified that he was not finished and would return.

It could be said that Jesus left the folded napkin at the gravesite to let those who would find it know that He would return. He was not finished.

At the same location a short time later, Mary Magdalene got back to the tomb, but the others had left. She hadn't passed them and hadn't heard. She still doesn't know any more than before. As she waits, alone, broken with grief, and now wracked by uncertainty, she can no longer hold back her tears. John says angels minister to her. "Why are you weeping?" "Because they have taken away my Lord" (John 20:13, RSV). She snaps. By that time, anger and frustration have pushed the grief from the forefront.

But suddenly, another voice, a different voice, totally unexpected, has the same question: "Why are you weeping?" And then, it asks, "Whom do you seek?" (v. 15, RSV).

She turns and looks at the Speaker but doesn't know who it is. For an instant, she stares at Him and doesn't recognize Him. Maybe the tears blinded her. Love can blind you, they say. So can grief
  and anger
    and frustration. Maybe He was standing in the shadows . . . or in the dark; it was still early morning. Or maybe there are some things about the resurrected body that transcend our comprehension.

At any rate, she thinks it is the gardener until He calls her by name: "MARY." John says that's what did it.

Someone has called this moment the greatest recognition scene in all literature. There have been some other memorable ones—Joseph's confronting his brothers in Egypt when the tables were turned, Ulysses's coming home from the sea to his faithful Penelope, Stanley's going down to Africa to meet Dr. Livingstone—but NONE OF THESE TOP THIS. It is when He called her by name that she believed. That's when the scope of what was going on first hit her.

From then on, the story goes quickly. The word spreads like wildfire. Mary, privileged to be the first to see Him, carries the word to the rest of them. "I have seen the Lord" (v. 18, RSV). How simple and direct. How *anything* but flamboyant. Notice, it's not argument she takes with her, nor is it proof, or analysis, or even explanation. It's not even evidence; she really has none. It's simple witness to what she has experienced. "I have seen the Lord."

That very night, the evening of that same first day, John says others saw Him, too, when He came to where they were, still cringing in fear, still paralyzed in fright over the experience of the preceding Friday.

Presumably it was in the Upper Room, behind closed and locked doors. Suddenly, somehow, He appeared and stood among them, saying, "Peace be with you."

Boy! What would you give to have been there? I have never been invited to an annual conference but am aware of some of the proceedings. This resurrected meeting of Jesus and the disciples sounds pretty much like an abridged annual conference meeting. They had just finished the hymn of praise and taken up the offering when He passed out the appointments. "As the Father has sent Me, even so, I send you." Yeah. I would've liked to be there.

Forgive me if I'm reading more into it than is there, but I think that's what did it. I think that's what confirmed it. It was certainly exhilarating when they saw Him—you bet it was. It was glorious when He appeared in their midst. Of course, it was! It was downright beatific when He said, "Peace be with you." But it was when He gave them jobs to do, when He gave them their assignments that they truly believed. That was when the scope of what was going on really hit them.

Now, that's how John tells the Resurrection story. Compared with the rest of John, it's remarkably subdued. Oh, there's drama in it, to be sure, and movement, and shading, but on the whole, there is very little here that exaggerates, stretches, or seeks to add extra decoration to the event itself.

There is certainly no superfluous gilding of the Easter lily. That's not John's emphasis. The true Easter miracle, he seems to be saying, is not represented by bombast or fanfare, or by spectacle or extravaganza, but by the change that takes place inside of people when the reality of Resurrection faith gets ahold of them.

What is most important about Easter is the effect of it. The Resurrection is an event, all right—something certainly happened—but the real significance of that doesn't occur until He comes alive in . . . *me.*

So how can we know Christ lives today? How can we know we serve a living Savior? Can we? Can we point to proof, to a corroboration, to evidence that will convince people, will convince a fair-minded skeptic of the truth of this claim on which our faith stands?

We cannot. We really cannot. No such tangible, incontrovertible proof exists. In fact, I think in honesty, we have to say there is probably at least as much empirical evidence available to support a position of *no* faith as to support faith itself.

So, what are we to say? Are we just left hanging at this critical point, mute and dry? I think we say what John says. We know the TRUTH of the Resurrection by the *effect* of the Resurrection. We know its power by what we see it doing. We know He's alive because we see the difference He makes in changed and transformed lives.

John's very reticence in reporting the event gives us our best clue. Look again at those brief scenes he paints for us with his inspired, divinely restrained pen.

Here are our best Easter messages. First we have the linen napkin from the tomb. John says the disciple whom Jesus loved believed that he saw that napkin neatly folded and laid aside. What a detail. Why would John want us to know that? Could we take it as a symbol? Was he saying that this was the first thing the resurrected Christ did when He awakened? Was this His first act as the risen Lord? *Straightening up?*

The battle is over. The victory is won, and the day of eternal jubilee has come. But before He appears in triumph, He takes time to make up His bed, as it were. He performs that simple, mundane housekeeping act. He folds the burial napkin and neatly lays it in place.

Apparently, that is what grabbed the disciple. That's when it hit him. He recognized the gesture. How typical and in character. The Master would do that.

How do we know He's alive? We know He's alive when we look at people and see *transformation*—when chaos is transformed into coherence, when hatred is transformed into harmony, when disorder and disarray are transformed into disciplined devotion.

We know He's alive when we see purposeful design in the lives of those who follow Him. They don't have to wear a badge to be identified; they don't have to scream for attention or wave a flag to make it clear He lives within them.

The surest evidence of the reality of the resurrected Christ is the whole and harmonious witness of a resurrected life. *We know He's alive when the effects of His Resurrection are too obvious and too winsome to ignore.*

Secondly, we have the naming. Mary didn't recognize Him in the garden for several moments. She was with Him. She saw Him and spoke with Him, but she didn't know who He was. The reality was there—the event had taken place; the historical had occurred. But nothing was different for *her.* Maybe it's so with some of us.

Then He called her by name . . . and she knew. Isn't John saying this is how it is; this is how Easter faith works? Now, I know we're in a realm of the subjective here. But aren't we always when it comes to the really crucial issues?

The person determined to keep the door shut between him or her and the divine Intruder, or the person so insensitive or so preoccupied that he or she has never taken time to listen may never have heard the voice.

But if you have ever, even once, felt His eyes bearing down on you, burning a hole through the center of your heart, if you have ever had your conscience wrenched until you thought you were going to die, and then if you have ever been forgiven, when He lifts the unbearable burden of guilt from your shoulders, lifts it and throws it away, you know that Resurrection is no fairy story.

"How did you know you were converted?" someone asked Dwight L. Moody one time. "How do I know?" he replied. "Why, because I was there when it happened." It's hard to argue with that. It's not a matter of proof, I don't think. It can't be proved. But when it grabs you by the throat, it's too big and too real to deny.

It happened to Mary in the garden, and it's what John wants everybody to experience. This is the truth of the Easter message. We know He's alive when He calls us . . . *by name.*

When did they know? When did it hit those disciples, locked away in fear and trembling, in the Upper Room? When did it get to them, the full scope of this thing that was so unprecedented and inexplicable? When did the power of it begin to be expressed in their hands and feet and bones?

Not just when He appeared, if there had been nothing more than that, they could have stayed on fire in the Upper Room until doomsday, and the world would never have known. Probably *we* would never have known.

It was when He sent them out that the Resurrection came alive. The power of the risen Christ is what He makes us do . . . for His sake—witness,
                                        serve,
                                        give,
                                        share. That's what John wants us to see.

The proof of Easter is not when we dress up and come together . . . not even in unusual numbers. Instead, the proof of Easter is when we go *out*, armed with basin and towel, to wash and wipe the feet of the needy of the world.

How do we know He's alive? *We know He's alive when the spirit of mission is alive and burning in our hearts.*

So that's the story according to John. That's how it was that day. "He is risen."

Is it history? Yes, sure; that's part of it. It's something rooted in an event.

But is there more? Well, I ask you: Is there?

12.30.12

Chapter 25

OUT OF THE
DEPTHS

That if thou shalt confess with thy mouth the Lord Jesus, and shalt believe in thine heart that God hath raised him from the dead, thou shalt be saved.
Rom. 10:9 KJV (see also vv. 8, 10-17)

Her eyes are staring off into the distance, like those of someone lost in contemplation. The pale moonlight reveals a soft countenance, milky white, with just a hint of a smile. She has a ribbon around her forehead, and her hair is up, but a few disobedient strands have broken loose and lie on her shoulders. A sudden puff of wind raises a cloud of dust around her, but her hair doesn't move—nor could it; it's made of marble, as are her bare arms and the hundred folds in her gown. The sculptor who crafted her used one of the world's most precious marbles, fixed in stone the likeness of one of the Romans' most revered deities: *Mater Matula*, "the mother of good auspices," the goddess of fertility, of the "beginning" and of dawn.

The statue has been here for many years now on its imposing marble pedestal, presiding over a neighborhood intersection. She is surrounded by darkness, but the diffuse pallor of the moonlight reveals the presence, beyond her marble arms, of a wide street lined with shops on both sides. One of the striking things you'd encounter is the quietness, an unreal silence that is broken only by the cascading water of a neighborhood fountain a few yards down the street. The fountain has a very simple design. Four thick slabs of travertine marble form a square tub topped with a short, squat column. The moonlight, struggling to break through to the street between the buildings, reveals the face of yet another deity carved on the column. It's Mercury with his winged helmet and a stream of water flowing from his mouth.

This is the Rome where Paul has found himself in A.D. 56. The Roman Empire had achieved its greatest geographical expansion. The Empire's perimeter was more than six thousand miles, almost a quarter of the earth's circumference. The Empire stretched from Scotland to the edge of Iran, from the Sahara to the North Sea.

Its inhabitants were drawn from the most diverse populations, from the blondes of northern Europe to the dark-haired peoples of the Middle East, from Asians to North Africans. Walking from one end to the other, you would have encountered icy seas with seals and sea lions, immense forests of fir trees, prairies, snow-capped mountains, huge glaciers, and lakes and rivers leading you down to the warm beaches of the Mediterranean.

No empire in all of history has included such a variety of natural environments. Everywhere, the official language was Latin. Everywhere, payments were made in sestertii. Everywhere, there was only one law: ROMAN LAW.

Paul had never been in Rome when he wrote this letter from Corinth about twenty-six years later. But he knew quite a few of the Christians there, as we see in chapter 16 when he addresses many people by name. Christianity possibly reached Rome when the Jews from Rome were converted in Jerusalem on the day of Pentecost and then carried back the Good News (Acts 2:10).

In those days, Christians were people on the move, whether as a result of persecution, because they were heralds of the Gospel, or due to the ordinary course of their work. These Christians in Rome were from both Jewish and Gentile backgrounds. The book of Romans has always stood at the head of Paul's letters, and rightfully so. Because Acts ends with Paul's arrival in Rome, it is logical to have the epistle section of the New Testament begin with the apostle's letter to the Roman church, written before he visited the Christians there. More decisively, Romans is the most important book theologically in the whole New Testament.

Historically, Romans is the most influential of the Bible books. Augustine was converted through reading Rom. 13:13-14 (A.D. 380). The Protestant Reformation was launched when Martin Luther finally understood the meaning of God's righteousness, and that "the just shall live by faith," in 1517. John Wesley received assurance of salvation through hearing the preface to Luther's commentary on Romans read in a Moravian house church on Aldersgate Street in London in 1738. John Calvin wrote of the book of Romans, "When any one understands this Epistle, he has a passage opened to him to the understanding of the whole Scripture."[1]

All these and other originators of different Christian movements are not worshiped—maybe that's important to say—but their respective stories and legacies are important to hear. Each had struggles. Each had doubts. Each had frailties. Yet their stories are magnificent, rich, and instructive. To me, the story that stands out as spot-on to my faith journey, and possibly many others' journeys, is that of John Wesley, the founder of the Methodist Church. His was a life and experience of turmoil and spiritual uncertainty before it came together for him that night in 1738, almost three centuries ago.

He had to get to the place where he recognized his own spiritual resources as inadequate. He had to be made to see that the heart of authentic religion is not striving and not straining after God, but SIMPLY ACCEPTING FOR OURSELVES THE LOVE HE BESTOWS.

Isn't this, after all, the significance of our "Aldersgate" moment—the recognition that salvation is a gift, a right relationship with God is a gift, the empowering of God to help us to live is a gift?

For thirty-five years of his life, Wesley had missed the point completely. And it is easy to miss. Personally, I know this for a fact. Some people have to reach the bottom before they'll stop kicking. It takes that kind of experience to bring some people to a realization of need.

Dr. Tom Price tells a story of a church member who asked him to "put the essence of Christianity into one sentence." He said he couldn't. *It was simply too big!* But after a period of contemplation, Dr. Price said, "The best I've been able to come up with so far is THE ESSENCE OF CHRISTIANITY, IT SEEMS TO ME, IS THE ADMISSION, THE HONEST ADMISSION, OF UNWORTHINESS BEFORE THE GOD OF JESUS CHRIST, BUT THE JOYOUS RECOGNITION THAT HE LOVES YOU IN SPITE OF IT."

Now, admittedly, this isn't complete theology. Of course it isn't, but it strikes the note of why we call it "Gospel," "Good News."

What a sense of release that can give a person. What a sense of unshackling it can bestow. Sure, there's a place for striving and sweating and straining, but it's no longer for SELF-JUSTIFICATION. THAT'S THE POINT. That's already been taken care of from the other side. Paul is saying, "If God loves me and claims me as His own, regardless of my intrinsic worth and value, then I am FREE, free to grow."

On May 24, 1738, in a little prayer meeting in a building on Aldersgate Street in London, led by a person whose name is forever lost to us, THE MIRACLE CAME INTO A LIFE. "In the evening," Wesley wrote, "I went very unwillingly to a society in Aldersgate Street, where one was reading Luther's preface to the Epistle to the Romans. About a quarter before nine, while he was describing the change which God works in the heart through faith in Christ, I felt my heart strangely warmed. I felt I did trust in Christ, Christ alone, for salvation; and an assurance was given me that He had taken away my sins, even mine, and saved me from the law of sin and death."[2]

How do you account for what happened to him? Had God changed? Had Christ changed? Had the power of love suddenly turned on its heels and gained momentum? Of course not. It was Wesley's attitude that had allowed something to happen to him.

The admission of need and the willingness, finally, to accept God's acceptance brought Wesley *out of the depths*. He had experienced grace, and you can't argue with that. That's the word of hope that still stands . . . regardless of the generation. Someone asked Dwight L. Moody one time, "How do you know you've been converted?" Moody said, "Because I was there when it happened."

What Paul was saying to the Romans in his epistle was that God can do anything if He has the tools, and the tools He requires to work in a life or in a church are simply . . . the reins. He needs the control of that life or that church. And I think if we listen closely, we can still hear Luther, Calvin, and Wesley say to each and every one of us: "What's to prevent you from giving Him the full control of your life? There really is not security in life except in the insecurity of complete abandonment. But in that abandonment, there is peace, and there is assurance. I ought to know because I was there when it happened to me."

Chapter 26

THE RECOVERY
OF HOPE

It is by the name of Jesus Christ of Nazareth, whom you crucified but whom God raised from the dead, that this man stands before you healed. He is "the stone you builders rejected, which has become the capstone."
Acts 4:10-11 (see also vv. 5-9, 12-20)

The place was Buchenwald. Even today, the name sends shivers up and down the spine. All that was horrible and ghastly, all that was physically and emotionally and spiritually debased took place there. For the rest of history, I guess, it will be remembered as one of the degraded places of the human experience.

At Buchenwald, along with numerous other such camps, a group of medical doctors was imprisoned. Some were Christians; some were Jewish; some were nothing at all in the way of religion. They were thrown into the same compound with the rest, indiscriminately, with no distinction being made, no preferential treatment given.

Just like all the rest, the doctors were starved, beaten at times, overworked. The same treatment was inflicted on them as on every other prisoner in the camp.

But at night, when the others had dragged themselves off to bed, this little group of physicians met and talked. They talked about medicine.
They talked about cases.
They swapped observations and diagnoses.
They organized within the prison camp a little medical society and did what they could to improve health conditions.

They began smuggling in materials to make, of all things, an x-ray machine. The pieces for it had to be found somewhere.
They had to be located.
They had to be stolen.
They had to be concealed.
They had to be carried back to the compound and slipped in, either by fooling or bribing the guards.

It took weeks, and there were all kinds of disappointments. But little by little, they did it, working for the most part into the night while others were sleeping, over and above everything else the routine demanded.

And they actually used that crude instrument in Buchenwald, a prison camp x-ray machine, to help take care of their fellow prisoners.

Dr. Karl Menninger, the famous psychiatrist of the Menninger Clinic in Topeka, Kansas, tells this story. He visited Buchenwald in 1945, just a few days after it was liberated, along with a group of army doctors. They got it firsthand from some of the ones who had participated.

What made them do it? What prompted that kind of devotion, stubbornness, and perseverance? What made them so dedicated to medicine and humanity that they would work like that, under those conditions, for so long? Dr. Menninger concludes that the one ingredient in the situation, the one factor that made it not only possible, but plausible, was the quality of HOPE.

They simply never gave up HOPE. They clung to it tenaciously, and even when external conditions threatened to crush them, that hope made out of them something that tragedy simply was not able to touch. They transcended it and gave both to their profession and to humanity at large a dignity that I think has not often been equaled. There's almost a biblical quality about it.

In east Tennessee, the Tennessee Valley Authority has been erecting dams since the 1930s for purposes of conservation and electricity. There are lots of them now. One particular dam was built on the Little Tennessee River. It's called the Norris Dam, and when it was built and put into operation, the water that was backed up by the dam flooded a whole section of bottom land, turning some good, rich property into a lake. Sara and I now own property near its shores. We ride our little pontoon boat on its waters, and gaze down into the depths of the water. Some say they have seen rooftops of the homes from days gone by.

Some people lived on that land. They had lived there for years. Their fathers and grandfathers had lived there before them and had farmed it for decades. It was home. When the government condemned the land, showed them charts and maps, explained to the inhabitants what was going to happen, and finally paid them, really quite generously, for their property, LIFE ALMOST STOPPED ON THOSE LITTLE FARMS. For a while, you couldn't see it, as it took several years for the inevitable to happen.

But long before that, everything had changed. Outwardly, nothing seemed so different, but inwardly, a whole new mood prevailed. Life pretty much ground to a halt. Building stopped. Fences were left unmended. Repairs were not made. Weeds grew up. What was the use? What was the point of fixing up a place if within a few months, it was going to be flooded?

One man had lived down in the bottom for all eighty years of his life. He was known throughout those parts as Uncle Ephraim. Commenting on the situation, Uncle Ephraim said with a kind of native, untutored wisdom, "You know, when there ain't no faith in the future, there ain't no power in the present."

And that's right. Uncle Ephraim almost could have been an Old Testament prophet. Both of these stories are about the same thing. One comes at it from one side; the other, from the opposite side. But they both illustrate the same point, and it's as solidly biblical as you can get: HOPE.

Strengthen hope, and almost nothing is impossible . . . even x-ray machines in Buchenwald. Eliminate hope, and you eliminate motivation, effort, desire, and after a while, even the will to live. But hope does something for each of us. It gives us something to cling to; it gives us something out there in which to anchor. When there's faith in the future, there's hope in the present. Uncle Ephraim may have said it backward, but he couldn't have been more in harmony with the basic biblical perspective.

My point is something that probably hasn't been said frequently enough from Christian pulpits: THE BASIS FOR CHRISTIAN HOPE IS NOT TO BE FOUND IN EXTERNAL CONDITIONS. IT'S ROOTED IN THE FAITHFULNESS OF GOD AND IN HIS REDEEMING ACTION IN JESUS CHRIST.

Our hope as Christians, our confidence in the future, whatever it may be, doesn't depend primarily on what's going on around us. Hope isn't determined by the *CBS Evening News*, or a Gallup poll, or by Secretary of State Hillary Rodham Clinton. If godliness seems to be on the decrease, it doesn't mean that the Almighty is incapacitated or home with the flu.

One of the oldest pieces of writing in the world was dug up on a clay tablet a few years ago in Iraq, of all places, what used to be the country of Babylon in the Middle East. There, ancient cuneiform characters scratched in the clay, when they finally deciphered it, read, "Alas, alas. Things are not what they used to be." Paul, as usual, summed it up best. It was a world, he said, "without hope and without God" (Eph. 2:12).

So, what are we left with? What were they left with? What, then, is the basis for HOPE in the Christian sense, if it's not rooted in external conditions, if it's not rooted in inevitable progress? Maybe the answer is transparently simple. THE BASIS OF CHRISTIAN HOPE IS A RADICAL COMMITMENT TO THE FAITHFULNESS OF GOD AND TO AN ABIDING TRUST THAT HIS PROMISES TO HUMANKIND CANNOT AND WILL NOT FAIL.

Our hope is not rooted in things.
  Our hope is not rooted in events.
    Our hope is not rooted in the times.
      Our hope *is* rooted in God and in His power to remain true to Himself. If we believe that, there is hope, regardless of what happens, and there is a motivation for "hanging in there" in absolute scorn of consequence.

Now, let's look at Acts chapter 4. It's a wonderful old story; I'm sure you remember it. It's the account of those two intrepid, bullheaded, Spirit-filled disciples who were hauled before the Sanhedrin on the charge of stirring up the people with their preaching. Imagine!

The authorities laid it out to them in unmistakably clear directions: CUT OUT THIS NONSENSE . . . OR ELSE.

They might just as well have been talking to two rocks . . . or maybe they were. Peter and John took a deep breath, I suspect, remembered Easter, looked the Sanhedrin officials square in the face, and then said: "Hey, whether it's right to obey you or God is something every man and every woman has to work out alone. All we know is something has happened in the world that never happened before. Regardless of you, we can't help but speak of what we have seen and heard."

I guess there are some things in life that nothing else in life can touch. To put those things first is to know HOPE. As the old hymn "The Solid Rock" says, "All other ground is sinking sand."

Chapter 27

LET'S ROLL

For just as the body is one and has many members, and all the members of the body, though many, are one body, so it is with Christ. For in the one Spirit we were all baptized into one body—Jews or Greeks, slaves or free—and we were all made to drink of one Spirit.

1 Cor. 12:12-13

Wallace Hamilton wrote a true story in one of his books about Dr. Gordon Torgerson, a well-known Baptist minister in Massachusetts, who crossed the Atlantic Ocean one summer a number of years ago. On shipboard, he noticed an Asian man who sat every day on a deck chair, reading the Bible.

He became curious about him, and one day he sat next to him and finally said, "I hope you'll forgive my curiosity, but I have seen you come here every day and read the Bible. I'm a Christian minister, and I assume that you are a Christian as well, and I am interested to know how you became one."

"Yes," said the other man, the Asian. "I'll be glad to tell you my story. I am a Filipino. I was born into a not very religious home in the Philippine Islands. We had some nominal Christian training along the line, but I'm afraid it was pretty perfunctory. Several years ago I came to America to study in one of your fine universities. I was planning to study law. On my first night on campus, a student came to see me. I had never met him, or even heard of him, but he was an upper classman, and he said, 'I just wanted to welcome you to the campus and to say if there is anything I can do to make your stay here more pleasant, I will be glad if you will call on me.' Then he asked me where I went to church, and I told him the name of the denomination.

"'Well,' he said, 'I can tell you where your church is. It's quite a distance from here and not too easy to find. You go down this street and turn . . . . No . . . you go this way and . . . . Here, let me draw you a map.' And so he outlined the way to the church and left.

"On Sunday morning when I awoke, it was raining and cold, just pouring down rain. So I thought to myself, *Well, I certainly am not going to church in this kind of weather. You know the minister will forgive me for not attending the first Sunday I'm here in this country. It's raining hard, the church is hard to find . . . . I think I'll just roll over and go back to sleep.*

"Then there was a knock on my door. When I opened it, there stood that upper classman, the same one who had welcomed me earlier in the week. He had on a raincoat, and on his arm there were two umbrellas. 'I just thought,' he said, 'that you might have a hard time finding your church in the rain. So, I'll walk with you and show you the way.'

"What was I to do? I had to be polite. As I dressed to go, I thought to myself, *What kind of person is this anyway?* And as we walked along together through the downpour, under the two umbrellas, I said to myself, 'If this upper classman is so interested in my religion, maybe I ought to find out something about his.'

"So I asked him. 'Oh,' he said, 'I'm a Methodist, not that the denomination makes that much difference. My church is just around the corner.' So I said, 'Suppose we go to your church today. We can go to mine next Sunday.'

"So we went to his church that day. And I've never been back to my own since. I found something in that group of people that I'd never before experienced. There was warmth, and a caring quality, a vitality that was catching. They accepted me and liked me. After four years there, I decided law wasn't for me; it was theology. I went off to Drew Seminary and was ordained as a minister and received an appointment to a little church in my home island. I am Bishop Jose Valencia, bishop of the Methodist Church in the Philippines."[1]

Now, I didn't tell this story to convert anyone to Methodism. You can find these types of people in any Christ-based church. But I do think it's important to focus on *the* most important person in the story—not the bishop, though he is important, especially in his own country. I'm talking about the man with the two umbrellas. He's *the* most important person in the story. Do you know his name? I think if you look close enough inside, you just may find him.

The apostle Paul was on a roll when he dashed off this chapter in 1 Corinthians, I'm pretty sure. He was churning it out. He didn't know he was writing a chapter; of course, those chapter and verse divisions came centuries later. He didn't even know he was writing 1 Corinthians. We call it that now, but in it he mentions having written them before. Heck, he didn't even know he was writing Scripture—God did, but I don't think He let Paul in on it at the time.

Think how nervous, how self-conscious you would be if you knew in advance that what you were putting down had to be durable, forever, that people would be poring over it and studying it twenty centuries down the line.

My stars, it would scare the spontaneity right out of you. Paul was writing a letter, basically at white heat, which was about the only way he ever wrote and about the only way he did anything.

There is power here in the spontaneity
                      and the freshness
                         and the intensity of a man committed to God so that
something bigger even than he is aware of is able to emerge—GOD'S SPEAKING THROUGH A MAN GRAPPLING WITH THE IMMEDIATE and timeless, packing down and overflowing with the timely. You can feel the electricity of it even from this distance.

Paul was on a roll when he wrote this. HE MUST HAVE BEEN . . . full of himself, full of his subject, full of a sense of concern for these people he knew so well and about whom he was so anxious.

They had written him first, you know. That church. Those Corinthians. That's the setting for the form of 1 Corinthians. In some ways, it's like listening in on one-half of a conversation. We can tell from what he says, what he writes, what they had invited his comments on. Wouldn't it be interesting to have their letter for comparative purposes? Don't you hope archaeologists dig it up someday or uncover it wrapped up in a crumbling jar somewhere? You never know.

Somehow they got word to him. "Tell us, Paul. Help us with some problems we're having here in the church. You're our father in the faith. You started this congregation. Help us. There's trouble in River City.

"What do we do about divisions that threaten to pull us apart? How do we handle immorality within the membership? Just wink at it and let it go? Can Christians eat meat that has been sacrificed on the altar of pagan gods? What are the ramifications of that? How about proper dress for church? Is what you wear important? Come on, man, help us out here."

Wow. And we think modern churches are the only ones that ever faced inner turmoil? First Baptist/First Methodist/First Presbyterian Corinth was the toughest appointment any minister could be sent to in the Peloponnesian Conference. Paul had a tiger by the tail.

But it was probably this PARTICULAR question that was most potentially divisive of all . . . the question of "spiritual gifts."
  Who are the most important people in the church?
    Would it be the Sunday school teachers?
      Those who count the collection each week?
        The exhorters?
          The healers?
            Those with the prettiest voices?
            Those with the most money?
          Apparently some in Corinth had the gift of speaking in tongues and would display that gift in moments of religious ecstasy. Does that indicate superiority? Are some gifts better than others?

It made Paul heartsick. He loved that church. He lost his hair over it, but he LOVED it. And he loved *the* church. So he sat down and wrote them a letter. Thank goodness air travel wasn't available because if Paul could have gone in person, he would have, and we wouldn't have this magnificent correspondence.

HE WAS ON A ROLL when he wrote this. The greatness of Paul was that when he dealt with a problem, he simply addressed it on the level it came to him.
  They asked about meat served to idols, and he answered about influence.
  They asked about clothing, and he answered about seemliness . . . always raising it high.

And here, you want to talk about spiritual gifts in the church? All right, then, let's talk about the CHURCH ITSELF, the body of Christ. He seemed to like the metaphor.
  Who are we, as members of this body?
  What are we CALLED to be about?
    What is our identity and purpose? Get that straight, and the question of the gifts will fall into place.

Paul wasn't writing to us. He didn't know us. He was writing to Corinth. Yet what he says to the church is so telling and so perennially pertinent that we should let him say it to *us*, so we can feel, as they probably did back then, the strength of his message.

It's as if he's simply saying we don't have to be alike in the church. Christians don't all have to be alike. WHAT A RELIEF! God doesn't call us to conform to a cookie-cutter mentality. Paul gets almost repetitive in his insistence on it. There are varieties of gifts;

> there are varieties of service;
> there are varieties of working, he says.

HE WAS ON A ROLL.

Just because one person stands out in one particular area, or has skills to do one particular thing well, doesn't mean everybody has to do that, too. The Christian life isn't a matter of all walking together in lockstep or keeping perfect cadence.

There is probably more room for diversity in the church than in any other organization I know about. God can use all kinds of talents and skills. Your skill doesn't have to be a carbon copy of somebody else's. IT JUST NEEDS TO BE AUTHENTIC AND AVAILABLE.

In my infancy in the faith, like most new converts, I was joining any and all church-sponsored activities that would allow me to join. I was on fire . . . but burning headlong at both ends and going absolutely nowhere. One night I had a visitation from the Lord. He was polite, maybe a little embarrassed, but persistent. I'm not sure now about all the details; I was asleep at the time. But the gist of what He said was, "Dale [that's what He called me; He always calls me by my first name], I just want you to know, I'm never going to ask you why you weren't Paul. But I may have to ask you why you weren't . . . Dale."

There are varieties of gifts,
  varieties of service,
    varieties of work, the apostle tells us. The good news about church membership (well, part of the good news) is that we don't have to be like somebody else to be active, productive members.

What a dull place church would be if it were *not* that way. Diversity is a given. What's more, it's God-given. That we're different is not an obstacle to be overcome but a resource to be used. There's a place for us all, Paul is saying. Whatever talent you have to bring, there's a role for you.

But in his inimitable fashion, Paul doesn't just leave it there with diversity. Oh, no. He partners it with a cognitive word (I learned "cognitive" from my wife, Sara), UNITY. They go together, not as contradiction, but as counterbalance.

Paul is saying diversity keeps us open,
        keeps us growing,
          keeps the heart pumping,
            keeps us from becoming monotonously stagnant. But diversity
unrestrained would become chaotic. We'd have no center.

It's like the fellow who ran out onto the street, hailed a taxi, jumped inside, and said, "Take off." The taxi driver said, "Where to?" The man said, "Anywhere. I got business all over the place."

Those diverse gifts Paul was talking about *are* related, whatever their differences. When the church is the church, they are joined back at the Source. Paul likens them to anatomical appendages, individual organs in a human body. They may be distinct and separate; they may be wildly unalike in appearance and function, but THEY ARE STILL A PART OF THE BODY. THEY HAVE UNITY.

Isn't Paul saying here that when the church is true to its calling, to its nature, to its essence, while there may be a lack of uniformity with respect to individual function, there is oneness at the point of BELONGING?

In reading 1 Corinthians through, Paul's responsive letter to their letter, I believe the Corinthians needed to hear that. They were a collection of people drawn from a wide spectrum. The city of Corinth itself was a mixed bag, and the church reflected it. Members came from all over the place, from the north and south, from the city and the country. Some were rich, and some were poor. Some were educated; some were not. Some had BMWs; some rode bicycles. Some came out of a Jewish background; some came from pagan religions; and some, from no religion at all. Very few had been raised in the Methodist Church.

Paul celebrated that multicolored texture. He applauded their individualism. But he reminds them that their individual talents and gifts only have enduring value when they are committed to the welfare of the whole.

Which gifts should be more coveted? THOSE THAT BUILD UP THE BODY, THE TOTAL BODY. The church is not a body of Christians for Paul. It's the BODY OF CHRIST.

Paul's message out of all this is that Christ loves the church, and that it's God's church, called into being by His Spirit. It's God's church, the body of Christ.

This precious gift into which we're called deserves the best we have,
                                                   the finest we can bring to it,
                                                   whatever the nature of the
particular gifts we have to offer.

We can't bring equal amounts of talent, BUT WE *CAN* BRING EQUAL LEVELS OF DEVOTION.

Let's bring our diversity together in unity, for we are all of one accord in the BODY OF CHRIST. LET'S ROLL . . . and bring an umbrella or two.

Chapter 28

12.11.12

SURPRISED
BY LIFE

But Christ has indeed been raised from the dead, the firstfruits of those who have fallen asleep. For since death came through a man, the resurrection of the dead comes also through a man. For as in Adam all die, so in Christ all will be made alive.

1 Cor. 15:20-22

Recently, I had a dear friend go to be with the Lord. His valiant battle with cancer was finally lost, and now his family and friends grieve that loss. We began our acquaintance at a small high school in a farming community in and around St. Paris, Ohio. St. Paris was dubbed with the moniker "Pony Wagon Town" due to the blacksmith shop on the outskirts of town that produced horse-drawn carriages and wagons. Apparently, they were produced in such abundance that the town became "famous" for its mass production.

Graham High School was the final "funneling" point of all the satellite middle and junior high schools in that area, where all "foreign" students melded into one class. Ours was the class of '67. And Rodney and I were individually collected into that large-mouthed funnel and tumbled together into the collection jar.

We had a few classes together and commingled at several sports that Graham offered: football, track, baseball, and wrestling. Our four years came and went so quickly, as youth has wont to do. The last time I saw him was at the cap and gown ceremony as we both received the coveted high school diploma from Graham High School, which ceremoniously closed one chapter of our lives and opened another. My life-journey took me away from St. Paris, and his chose to remain grassroots-bound.

I never had any more communication or contact of any type with Rodney until this past winter, when I received a call from Sharon (Berry) Burroughs, a fellow '67 alumnus. Sharon told me of the seriousness of his condition. She attempted to fill in forty-two years of a missed relationship within a fifteen-minute telephone call. One story that affected me the most about him was his love for and his faith in his Lord and Savior, Jesus Christ. He loved to sing in the church choir and had incredible delivery when he sang his solos. What a gift God had given to him to share with others. I'm sorry that I never had the opportunity to hear him.

I know we've all been affected in our lives with the loss of friends and family, and I don't claim that this passing is any more painful or unique than others. It's just personal, especially on a day such as Easter. But I'm told that he knew where he was going and knew it was time to get started . . . on the next page of his LIFE. I'm told he had that kind of faith.

Just northeast of Los Angeles, California, lies a desert gorge, which goes by the foreboding name of Death Valley. It's the hottest spot in the United States. The official maximum temperature reading is 134 degrees Fahrenheit. Practically nothing lives there. A few little rivulets run down from the surrounding mountains into Death Valley and just disappear into the sand. The average annual rainfall is only two and a half inches. But a while back, an amazing thing happened out there. It was completely unseasonable,
completely unexpected,
and completely out of character for that region of the
world. But for some reason, it began to rain in Death Valley, and it rained for nineteen straight days.

Nobody in living memory had ever seen anything like it. Suddenly, out of nowhere, it seemed, all kinds of seeds that had been lying around dormant, apparently for years, burst into bloom, filling the whole area with color and beauty. Those who resided nearby called it a miracle. In a valley of death, people were surprised by life.

THE CRUCIFIXION IS THE DEATH VALLEY OF THE NEW TESTAMENT.
  It's the lowest spot on the biblical continent.
    It's the desert floor of human existence,
      where all the trails run out,
        and there is no place left to turn to for shelter.
        IT'S THE END OF THE ROAD.

But on Easter morning, the showers of God's grace fell down on the world, "showers of blessing," the old hymn calls it, and suddenly, new life burst forth before people's eyes in this old, dead gorge of human history.

The Resurrection accounts in the Gospels differ from one another in detail, but basically they all tell the same story: PEOPLE EXPECTING DEATH WERE SURPRISED BY LIFE. For example, Mark tells how three women went early Sunday morning to the tomb to anoint a dead body. That's what they thought they'd find. That's what they expected to find. It was all they had left. BUT THEY WERE SURPRISED BY LIFE. HE IS RISEN!

John tells how Mary Magdalene stood at the mouth of the grave with tears running down her cheeks until she heard a voice that was strangely familiar calling her by name: "Mary, Mary . . . Why are you weeping?" IT ABSOLUTELY TOOK HER BREATH AWAY.

The twenty-fourth chapter of Luke tells of two disciples who were walking along the road to the village of Emmaus. As they walked, they poured out their hearts to a stranger who had joined them. Then evening came. They all went inside for supper. When the Stranger broke bread, was it the way He did it? Some gesture they recognized? Could it have been the nail wounds they saw then in His hands? SOMETHING HAPPENED. Something about the way He broke the bread opened their eyes, and they dropped everything and ran . . . RACED . . . all the way back to Jerusalem to tell the others how, with eyes for death, they had been SURPRISED BY LIFE.

Over and over again, Jesus came upon frightened groups of followers and transformed their existence from one of living death to one of radiant . . . *life*. In a way that is almost explosive in nature, God's grace and power fell into the Death Valley of their souls and caused new life to spring and bloom.

The cold, pallid darkness of Good Friday turned into *the* most radiant surprise this old world has ever known, and who would have believed it possible? I feel there is a good chunk of the Easter message right here. Don't be too sure about things—don't judge too quickly. Don't think we have to evaluate all of life by the immediate, bad circumstances because that may not be the whole story.

Judging from the Gospels, it may come when you're on your way to anoint a dead body. It may come, as it did to Simon Peter, when you have given up and are on your way back home to forget it all. It may break in on you as you stand with the broken pieces of your shattered dreams in your hands. You never know.

When John Keats was twenty years old, he was a medical student in London. He was a decent enough student, they say, but somehow his studies weren't satisfying to him. He was just going through the motions.

One day a friend gave him a copy of George Chapman's translation of *The Iliad*, Homer's great classic. As he read through that book, it was sheer magic to him. He tells us, "Then I felt like some watcher of the skies when a new planet swims into his view." Forgetting all about medicine, John Keats found new life breaking forth from poetry and a dusty, old book.

Dr. Benjamin Dugger was the discoverer of a modern wonder drug. During his later years, everywhere he went, he would scoop up a handful of soil and send it back to a laboratory in New York. People who were with him, or saw him often, thought he was out of his mind. But Dr. Dugger remembered that such a handful of dirt, scooped up from a farm in Missouri, had hidden within it the golden mold that produced the drug Aureomycin.

"You never know," he said, "where a better drug will turn up."

And Easter reminds us that we never know where life will break forth—maybe from a dusty old book, maybe from a handful of dirt, maybe in a desolate tomb in Death Valley.

On Good Friday, the forces of evil did their very best . . . AND IT WASN'T ENOUGH. Easter means no situation is past redemption, and the breakthrough may come from almost any quarter.

New life may be all around us right now . . . in a flower,
> in the song of a bird,
>> in some job that needs to be done,
>>> in some person nearby who needs our

ministry. In some act, some deed, some moment of self-forgetfulness, you may be found by Him, slipping up on you, and almost before you know it, you discover that you're vibrantly and radiantly alive. *because He is alive in me*

Oftentimes we think, though, that there is something we must do to take advantage of the Easter surprise, the surprise of new life. But what we must realize is that God gives it . . . FREELY, out of His prodigal grace, but it's up to us to appropriate it. We must claim it. We must accept it.

God is a wonderful Gentleman, with impeccable manners. He simply doesn't go around bludgeoning people into submission. He can be all around you and be unrecognized.

In the garden, Mary looked right at Jesus, talked with Him, and continued to think He was the gardener . . . until His voice revealed His identity. SHE WAS RIGHT THERE WITH HIM AND DIDN'T KNOW HIM.

On the way to Emmaus, the disciples walked along and conversed with Him and didn't know who He was. They were with Him and didn't know Him. All around us, there may be wonder, new life. My gracious, if only we would have eyes to see.

I read a story once of a man who was on a Greyhound bus tour of the Colorado Rockies. It was his first trip to the Rockies, and he reports: "They were awesome in their majesty and grandeur. The aspens were still golden and luminous; the huge boulders up close were overwhelming. And on the mountaintops, in the distance, you could see the snowy peaks. . . . They almost took your breath away. IT WAS SPECTACULAR SCENERY. Every bend in the road brought a fresh gasp of amazement."

But there was a young man on the bus near him who wasn't paying any attention to the scenery being displayed right outside the window. He had his eyes glued to a book he was reading . . . he was focused in intense concentration. He recognized the book because he had a copy of it on his own bookshelf in his office. He was reading *Making of Heaven and Earth,* by Langdon B. Gilkey, a study of the doctrine of Creation.

The man thought, "HERE IT WAS, at its most majestic, all round him . . . the magnificent handiwork of the Maker...AND HE HAD HIS FACE BURIED IN A DESCRIPTION OF IT." Upon suggesting to the studious bus companion that he was missing some incomparable scenery, he dismissed the suggestion with a curt wave. "Don't have time for that now," he said. "I've got to study this material for an exam."

Often we can miss more than scenery if we're not careful. We can miss life itself, even when it's all around us. Having it as close as an open window, as close as a companion on the Emmaus Road, we can still miss it.

In reading this story, I couldn't help but think of the story of the philosophy professor who, when he got to heaven, was confronted by two doors. On one was written "THE KINGDOM OF GOD," and on the other, "A DISCUSSION ABOUT THE KINGDOM OF GOD." You can guess which one he chose.

Easter is a reminder; it's a piece of string tied around the finger, if you will, that says, "Keep your eyes open." You never know where new life will break forth. God has done something, something BIG, and absolutely unprecedented, turned Death Valley into a garden by the exercise of His grace and power. What's more, that reality is FREE, AVAILABLE, and WAITING now to be appropriated by any person in the world who wants to claim it.

A number of years ago, John Masefield wrote a play titled *The Trial of Jesus*. In the play, he conveys a sense of the strange power the silent Jesus held over His captors. The one most impressed was Procula, the wife of Pontius Pilate. She tried to save His life, but when she couldn't do that, she inquired about His death:

"Did He suffer much?"
  "Were His relatives present?"
    "Did His family have need?"

But one question especially burned in her heart: "What do you think of His claim?"

Longinus, a Roman soldier who was at Calvary, answers her: "If a man believes anything to the point of dying for it, he'll find others to believe it."

"Yes," says Procula, "but that's not what I'm asking. Do you think He's dead?" "No, lady, I don't." "Then where is He?" And the tough, hardened soldier answered, "Let loose in the world, lady, where neither Roman nor Jew nor anyone else will ever be able to stop His truth."[1]

This is the faith of Easter. This is the faith on which I'm told Rodney had based his whole life, this life and the next. This same Jesus who came to the disciples in the midst of their Death Valley and surprised them with life has been raised from the dead.

His Spirit, let loose in the world, can never be stopped, not by bullets
                                        or armies
                                        or parliaments
                                        or ideologies
or anything else in all creation.

His Spirit, let loose in the world, can reach down and lift us out of despair and futility and meaninglessness and any other human predicament. His Spirit, let loose in the world, can claim us and change us and make us what we were meant to be all along, for time and for eternity. That's the Easter message. That's what He wants for each one of us.

"For as in Adam all die, even so in Christ shall all be made alive. . . . Thanks be to God, which giveth us the victory through our Lord Jesus Christ" (1 Cor. 15:22, 57, KJV).

statement referring to the Pharisees

letter of the law

Jesus - spirit of the law.

"what do you think?"

Conscience can be developed to
rationalization

PBS - The ~~Abolitionest~~
Abolitionists

"The Five thousand year Leap"

Chapter 29

THE NEED FOR STANDARDS

And the peace of God, which passes all understanding, will keep your hearts and your minds in Christ Jesus. Finally, brethren, whatever is true, whatever is honorable, whatever is just, whatever is pure, whatever is lovely, whatever is gracious, if there is any excellence, if there is anything worthy of praise, think about these things.

Phil. 4:7-8 RSV

We've been awfully hard on the Pharisees through the years, along with drunks, drug addicts, and used-car salesmen. Pharisees are our favorite enemy. They're so easy to caricature, so prim and self-righteous; they've made perfect targets for ridicule. Describing someone as "pharisaical" is about as ugly a thing as you can say. It blackens the person with the tar of hypocrisy. It connotes a falseness at the center. It suggests a topsy-turvy set of values.

Those are wonderful balloons to puncture, and there's nothing we enjoy more than sticking in the pin and hearing the air rush out. Pharisees are the ideal folks for pulpit jousting. If a preacher has nothing better to say on a given Sunday, it seems he or she can always kick the Pharisees around for half an hour.

Now, it's true that Jesus also was tough on the Pharisees. The Gospels are transparently clear on that. Some of the most scathing things He ever said, some of the most scathing words ever uttered by human lips, were words Jesus directed toward pharisaical priorities and excesses. "Woe to you, . . . Pharisees, you hypocrites! . . . Blind Pharisee!" (Matt. 23:25-26). That's pretty strong language. "You are like whitewashed tombs, which look beautiful on the outside but on the inside are full of dead men's bones" (v. 27). YOU COULD HARDLY CALL THAT A RINGING ENDORSEMENT.

But I wonder if it isn't easy to exaggerate the enmity between Jesus and these men, who are so prominent in the Gospel story. For us, they've become caricatures,

almost cartoon characters,

straw men. THE REALITY WAS

A GOOD BIT MORE COMPLEX. The Pharisees were the people in Jewish society most closely akin to the very things for which Jesus Himself stood. They were scrupulously moral, fastidiously

fundamentalists

Pharisees focused on the seen,
Jesus taught the unseen. Paul Knee

ethical. They performed good deeds. They made generous contributions. They were upright, decent, highly religious people.

Far from being hypocritical, they took their religion with the utmost sincerity. The reason Jesus was so hard on them is precisely because they were so close, so very close to the kingdom . . . almost there. THEY WERE ISRAEL'S BEST HOPE.

Paul Knee

When Jesus talked about their scrupulousness, their rigid, even stubborn, adherence to the Law, to the code requirements, He didn't criticize their rigor in observing them. All those things they should have done, He said. He faulted them only on the spirit with which they went about observing them.

He had no quarrel with their standards, only with the narrowness of their attitudes toward those standards. "THERE ARE SOME WEIGHTIER THINGS YOU ALSO SHOULD BE SCRUPULOUS ABOUT," He was saying. "Let Me show you. Let Me lead you into a bigger room." *the unseen*

They made almost a fetish out of standards. If anything, they had too many, and they had difficulty in distinguishing the more important ones from the lesser important ones. All that is true, BUT AT LEAST THEY HAD STANDARDS. They recognized them and took them seriously.

If we truly look at our diluted morals found in our movie theaters and on our TVs in our own living rooms, I'm afraid we'll see our problem is that we have too few. We could probably benefit from the presence of some scrupulous Pharisees in our midst.

From "nothing is permitted" and "nothing goes," we've swung to the opposite pole of "everything goes," an ethic just as bad, probably worse. Without appearing to be judgmental, I wonder sometimes if we have gone too far.

I probably wouldn't have written on this subject forty years ago. I'm aware of that, and I thought about it as I was researching this piece. Back then, I probably would not have selected such a topic. My parents probably would have, but not I, forty years ago. My parents—knowing the kind of music I was listening to, the clothes I was wearing, the places I was frequenting, God only knows the things I was doing late into the night—would like to have had a platform such as this writing to express their concerns about what was going on with *that* generation, *my* generation, forty years ago.

I'm not sure how much times have changed, or is it how much I have changed? In an earlier day, or when I was younger, any talk about standards, unless approached very obliquely, would have had the effect of chilling me out completely.

I guess the young are made that way. Standards? They smack of rules and regulations and guidelines and inhibitions . . . negative stuff, all that closes down on life and keeps it from flourishing.

I said that. Speak of fulfillment, and I will listen.
    Speak of freedom
        and self-expression
            and liberty, and I will dance right along with you. But don't burden me with this old-

fashioned, barnacle-laden stuff about standards. WHAT A DRAG. I want to take my life in my own hands. Why, Frank Sinatra came up with a song along those same lines. MY WAY—that's how I want to do it. My way. I want to live apart from the time-worn, suffocating pattern of conventional conduct, and so on and so on.

I remember saying that, inwardly, of course, in almost those very words. I even thought—gosh, this is so funny now—that I was probably the first human in history to say it. Then someone showed me this A. E. Housman poem, written more than 120 years ago:

> The laws of God, the laws of man,
> He may keep who will and can.
> Not I. Let God and man decree
> Laws for themselves, and not for me;
> And if my ways are not as theirs,
> Let them mind their own affairs.

Housman wrote it when he was still in his twenties. Not surprising, is it? You certainly can't call him a Pharisee. BUT YOU CAN'T CALL HIM WISE AND INSIGHTFUL EITHER.

His very rejection of any outside standard, his very denial of any fixed, abiding value bigger than himself only made him servant to a terribly small god . . . nothing more than his own whimsical emotions. *Find the book - Your God is Too Small*

The truth is we do live in a world where there are standards, something we deny or ignore at our own peril. Deep inside, I think we know it and resonate with it. It really represents our hope. There may be relative differences with respect to the details of those standards between cultures, ages, races, genders, and periods of history. That is, what's considered appropriate in Samoa or Kenya may well be in terrible taste in Vicksburg. But if the Bible is unambiguous at any point, it is regarding the fact that at the center of creation, there is a moral core. It's just there; that's all. The Bible doesn't argue about it. It doesn't debate it. It assumes it. IT TAKES IT FOR GRANTED. Right and wrong do have meaning.

They are not illusory human constructs. And while Christianity denies that a right relationship with God can be realized through performance, the Pharisees had trouble with that; they were adamant in their insistence that grace is meaningless if separated from morality.

We need standards, not to worship as ends in themselves, but for foundation and direction, to point us toward the higher way. *Kneeling in prayer faded thanks no*

The truth is, we can't live without standards. You wouldn't let a plumber work on your plumbing if you didn't think he maintained at least a minimum standard of competence. If he said, "Today, I feel like expressing myself, and I think I'll repair the hole in this pipe with purple tissue paper," you'd throw him out on his Ridgid pipe wrench.

You select a doctor with utmost care. At the first hint of sloppy standards, you'd change doctors in a heartbeat. AND YOU'D BE WRONG NOT TO DO SO. There have to be standards.

AND IT'S TRUE INTERNALLY AS WELL. We all know deep down inside that we ought to keep our personal standards high, that we ought to do right and shun wrong. We know those standards are there, and I suspect we're not as mixed up about what is right and wrong as we're sometimes painted by the so-called experts.

There is something in us, I think, something implanted within—an instinct, a gut feeling, a conscience . . . call it what you will—that tells us pretty clearly what we should and shouldn't do.

In one of his most beautiful passages in the New Testament, Paul urges us to focus on the things honorable, true, just, pure, lovely, and of good report. We know that when we do, we feel better, and WE KNOW WHEN WE DON'T, WE FEEL WORSE. A sour taste comes in our mouths, and an unclean, ashamed feeling comes over us when we take the lower way.

Part of it, of course, is training, heritage, what we learned as children from our parents, our teachers, and the church.

But it's deeper than that, isn't it? The moral sense, the conscience, the affinity for standards seems to be native to us. It can be undeveloped.
> It can be distorted.
> It can be twisted.
> It can be dulled. But it's virtually impossible to eradicate it.

Someone once said, ". . . brushing all debate aside, the moral nose should be the instant guide." God has made us with the "moral nose," as it were. Before becoming a Christian in my adult years, I was always aware of His beckoning. He always prompted me to distinguish the honorable things, the decent and upright things, from those less so, and He expects us to heed what this innate sense tells us.

Jesus appealed to it . . . over and over. Have you ever noticed how much Jesus in His teaching relied on basic common sense, on the basic moral judgment of His hearers? He treated them with enormous respect. It's one of the most beautiful things about Him. He knew they knew right from wrong, and He built on that.

"WHAT DO YOU THINK?" He would ask, when presented with a moral dilemma. "What do you think?" That's why ordinary people responded to Him so warmly. That's why they heard Him gladly. He didn't patronize them. When they listened to Him, they felt that what He said made sense. He struck chords that echoed within them. He put into words what they intuitively knew was true.

Which of you, if your son asks for bread, would give him a stone? If he asks you for a fish, would you give him a scorpion? OF COURSE NOT. NEITHER WOULD GOD.

I think the whole point of the appeal of the story of the Good Samaritan is innate moral decency. Who is my neighbor? Look at how this outsider, this most unlikely person, this Samaritan behaved toward a total stranger.

THAT'S WHAT YOU SHOULD DO. You know it.
> You know it perfectly well.
> It's inside of you. NOW ACT ON IT.

I read a story once about a missionary who had been working among some Andean Indians in Ecuador, remote people, people who had never heard of Jesus. He told how he expounded the story of the passion to them in the simplest terms he could command. He said he just let the old story tell itself. He told them how this Man who loved people, even His enemies, was put to death in an excruciatingly horrible way, yet never ceased to love, even as His life's blood dripped on the ground, and how God raised Him up again and turned Him loose to live and reign forever.

HE JUST TOLD THE STORY, IN ALL ITS POWERFUL SIMPLICITY. When he had finished, he was surprised to hear an old woman say, "I knew it. I knew it. Somehow I've known it all my life. I just never knew His name."

You see, there is something there, something built-in and instinctive, that makes us know there is a difference between superb and shoddy,
> between meaningful and mediocre,
> between the best and the base,
> between right and wrong. We're made to respond to it.

John Bergland tells the story, I suppose apocryphal, of an old hermit who lived in a cave in some mountains in central Asia. He had a reputation for wisdom,
> for kindness,
> for sanctity. People would come from great distances to seek his counsel. It was said he could give you whatever you wanted if you went to him and asked him and would do so with cheerfulness and generosity.

One day a greedy, covetous man made his way to the hermit's cave in the mountains. It was a long trip, over land and up tremendous heights, but he got there, exhausted in body but flushed with anticipation. He rushed into the cave, where the old man was engaged in prayer, and cried out to him, "Give me the stone. GIVE ME THE STONE."

"What stone?" asked the hermit. "What do you mean? What are you talking about?"

The man said: "I had a dream. An angel came to me in the dream and told me to go to the cave of the hermit in the mountains and ask him for the stone. The angel said if I had the stone, I would be rich forever."

"Oh," said the hermit. And he reached into a pocket in his rough tunic and pulled out a huge diamond. It was as big as his fist and sparkled with a brilliance that dazzled the eye. "You must be talking about this stone. I found it one day on the path and stuck it away. Maybe this is the stone the angel meant. Here, take it. I'm glad to give it to you."

The man grasped the diamond in his hand. It was so large that he couldn't close his hand around it. The brightness of it nearly blinded him, so he couldn't enjoy its brilliance, its beauty. And he went away with the stone that would make him rich forever.

But that night, he couldn't sleep. He tossed and turned, clutching the precious stone, thinking about the man who gave it to him and about his own life. The next day, he returned to the cave. After making the long climb back, he went inside and said to the hermit, "Give me the wealth.

GIVE ME THE WEALTH."

"What wealth?" asked the hermit. "What do you mean? What are you talking about?" The man said, "Give me the wealth that makes it possible for you just to give away earthly treasure."

Les Miserables

Something in him made him respond to the act of selfless generosity.

There are standards inside each of us that are far higher than we can ever reach on our own, but the Master, through the power of His incredible grace, can lift us to meet them.

"Whatever is true, *I am in God, God is in me"* the Messiah *acknowledgem*
   whatever is honorable, *Father forgive them, they don't know.*
   whatever is just, – *the money changers in the temple.*
   whatever is pure, – *become like little children – pure trust*
   whatever is lovely, *lillies of the field*
     whatever is gracious, if there is any excellence, if there is anything worthy of praise, think about these things." – *responsibility to feed the hungry, the*

What key will I most reflect on from this chapter?
Jesus is the wealth that allows my eyes to see, my ears to hear, my spirit to listen and my spirit to speak. 1.24.13

Paul said – just because something is legal it ~~may~~ is not right w/ God. I no longer have an issue w/ gay marriage. God will decide, does

174

Chapter 30

IMITATION vs. ADULATION

I am reminded of your sincere faith, a faith that dwelt first in your grandmother Lois and your mother Eunice and now . . . dwells in you.
2 Tim. 1:5 RSV

Third generation—that's what he was, a third-generation Christian. We're fortunate to know that detail about Timothy. It explains a lot, and it's more than we usually get. We don't know that much about most of the personalities whose names appear in the chronicles of the early church.

In most cases, all we have is a name. That's it. In Acts, in the letters of Paul, in the pastoral epistles, personal references are spotted here and there; names are dropped, the names of individuals who were known to those on the inside, known to the first readers, but who are not known to us—Rufus, Alexander, Phoebe, Epaphras, Claudia—but just names.

Who were they? What were they like? THEY WERE PEOPLE, real flesh-and-blood individuals, about whom we know nothing beyond their names, except that they were members of the early Christian community.

Maybe someday in heaven, we'll get to meet some of those people and hear some wonderful stories. I almost said, "I can hardly wait," but that may be a slight exaggeration. I think I'll try to hold off a little longer. Someday, though, in God's gracious providence, they'll become more than just names.

We don't know a whole lot more about Timothy himself, Paul's young colleague and "son" in the faith. It's almost casual, almost as a footnote that Paul drops us a fascinating clue about his youthful apprentice. He was a third-generation Christian, and that triggers an intriguing line of speculation.

It gives us an intimate look from within at the church of that day and at one neophyte preacher of that day, through the eyes of a veteran pastor.

And one of the things we learn is because Timothy was A THIRD-GENERATION CHRISTIAN, he was not a recent convert,
    not a new inductee,
     not a raw recruit,
      not one just in from the cold, from the sea of paganism still raging out there.

Rather, he was a forerunner,
>>a pioneer,
>>>a progenitor in the faith, but it didn't begin with him. HE WAS A RECIPIENT, an inheritor, the beneficiary, in the beginning of someone else's faith. He was the spiritual heir of something that was there before he was born. We read this in the text: ". . . a faith that dwelt first in your grandmother Lois and your mother Eunice . . . "

Both of these women, Eunice and Lois, Timothy's mother and grandmother, respectively, were Christians before him, and they passed it down the line. It is a legacy from those with whom we are linked.

If we do our homework, we find one more fact about this family. It comes from the book of Acts. There we learn in a separate setting that Eunice was a Jewish Christian married to a Greek man, Timothy's father. Whether he was a Christian or not, we don't know, but that would certainly explain Timothy's Greek name. They all lived in the town of Derbe, in Galatia, where Paul went on his first missionary journey.

Questions abound at this point: Did Paul convert Eunice and her mother? Maybe. Not an unreasonable guess. Did Lois, the grandmother, become a Christian first and lead her daughter into the faith? Could be. Paul says, ". . . a faith that dwelt first in . . . Lois . . . " Is that why the daughter felt free enough to marry a non-Jew? That wasn't done very frequently.

We're building on a bare-bones outline, and gaps just have to be filled in with our imagination. We're reduced to speculation for much of this. At least for now. Don't forget to ask these questions when you get to heaven. Make some notes so you'll be sure to remember.

As we read this text, we don't want just to skim over it quickly and not fully grasp what is happening here. Rev. Gary Rideout has coined the phrase "Context is everything." And it certainly applies here.

This whole stirring scenario of the mother and grandmother could not have been tranquil and serene in *any* sense, but rather courageous and daring in *every* sense. This is first-century Christianity, after all.

If Lois was the first Christian in the family, she took a risk that's hard to exaggerate, even in today's Middle Eastern society among women. Undoubtedly Jewish herself, since we know her daughter was, she had to take a step of faith that could not possibly have been casual. It would have involved a break with her synagogue,
>>with her tradition,
>>with her upbringing,
>>>with her family. You don't make that kind of decision lightly.
You don't make it on a whim, and for Lois to take that radical step, probably alone, without male support or sponsorship or protection, which women typically had to rely on in the society of that day, LOIS HERSELF MUST HAVE BEEN A VERY SPECIAL WOMAN.

You know, Christian historians, or the pulpit, for that matter, have never done justice, I don't think, to the decisive role women have played in the propagation of the faith. Maybe it's because most historians are male, and the record is somewhat clouded by that fact. But if you read it carefully and look between the lines, you'll find the contribution of women from beginning to the present day to be far out of proportion to the credit they've received.

To paraphrase Alfred Tennyson, more things are wrought by women than this world dreams of, or at least more things than about half this world dreams of.

AND HERE IT IS. A man brought the Gospel to Lois, but it was she who grasped it,
embraced it,
claimed it,
nurtured it,
acted on it,
and lived it so that others wanted it. It was through her that it passed to daughter to grandson and on from little Derbe to across the Roman world. It was in *them* before it was in *him*.

It was bequeathed to him through people who loved him,
believed in him,
cared for him,
and spent something personal of
themselves in him.

Now we come to it, the question of the day: Is Timothy's case an isolated one? Is his experience unique? I don't think so.

Doesn't your experience and mine pretty much parallel his? Most of us, too, I suspect, have inherited a good part of our faith, certainly the initial foundation. We didn't make it up; we received it . . . from somebody who believed in us and in whom we came to believe. MOST OF US, IN TRUTH, WERE *LOVED* INTO THE FAITH. That was our initiation, and it's probably the most effective kind of Christian propagation we can have. I truly believe that's why women make the best evangelists.

Most of our choices, especially the significant ones, the life choices, are really made more with the heart than with the head. Our decisions and conclusions are deeply influenced by emotion, sentiment, our likes and dislikes, and even our prejudices.

Consider the old story of the college math and philosophy major who was all logic and no sentiment, all rationality and no emotion—at least he thought he was. One day, though, something alien, something strange and new got into his bones, and he had an inescapable yearning for companionship with a female.

He happened to know a young lady, so he decided with logical deduction to ask her out. He went to her home and began his approach: "Premise number one: I am a boy," he said. "Premise number two: You are a girl." And finally, "Premise number three: It is customary in our North American cultural milieu for boys and girls to get together from time to time for purposes of social interaction."

Before he could say another word, she broke into the monologue briskly and told him to GET OFF THE *PREMISES.*

We don't live on a purely logical plane. We don't reach all our conclusions on the basis of pure logic. Why are we Methodists or Baptists?

Why are we Republicans or Democrats or Libertarians?

Why are you a Wolverine? (Yeah, why in the *world* would you be that?) I think we would be surprised to know how many emotional factors entered into such decisions, as was the case in the story of Timothy.

His decision probably started, as it does with many of us, when he was very young. He saw it first in Lois and Eunice, and I'm certain he saw it before he understood it. He witnessed it before he comprehended it. He experienced it before he was able to analyze it.

I know we can't be sure, but don't you imagine that as a child, he was rocked to sleep with Bible stories, recollections and retelling of the time Paul came, and wonderful accounts of this Man they called Jesus.

Maybe they sang Sunday school songs in the home. I bet they said a blessing before they ate. And I bet they taught him early to say his prayers at night.

Silly and sentimental?

Naive and unsophisticated? Well, call it that if you want to. THIS WAS A HERITAGE BEING PASSED ON, A LIFE BEING FORMED, just like yours and mine were. Why would we suppose it any different?

As he grew, the faith in him grew. In time, he learned about the courage of his grandmother and her resoluteness in holding on to her convictions against terrible pressures from the outside.

Here was his grandmother and his mother taking this business seriously, living their faith before him, representing daily in his presence a texture of womanhood that was above the norm of that community. Timothy saw Lois and Eunice *being* Christian, not just talking about it. I'm sure no single act did it. Instead, it was the accumulation, the seamless bringing together of belief and behavior,

theology and life,

being and doing.

SOMEWHERE ALONG THE LINE, THEIR FAITH, LIVED WITH AUTHENTICITY, DREW OUT THE BEST THAT WAS IN THE YOUNG MAN AND MADE CONVERSION TO THE GOD WHO WAS THE SOURCE OF IT EASY, MAYBE INEVITABLE.

The heritage was passed on. I believe it's how nearly every person is won for Christ.

Now, I apologize if I've spun more explicit details than the evidence in the text warrants, but isn't the essence of it at least implied? "I am reminded of your sincere faith, a faith that dwelt first in your grandmother Lois and your mother Eunice and now . . . dwells in you."

If the individual "conversion" stories of the readers of this chapter were made known, I dare say there would be a Lois and a Eunice hidden in the shadows. My wife, Sara, took me by the hand, led me to the church doorstep, and allowed me the dignity to figure it out.

I feel that the best gift we could ever give our personal benefactress—mother, grandmother, wife, or other—is to maintain our faith and keep it in tiptop condition. IMITATION IS A BETTER GIFT THAN ADULATION . . . and, in the long run, an even greater tribute.

I also feel that, regardless of our time in the faith, we are all young, inexperienced, and not totally self-assured about our role and the calling God has for our lives. THERE ARE ALWAYS MORE TIMOTHYS THAN PAULS IN THE CHURCH.

But the wonderful assurance of the Gospel—it's just about the most encouraging thing I know— is that when it comes to heritage sharing, we are not required to succeed; we are just asked to *try*. Someone tried for me, AND I THANK GOD FOR THAT.

Chapter 31

12.6.18

FAITH IN
ACTION

Be ye doers of the word, and not hearers only.
James 1:22 KJV

The First United Methodist Church in Winter Park, Florida, where my wife, Sara, and I worship and serve took this passage in James quite literally one Sunday morning. From the pulpit, it was suggested that in lieu of a normal Sunday church service, each member choose for himself or herself a community service project to personally participate in either on Saturday or Sunday.

The church provided a list of services, which included donning a dust cap and an apron and cleaning the chapel, repairing and dispersing bicycles to needy children and adults at our Bicycle Blessing Ministry, re-striping the church parking lot, and assembling Street Eat bags to be passed out to the homeless. On and on the list went. Or members could come up with their own community service project in which their entire family could participate. It was our choice. We just needed to put our FAITH INTO ACTION, or, as James said, "be . . . doers of the word, and not hearers only."

You're probably familiar with the expression "much-maligned." We say it about someone whose name is besmirched but who we know underneath is decent and honorable: "He or she is much-maligned." We mean the bad rap on them is undeserved.

I've heard it said about Harry Truman when he was president, before his true stature became fully evident. I lived through it and was there when they said it about most of the early civil rights leaders in the '60s and '70s . . . and today. Any baseball commissioner who takes a stand for the good of the game and refuses to pander either to the owners or the players is virtually asking to be much-maligned.

In addition to people, books, too, are sometimes much-maligned. And if any book of the Bible has been the recipient of that treatment, it surely is the book of James. It bears the burden of a besmirched reputation.

Martin Luther started it back in the sixteenth century. He labeled James rather cavalierly "an epistle of straw," hardly a glowing compliment. His assessment was based primarily on the verse in chapter 2 that says, "Faith without works is dead" (v. 26, KJV). Luther saw that as undermining the great Reformation principle of "justification by faith alone." Because it wasn't theological enough for him, he dismissed James as "of little importance."

James is really a very down-to-earth, practical book, one that deals with practical theology. G. K. Chesterton used to say, "There's nothing quite as practical as a good theory." And James certainly does demonstrate that. It *is* theological, just not abstractly so. My friend Dr. Brian Russell says theology students in his class are introduced to the term *practical theology*, a phrase that means exactly what James is all about: LIVING THE CHRISTIAN LIFE, DAY BY DAY, IN THE REAL WORLD. It means hands-on theology, putting it into practice in specific, concrete ways. James is a how-to book, one that focuses not on the theory behind the application, but on the application itself.

Any Christian who takes his or her faith seriously, who wants to be a better disciple, needs that. We want to know what our belief means for daily living, how we're supposed to act as a result of what we profess, and how we go about getting into it.

The book of James has some very wise and practical things to teach us along those lines, especially in this passage. He makes a number of pointed observations, maybe in somewhat rambling fashion, but on target for the growing and beginning Christian: the importance of listening, the value in keeping your anger under control, the need to care for the weak and defenseless . . . all practical experiences of faith.

He reminds us, his readers, that although life is fragile and in a constant state of flux, God is not. In Him "there is no variation or shadow due to change" (James 1:17, RSV). And he lays on us the charge that emanates from that permanence: If the God of perfect love is faithful to Himself and to His purpose, our response must be to let His purpose flow through us in deeds of love and service.

"Be ye doers of the word" is his ringing theme. It's not a denial of good theology but an expression of it. James knew, presumably out of his own life and experience, that faith, virtue, and truth wither when they're enclosed,
when they're bottled up,
when they're guarded and held closely. They, and life itself, only become
real when they're laid on the line and expended.

I wholeheartedly agree with James in that Christians need to get their faith out of the ivory tower and out onto the street. I think that quite often, we come at this discipleship business from the wrong direction. We think we have to understand everything first. We think we have to get all our theological ducks in a row, get our beliefs all in order before we move out and put them into practice.

However, James reminds us it doesn't have to be so. The direction of disciple-making is not always from heart to hand; sometimes it moves from hand to heart. It's not always the change of heart that produces the change in our Christian behavior; sometimes it's the change in behavior that produces the change in heart. Engaging in service makes for larger service orientation. Expressing love makes you more loving. You just do it, and it begins to happen.

An old theory in psychology, the James-Lange Theory, named in part after the great psychologist and philosopher William James, is a pretty interesting hypothesis. It says, in essence, that an emotional feeling is not the cause of a physical body response; it's the reaction that produces the feeling.

That is, your knees don't shake because you're scared. It's the other way around. You're scared because your knees are shaking.

Now you scoff, you smirk, you say, "Pooh-pooh" to the idea, and admittedly it does sound pretty strange, but let me tell you, there's something to it. The other day I was in a terrible mood. I mean, just a terrible mood. My wife knows about these things, and she can vouch for it.

Everything had gone wrong. The coffee was too weak. I cut myself shaving. I got soap in my eyes in the shower. And the showerhead spewed water . . . well, that's another story; I don't even want to get into that.

The only clean pair of underwear in the drawer had a bunch of wolverines on them from the University of Michigan. They were bestowed on me as a gag gift, and I wasn't about to put those things on in case I got into a car accident. I listened to my mother.

Then I spilled Cheerios on the floor at the breakfast table, bumped my head reaching down to pick them up, and was still nursing that wound when Sara bounded in with the announcement that not only had the neighbor's dog chewed up the newspaper, but one of the car tires was suffering from a pronounced flatness.

IT WAS ONE OF THOSE DAYS. You can probably relate. And right in the middle of this scenario, on top of everything else, this sweet, treacly, smooth, and mellifluous voice, just nauseatingly pleasant, came over the radio, that little transistor thing we have hanging around, and it said—I promise—"Are you downhearted? Well, then, smile!" That dumb radio never knew how close it came to being belted into smithereens. I almost . . . but then, for some reason, I had a second thought. I said to myself in as sincere a tone as I could muster, *Dale, what have you got to lose?*

And I forced the corners of my mouth into a kind of cheerful grimace. AND THEN, BY GOLLY, I DID FEEL BETTER. It was practically amazing. It really worked. No sooner did I make myself smile than a sense of beatitude went surging through the corridors of my morose body. Everybody in the house relaxed just a bit. Even the showerhead seemed less inimical.

It wasn't the feeling that produced the reaction. It was the reaction that produced the feeling. It's this way in dealing with people . . . like husbands and wives. Before they're married, all they can think about is expressing affection. They go around kissing and carrying on. You've observed that, I'm sure. *After* marriage, I'll tell you, it tends to taper off after a while, and you say to a man, "How is it that when you come home from work in the afternoon, you don't plant a big smacky-lou kiss on your wife's lips anymore, the way you used to?"

If he's like most husbands, he says, "Well, I'm too busy. I've got too much on my mind . . . all these reports to make, all this work to do . . . " And you say, "Yes, but you really ought to kiss your wife, you know." And he says, "But if I kiss her when I don't feel like it, I'm not being sincere."

Well, you want to know something? As far as Christianity is concerned, sincerity is an overrated virtue. Now, don't get me wrong here. Don't misquote me and go running to Rev. Jayne Rideout and tell on me.

Sincerity is fine . . . in its place. It's a perfectly good, upstanding characteristic, but I don't think it's the most important quality in the Christian hierarchy of values. A person can be perfectly sincere, overwhelmingly sincere, and be sincerely wrong, sincerely mistaken. I suppose no people in history were more sincere than those who burned Joan of Arc at the stake or crucified Jesus of Nazareth.

Therefore, sincerity is not enough by itself. It really is overrated. In interpersonal relations, the important thing is to do deeds of love, to put them into practice in concrete situations.

When the husband comes home from work, whether he feels like it or not, he ought to kiss his wife, and the beautiful thing about it is when he's done it, he'll feel more like doing it again. That is because it's not the feeling that produces the reaction; it's the reaction that produces the feeling.

It's the same with our faith. Put it into practice, and the behavior will pump up the motivation. If need be, make yourself do deeds of love, and after you've done a few, see if something isn't happening to you. See if you aren't more excited about future possibilities than you've ever been before. I BELIEVE JAMES HAS SOMETHING HERE.

One of the most exciting things about the Gospel is that anybody who really wants to can begin to live it, starting wherever he or she is at that particular moment.

Of course, you won't be a Mother Teresa overnight. Even Mother Teresa wasn't Mother Teresa overnight. Nobody becomes theologically and spiritually mature in just a few hours. But we can begin; we can start.

Look at how Jesus went about calling people. He didn't first test them on their theological knowledge; that's not how He began. He didn't make them show their confirmation certificates or their SAT scores.

For Him, Christianity was a way of life. It was an attitude,
                                        an acceptance,
                                        a relationship,
something you did and thought and practiced.

One day, He saw James and John on the shores of Lake Tiberius. They didn't have anything much to recommend them. They were just fishermen, with no training, no education, no Bible courses under their belt. They were just FISHERMEN, with a well-disguised aptitude, apparently, for the spiritual life. And He merely said to them, "Come, follow me" (Matt. 4:19).

One night, He was having supper with a sawed-off little tax collector named Zacchaeus. He didn't have promise. Tax collectors were worse than . . . politicians. They almost weren't even human beings. They were traitors, Roman puppets who sold out and bled their own people just to get a dime. Jesus said to Zacchaeus: "You're not leading the best kind of life, and you know it. You're selfish and greedy and, on the whole, thoroughly contemptible. You know it as well as I do. Why don't you give it up and try it My way?"

Remember what happened then? Zacchaeus gulped and made his decision. "All right, Lord, I'll do it. The half of my goods I'll give to the poor, and if I've defrauded anybody, I'll repay it 400 percent."

Jesus said, "Good for you, brother. That's a great beginning. Today, salvation has come to this house."

Now, don't misunderstand. I'm not suggesting that what Zacchaeus said and did that day is all there is to Christianity. Of course, it's not. There's more to this faith of ours than any of us knows. There's depth, height, and breadth to it that I suppose we'll never comprehend, even if we live to be a thousand.

But you don't have to comprehend all of Christianity to begin or to grow in it. You don't have to understand all of it to start living by it. You can start right where you are. Even if you limp or stumble at first, see if you don't begin to want to pick up speed. THERE IS NO BETTER WAY IN THE WORLD TO COME TO KNOW GOD THAN TO GO TO WORK FOR HIM.

"Be ye doers of the word," James insists.

If you have not read William Barrett's novel *The Left Hand of God,* I highly recommend it. After it was published, it was made into a movie starring Humphrey Bogart. It's the story of an American flyer, Jim Carmody, who finds himself in China during those terrible days of Communist takeover after World War II.

Carmody is not a religious man. In fact, he's a rather embittered cynic, but to escape detection and capture by his enemies, he assumes the role of a murdered Roman Catholic priest, a man who, before his death, had been the rector of a little mountain mission. Carmody dresses himself up in the dead priest's robe and cassock, totally changing his identity, and goes through the motions of performing the priestly functions, as though he were the priest.

This masquerade has no effect on him at first. He had been raised a Catholic, so he knew enough words and motions to get by. It didn't disturb his conscience; it was simply a matter of survival.

But little by little, something begins to happen to him; something begins to change inside him. He begins to think about those holy words he's saying and about those Sacraments he's dispensing.

He begins to remember some training he had back in his childhood. He begins to doubt some of his own doubts, and to wonder about the possibility of something better, something finer, something bigger than himself. He begins to brood on who he really is and what the purpose of being born is.

Then one night, in the visiting room of an old, dilapidated hospital, IT ALL COMES TO A HEAD. It happens as he waits with a distraught family, trying to share with them words of comfort as they sit agonizingly through an operation on the father.

As he is attempting to express love without once thinking of himself, THE LEFT HAND OF GOD, Barrett calls it, sneaks up on his blind side and enters into his soul with an overwhelming sense of peace.

Though it started through the playing of a role, even without conviction at first, through performing deeds of love in concrete situations, IT LED TO SOMETHING MORE PROFOUND, A MAN WHO WAS DOING THE DEEDS OF A CHRISTIAN FINDING HE HAD BECOME ONE.

Not everybody enters the kingdom that way, but some do, and if you're waiting around to get going on your Christian walk until a lightning bolt belts you into motivation, take heed of the counsel of a much-maligned, but surprisingly wise, practical theologian: Just do it. Get going. Act on what you do know. Be a doer of the Word and not just a hearer. You may be both surprised and excited about what it will lead to.

Chapter 32

WHAT TO DO WHEN SUFFERING COMES

Beloved, think it not strange concerning the fiery trial which is to try you, as though some strange thing happened unto you.
1 Pet. 4:12 KJV (see also vv. 13-14; 5:5-11)

Usually, the best place to start is at the beginning, especially if you ever expect to get to the end. This text of Peter, frankly, is a somber one, one you can't be light and flippant about—the old, perennial,
mysterious,
painful problem of human suffering. WHAT CAN YOU DO WHEN SUFFERING COMES?

It's important to note right off the bat that it's *when* suffering comes, not *if* . . . declarative, not conditional. The text spells it out very plainly and with solemn authority. W. H. Auden put it this way: "About suffering, they were never wrong, the Old Masters: how well they understood its human position."

The author of 1 Peter was nothing if not an "Old Master." He understood, all right, and just maybe if we let him, he can help us to understand this suffering and its benevolent Helper. It might be accurate to call 1 Peter a letter, or a treatise, or a position paper rather than the book of Peter. It's not very long, only five chapters, but it's an exquisite biblical gem.

Oh, questions abound about it, of course—historical questions: Where was it written? When was it written? To whom was it first addressed? And, of course, especially the question of whether Peter, the disciple, the big fisherman, could have been the author. It claims to have been written by him. But attribution to somebody famous often was made concerning writings of that day. An actual author frequently would latch on to somebody else's name, not with the intent of fooling readers, but with the intent of adding weight. It wasn't considered a crime; it was considered a technique. Just because it *says* Peter wrote it doesn't necessarily prove it. But . . . does it really matter?

John Calvin characterized it as "an epistle truly worthy of the chief of the apostles, full of apostolic authority and majesty." It sure does sound like a Presbyterian, doesn't it? B. H. Streeter called it "one of the finest things in the entire New Testament." That's pretty heady praise. Part of it sounds like it might have been written for a baptismal setting, when you sit and analyze it. References to water

and to belonging

and to dying and rising with Christ are found scattered throughout it. You could read it, just as it stands, at a baptismal service for adults, and the relevance would be quite striking.

The writing, apparently, is to people who have chosen to follow Christ,

who have made an initial commitment,

who are coming now into the church, into the

fellowship, into the body of believers.

The Old Master pulls no punches about what is involved—expectations, obligations, responsibilities—but he also lays out for them explicitly the resources of the faith that are available for COPING. He reminds them of some things they can hold onto to sustain them, and especially of some things they need to remember WHEN SUFFERING COMES.

For these Christians, he knows it will come. He knows it's inevitable. "About suffering, they were never wrong, the Old Masters" And what he has to say carries the ring of authenticity, of timelessness, even across the chasm of twenty centuries.

Being a Christian doesn't free you of the pain of grief when death strikes, or form a wall of insulation around you so you don't experience loneliness,

or hurt,

or physical pain. The Christian is heir to

those things, too, just like all people, because those things are human, universal experiences.

But that's not what he's talking about. He's talking about the suffering a person accepts, or is willing to bear, because he or she doesn't want to dishonor Christ. You will experience some, he says. You can take that to the bank, if you go through with this thing.

Can you imagine those new Christians Peter was speaking to, those confirmands, those newbies coming into the church? They had seen a vision

and had heard a call,

and were responding to a tug on their minds and their

hearts. Christ had laid His hands on them. Now it was crunch time.

"By your decision," says the Old Master, with exquisite kindness, but also with ruthless candor, "you can expect to face some special suffering, not in spite of the fact that you are a Christian, but *because* you are a Christian."

SO, WHAT DO YOU DO?
WHAT DO YOU LEAN ON WHEN THAT KIND OF SUFFERING COMES?

Will you see it as a sign of disrepute, as an indication of failure or rejection? Or will you see it almost as a kind of accolade? What will you hold on to in order to help you overcome?

It's not a light, flippant theme, but for those on the firing line for Christ, in whatever era or position of our respective personal journey, think of the resolve,

the strengthening,

the uplift of having something to cling to.

See how he spells it out. What do we do? How is the Christian sustained when suffering comes? Peter tells us just by not allowing it to surprise us.

"Beloved," he writes, "do not be surprised at the fiery ordeal which comes upon you . . ., as though something strange were happening to you" (1 Pet. 4:12, RSV).

It shouldn't be considered strange.

It shouldn't be considered exceptional.

It's part of the package. In other words, if you are going to strive to live a Christian life and live it with integrity, you can expect some suffering to ensue. Don't let it catch you off guard or tempt you to think *you* must have done something wrong for it to strike. On the contrary.

In this modern day and age, an honest profession of faith, a sincere, winsome expression of faith, may not cost you your life, as it very well could have in the first century, but it could cost you a promotion,

or a raise,

or entrance into some inner circle,

or the approbation of some special group. It could cost you a measure of popularity if your faith compels you to take a stand against something that is wrong in your school, business, or community.

It could cost you money if, because of your Christian principles, you cannot in good conscience take advantage of a person or a situation to further feather your own nest.

Suffering, even on this basic, beginning level, is a part of the Christian experience almost by definition because the world, in many respects, is out of sync with Christ.

Don't be surprised when faithfulness to Him brings rebuke. It will. It should. The Old Master is saying that remembering that may not reduce the intensity of your suffering, but at least it may keep you from being blindsided and can put you in a more stable frame of mind to receive it and handle it when it comes.

We need to remember that our suffering for Him is linked to His suffering for us and for all people. We also need to remember that it is a privilege, even if it costs something . . . and it will. And as with all truly worthy sacrifices, the benefit derived outweighs the expense.

The sheer loftiness of it as it is expressed in the text almost takes your breath away: "Rejoice in so far as you share Christ's sufferings, that you may also rejoice and be glad when his glory is revealed" (v. 13, RSV). Again, "If you are reproached for the name of Christ, you are blessed, because the spirit of glory . . . rests upon you" (v. 14, RSV). In both sentences, suffering and glory are juxtaposed.

Now, that's heavy. That's heavy and very easily misconstrued. Suffering *for Christ* is the key to it. Leave that out, and you have something entirely different. He's not saying all suffering is

Christian. He's not saying that suffering in and of itself should be an occasion for rejoicing. The Old Master certainly wasn't a masochist.

Some people believe that suffering for its own sake is somehow good, and some of them are in the church today . . . the "hair-shirt" people, who are never happy unless they're miserable.

I don't think that's what Peter is talking about at all. In no way is the author suggesting that we should find some kind of twisted delight in having to undergo pain. After all, Jesus Himself spent the bulk of His ministry opposing the kind of human suffering that most flesh is heir to. He did all He could to relieve the pain, the misery, and the hurt of the multitudes He found around Him. He didn't praise that kind of suffering or praise it for its teaching value. He fought it with all His might.

Suffering for Christ is something other than that; it's a two-way street, with the privilege and the honor of sharing in Christ's ministry met by His strengthening intercession coming back.

I must stop right here and tell you that this is beyond where I am in my own personal walk. Certainly, the heights and depths of it are. What a word of encouragement this is, though, to those genuinely serious about wanting to be faithful: THERE IS MEANING IN YOUR SUFFERING.

You can take pride when you are willing to endure for Him rather than give in to pressure. I know people on both sides of this fence. You can count it a blessing when you are able to hold on to a noble standard,
    to a principle,
      to a way of life without allowing it to be pulled down to a lower common denominator.

You are not doing it for yourself.
  You are not doing it for glory.
    You are not doing it for recognition. YOU ARE DOING IT FOR CHRIST, and He will sustain you in your effort.

Recently, I read of the death of an elderly English woman who had long been sorely crippled in almost every joint by rheumatoid arthritis. Even to get out of bed, she had to be physically lifted. In constant pain, she could not move her head or arms. She could not even look around to see who was coming into her room.

Yet such was the sparkle of her conversation, the brightness of her personality, and for those who came to see her, those visits became memorable and moving. Once she shared with a visitor the secret of her transcendent radiance.

Apparently, her disease had come from a germ she picked up years earlier while traveling in South Africa. As vigorous and alert as she had always been in body and mind, it was a long time before she found inward peace.

It had only come when she had learned to make a daily offering of her sufferings to the Lord. She asked Him to take her suffering and unite it with His passion and death upon the cross and with His intercession for the land and peoples of South Africa.

And she added a word of caution: "Tell people," she said, then paused for a moment before continuing. "Tell people that they must never try by themselves to make use of their sufferings in lifting people out of their troubles. That just tears the soul to pieces. I know, because I have tried. You must not reach sideways. Seek Him to take what you have to offer and make use of it what He will. That way alone brings peace."

I have an idea we're standing pretty close to an infinite mystery here. Suffering and glory juxtaposed? Rejoice in suffering? Can it possibly be? When our suffering is linked to His, it *can* happen. It may be the ultimate blessing. Blessing and being blessed merge into one.

We must be sustained as Christians when suffering comes, when we view our suffering in solidarity with *others* who suffer. Not only are we linked with Christ when we suffer *with* Him and *for* Him, but we are also with a fraternity of fellow sufferers, a strong and vibrant worldwide fraternity.

"Resist him, firm in your faith," says Peter, "knowing that the same experience of suffering is required of your brotherhood throughout the world" (1 Pet. 5:9, RSV).

What a powerful resource when suffering comes. We all know the relief we have and the strength we gain when we find others who have experienced pain in ways that we have. Knowing that we're not alone in our trial, that our experience is not unique, that others have been there, too, or are there now, fortifies us to hang on a little longer.

I'm told that a part of the enormous power of Alcoholics Anonymous comes out of the sense of corporate oneness. The participants are not alone in their struggle.

There is a man who lives here in Florida I wish I could know personally. I would count it a privilege to be acquainted with him. He's a Haitian Methodist minister named Alain Rocourt. He's educated,
> cultured,
> > and fluent in four languages. At the time of the overthrow of the "Baby Doc" Duvalier government, he was the leader of the Methodist Church in Haiti.

Because of his prestige and integrity, recognized far beyond church circles, he was named to the elections committee that was formed in the vacuum and given the assignment of preparing for free elections.

As you might remember, the military interim government came in, threatened by that process and not wanting free elections, disrupted those elections by force, and threw the country into new chaos.

At the time, people shot at the home of Alain Rocourt and his family. Bullets whistled through the window just above their heads and lodged in the wall. With the help of friends, they escaped and went into hiding and were shuttled from place to place for several weeks.

In writing of that experience, this man of God, who now heads up the Haitian work of the conference of Florida, said: "I think I understand better now something of what our ancestors in the faith endured. What sustained us during that awful period was the grace of God, and the

191

knowledge that you, our friends and fellow Christians, were with us in spirit. We knew you were praying for us, and we could almost literally feel the strength of your support."[1]

Suffering *does* come to Christians—sometimes even violent, dangerous suffering, suffering *for the faith*. But we do not suffer for Christ in isolation. He is with us, as are other Christians. Out of their support and sustaining concern comes our strength.

When suffering comes, we, as Christians, can be sustained by remembering that our suffering will not last forever. Someday it will end, and the cause for which the suffering is being endured will prevail.

Read the text of 1 Pet. 5:10: "After you have suffered a little while, the God of all grace, who has called you to his eternal glory in Christ, will himself restore, establish, and strengthen you" (RSV). I don't know of a more positive declaration of final victory to be found in the Bible.

Those who suffer for Christ's sake are not promised vindication and reward for their suffering in this life. Nowhere in the New Testament, that I know of, are we encouraged to look for the prize in the package. But there is the promise, sure and certain, that the things of God,

the will of God,

and the purpose of God will ultimately triumph. We hang our faith on that hook, and it sustains us, regardless of what happens.

What do we do when suffering—Christian suffering, suffering *for Christ*—comes? It may come to the church in America one day. It may come to *your* church. Why should we be immune? Or it may come to you personally because you believe. I don't think we will be surprised by it when it does come. Let it link you with Christ's suffering. And know that you are not alone in it. Finally, be assured it won't last forever.

Maybe that's all we really need.
  "About suffering, they were never wrong, the Old Masters: how well they understood . . . "

Are we immune from suffering? No.
  Is it difficult? Absolutely.
    Is it pointless? Not on your life.

ENDNOTES

THE GOOD NEWS OF FEARLESSNESS
1. Henri J. M. Nouwen, *Gracias: A Latin American Journal*, 1st edition (New York: HarperCollins Publishers, 1983), p. 87.

THE FAITHFULNESS OF GOD
1. Lewis Carroll, *Alice's Adventures in Wonderland* (New York: Macmillan Publishing Co., 1865), p. 132.
2. *The Green Pastures*, Marc Connelly (1930).
3. Marjorie Kinnan Rawlings, *The Yearling* (New York: Macmillan Publishing Co., 1939), p. 211.
4. Ibid.

A RECKLESS COMMITMENT
1. Martin Niemoller's quote, which is taken from the Holocaust Memorial Museum, stems from his lectures of the post-war period.

WHY DOESN'T IT GET BETTER SOONER?
1. *Love and Death,* 35 mm, 85 min. United Artists, Los Angeles, 1975.

THE INCARNATION ACCORDING TO MARK
1. Albert Schweitzer, *The Quest of the Historical Jesus* (London: A & C Black Publishers Ltd., 1906), p. 89.

LET IT GO
1. Paul Scherer, "Christianity Held World's Only Hope," *New York Times* (1942).

THE MAN BY THE SIDE OF THE ROAD
1. Hal Luccock, *The Interpreter's Bible* (Nashville: Abingdon, 1951), p. 177.
2. Malcolm Muggeridge, Malcolm Muggeridge Society, 2006.

LITTLE BROTHER
1. Martin Dugard, *Into Africa: The Epic Adventures of Stanley and Livingstone,* audio book (New York: Random House Audio, 2003).

OUT OF THE DEPTHS
1. John Calvin, Rev. John Owen, trans. and ed., *Commentaries on the Epistle of Paul the Apostle* (Edinburgh: The Calvin Translation Society, 1849), p. XXIV.
2. John Wesley, *The Journal of John Wesley* (Chicago: Moody Press, 1951).

LET'S ROLL
1. *Midnight Cry*, Wallace Hamilton (1963).

SURPRISED BY LIFE
1. *The Trial of Jesus,* John Masefield (1925).

WHAT TO DO WHEN SUFFERING COMES
1. Alain Rocourt, Doc. 9, Rev. 1, to the Inter-American Commission on Human Rights, 1988.

IF YOU'RE A FAN OF THIS BOOK, PLEASE TELL OTHERS...

- Write about *Looking Up to See the Bottom* on your blog, Twitter, MySpace, and Facebook page.
- Suggest *Looking Up to See the Bottom* to friends.
- Send my publisher, HigherLife Publishing, suggestions on Web sites, conferences, and events you know of where this book could be offered at media@ahigherlife.com.
- Purchase additional copies to give away as gifts.

CONNECT WITH ME...

To learn more about *Looking Up to See the Bottom*, please contact my publisher:

HigherLife Publishing
400 Fontana Circle
Building 1 – Suite 105
Oviedo, Florida 32765
Phone: (407) 563-4806
Email: media@ahigherlife.com

If you would like a personally autographed copy of this book contact me at: dale67cubs@aol.com or (407) 467-1186